Soul Mastery:

Accessing the Gifts of Your Soul

Soul Mastery:

Accessing the Gifts of Your Soul

For you Rebecca and your soul's emergence with great joy,
Susann

Susann Taylor Shier

VELVET SPRING PRESS

Published by

Velvet Springs Press

www.velvetspringpress.com

Boulder, Colorado

ISBN 0-9771232-0-0

Printed in the United States of America

Cover Design by Manjari

Photograph on back cover by James Barbour

Dedication

I dedicate this book to the beloved presence of our Creator from which my essence and existence springs. And to my sacred union with divine Love, which has given me the opportunity to know the glory of life and birth this writing.

I dedicate this book to the mission of reinstating the original Blueprint for this sacred Earth. It is a deep honor to participate in the fulfillment of this divine adventure with such a host of angelic friends at my side. These angelic friends are my beloved guides and teachers from the invisible realms that continually hold love and support for me. And these angelic guides are all of the clients, students, and friends who have inspired me as we walk together in the collective heart and Soul of Light for this world. We are a team in the manifestation of this book and in the unfolding of the glory of this dear journey called life.

May this knowledge from the Akashic Record Library contained in the chapters of this book open the doors to your Soul exploration, revealing to you its beauty and timelessness.

I join with the heavenly cast of thousands in dedication to your courageous journey of bringing your Soul gifts to this incarnation. May your reading of this book open the kingdom of your heart and Soul fulfillment. You are loved.

ACKNOWLEDGMENTS

On the top of my list is my acknowledgment of and appreciation for my editor, John Kadlecek. His editorial skills, feedback, and supportive presence throughout this whole process have allowed the birth of this book to carry a quality and excellence of articulation that are priceless to me. His partnership in the book's fruition allowed this labor of love to be the jewel that it is and that it may be for you. I am deeply grateful for my hundreds of clients and students who inspired and encouraged me to bring this wealth of knowledge from the Akashic Records of our collective of Souls to paper. Many have offered directly. This truly has been a team effort. May the Soul essence that each of you have brought into this book be magnified by your contribution in spirit and form.

I am so appreciative of the perfect book cover designed by Manjari. And thank you to my dear photographer friend, Jim Barbour, for the photo on the back. Also, Tam Hansen expertly did the artwork in the book. Thank you, Grayson Towler for your transcription of the interviews that speak of worlds that are certainly not part of our daily language. To Amy Bayless, for her joyful typing of my handwritten manuscript. Also, Kama Devi for her typing when I needed a push forward. And I so appreciate Haven Iverson for her eagle-eyed expertise in proofreading, along with Chad Morgan in his artistically knitpicky and methodical typesetting skills.

To all my friends near and far, who were cheerleaders for me on every step of the way, enthusiastically anticipating this birth as much as I have. And to my dear daughter, Courtney, who allowed me to retreat into writing and book space for endless hours. Last but not least, I am so very thankful for all the settings in nature in which my writing took place, which definitely contributed to the bringing forth of this creation. Nature itself and all the nature spirits were inspiring and collaborative in this endeavor in a grand way.

Arlen Bock was the initiating access point to uncovering the wealth of the Akashic Records for this particular knowledge of Soul Heritage and Archangel Realms. The Akashic Records are the records of all knowledge for all Souls for all time. His original vision to uncover the purpose and plans of Souls coming to Earth to help its evolution has ultimately yielded a treasure trove of information. By using the pendulum to divine the Akashic Records with specific, common sense questions, Arlen discovered not only the specific reasons that Souls choose to come to Earth, but also where they come from--that there are specific Soul Families to which they each belong, and that each family has distinctive qualities and gifts to offer. Through his painstaking investigations he gleaned detailed information about each Soul Family--their purpose, characteristics, and particular challenges. As he was divining the Akashic Records, he also gained an in-depth understanding of the knowledge of particular Archangel Realms that our Souls carefully chose. The attributes of each of these Archangel realms shape our Soul personalities while we are on the Earth and further articulate the nature of our Soul purposes. From this extensive research, he began to offer classes in divining the Akashic Records and doing Soul readings for individuals in order to reveal to them their own personal Soul heritage and to clear patterns on the Soul that no longer serve them.

Venessa Rahlston received Arlen's teachings and also began teaching this valuable information. It was through Venessa that I was able to reap the benefits of Arlen's harvest-diving knowledge about our Soul heritage contained within the Akashic Records. I have furthered this work through my own focus of desiring to bring Soul fulfillment and mastery to each one I touch. This book is a tremendous part of this harvest! The foundation laid by Arlen and Venessa has been invaluable to me as I have continued to expand my knowledge of the magnificent gifts and strengths that so many Souls have brought to this world for its evolution, at a time that is unparalleled in collective Soul history. My clients and students have opened vast panoramas to reveal the gifts of this and other Universes. They have been an extraordinary resource by telling their Soul's story and detailing the wisdom that now comprises this book. Their willingness to explore, create, and open the treasure chest of their Souls has brought immense joy and fulfillment to me. This book is a true expression of co-creation with those clients and students who desire to bring forward Soul Mastery in their lives. Their passion to bring the Original Blueprint to this world leaves me breathless.

And, you, reader, I am grateful for your desire to embody Light and to bring to fruition the seed that you were given. I sincerely hope that Soul Mastery: Accessing the Gifts of Your Soul unlocks the doors through which you will find the understanding you've always wanted and the affirmation of purpose for which you are here.

TABLE OF CONTENTS

PREFACE

We are each a master, here to bring forth our Soul's purpose, our heart's fulfillment, and our life mission. As a master, it's our job to understand why our Soul chose to come to Earth and how it is to bring Light into a world at a time when great darkness prevails. Each Soul has many helper aspects. It is innately connected to guides, angels, councils of beings, and Soul Families. Through our Souls, we belong to a collective, unified energy field that is working for all humankind. This appears to be true more than ever at this highly significant time in our universal history.

Each moment that we lead our life from our heart and Soul, we are aligned with our Soul's destiny and we are practicing Soul Mastery. As simple as it sounds, accessing the gifts of our Soul is the greatest offering we each can make to return the world to its Original Blueprint based on Love. It is the world that we all feel in our bones is possible.

FOREWORD

I met Susann in the mountains of Colorado. It was a summer evening. We sat on the couch in my cabin retreat, Susann's little dog Ollie between us, talking about life, love, science, mystery, spirit, and soul. Each piece of our conversation would come to expand this book. Each excited breath would eventually appear in these pages. As the hours passed and darkness began to fall, the cool wind stirred the curtains. We opened the cabin door to witness a torrential downpour, hail bouncing off the porch. Somehow, it seemed appropriate.

Susann and I share a passionate and highly energized view of life. We speak the same language, often without words. Out of a desire that sprang from deep within we had each begun our own study and practice of mastery of the Soul. We had to travel many miles to finally meet face to face. The journey was long and winding with many years full of experiences, and then our paths began to cross. Why wouldn't the elements match the energy that had been created by this union of like spirit?

We live in a world of strange contrasts. We can decode DNA. We can transplant organs to prolong the body's life. We can create life in a petridish, and clone stem cells. If you have no family history, you can get your DNA tested and learn what part of the world you are from. All of these things give meaning to people's physical existence, yet the world is still far from being freed from the grip of disease, poverty, or war. That is the world we live in.

Technical advances in science have created the ability to see beyond our planet in ways unimaginable ten years ago. We are reaching out to the stars and the galaxies for information about how we got here and what that means for us. Yet each scientific journal I read still admits to more ignorance than information. This is the world we live in.

With all the knowledge and information available to us, people are still searching for answers to what remains unanswered in the depths of their Souls. Through our consulting practices, Susann and I, along with other practitioners, have been privileged to bring our clients back into a realization of the part of them that is unique and immortal; the part in *all* of us that breathes life into form. The Soul. These physical bodies of ours are just temporary and could not exist without this amazing and powerful force. How much do you know about it? Put aside the life view you are experiencing by being temporarily alive in physical form in this particular point in the history of mankind. Go back to the beginning and consider that each one of us has always been in existence and look at what that means to you in particular. Where does your immortal Soul come from? What are your Soul gifts and challenges? Let that give meaning to each breath you take and each day you wake up to experience what life has in store for you.

Soul Mastery is a gift of awareness to those looking for the answers. It is a beacon of light to lead you to places where the Soul finds its truth, fulfillment, and peace. Read it with an open-hearted mind. Only as each one makes the journey back to their Soul truth, will the tide be turned for the world to be returned to Paradise.

—Mamie Wheeler, RNC
Intuitive Consultant

I

INTRODUCTION

We do not have to leave the room.

Remain standing at your table and listen.

Do not even listen, simply wait.

Do not even wait.

Be quite still and solitary.

The world will freely offer itself to you to be unmasked.

It has no choice.

It will roll in ecstasy at your feet.

—Franz Kafka

To the Reader

One of the deepest concerns of our heart and Soul is that we do not wish to die with our song unsung, with our gifts unwrapped, and, really, we do not wish to live in any moment that our spirit is not free to shine!

Do you remember what it was like when we were children and we lived from our openhearted love and purity, freely expressing our brightness and sensitivity? Each of us hold that memory in our Soul even if it was just for one brief moment at birth. At some point, our truth and sense of inner direction were overridden by someone else's idea of how life should be for us. The unique Light we came to bring into this world was not seen or understood. We lost our sense of knowing why we came, a sense that was declared in our first breath.

How do we get from where we are—which may not feel fully alive or abundantly wealthy in spirit and life expression—to that very state that we sense is possible, that we remember from once before, where we feel alive in every breath we take? Our Soul brought that richness with it, from its existence and experience before coming here. It holds the potential to be in full connection to the universal cornucopia of oneness and connection to the beloved all that is, every day, in every experience. Our Creator never meant for life to be otherwise. The Universe is abundant and freely wants to pour its riches through the vessels of human experience that planet Earth has been designed for by our Creator.

Yet I encounter many precious Souls in my counseling work who feel like strangers to this life. They tell me that in their hearts they feel that Earth is not their home. They long to know what they are homesick for. What is the piece that so palpably seems to be missing? These are questions that this book can answer because the answers are not mysteries. These longings for home can be fulfilled because our Creator meant for every Soul to be seen, known, and understood. We deserve to feel deeply connected to the Divine and the universal foundation of the home we are part of.

Many Souls have come to this precious Earth from other worlds to fulfill a mission. And at this ripe and precipitous time, that assistance is golden.

By connecting you to your Soul's heritage, this book will help you open the doors to your Soul's personal mission and give it expression in your daily life, bolstered by the divinity of your heart. You are not alone.

Many Souls like you have volunteered to come here with treasures of spirit to assist this world in returning to a Blueprint fueled by divine Love. In fact, Souls have been dedicated to coming here for up to 250,000 years from planets that are part of other star systems. These Souls have spent their existences there developing qualities of spirit that make up the Soul heritage you can experience in your daily life. In these worlds where our Souls originate, their true families knew them.

They have given us this memory of belonging, brought to us from their world to ours. The contribution that some Souls bring to Earth is relatively new, even though as Souls they are ancient in their existence in the Universe. Some Souls have spent time predominantly in one star system before coming here, while others have spent time in multiple places, gathering a variety of resources. Each one knows that this mission to Earth at this time is essential to the life of the entire galaxy.

The sense of feeling seen, known, and understood will burst forth in you as you read about the various Soul heritages and discover which ones you resonate with. During the journey of reading this information, allow yourself to connect with the frequencies of the various Soul Families and patterns. Feel the spark of recognition ignite into the light of remembrance deeply within your own heart and Soul. Let the spirit in the words speak to the unique fingerprint of your Soul, coaxing it to come forward safely and lovingly. I am, through this book, a witness to your Soul's existence, awakening you to your Soul's significance, just as an intimate partner is a constant witness to your life and its movement. You are seen, known, and understood by me. There are many others who share your Soul purpose and mission and love what you love. They have even come from the same places your Soul knows as home.

It is my hope that the divine outpouring within the pages of this book will reawaken all that you are as a Soul, that divine part of you that so generously came from other reaches of this grand galaxy. I thank you from all that I am for taking the journey to come here and spread the seeds of your Soul treasures to help bring back the Original Blueprint, fueled by divine Love.

The Gifts of the Soul

The Akashic Records are an energetic library. They are the records of the knowledge of all Souls for all time. In the spiritual world, they hold the record of all events, actions, and feelings that have occurred and will occur. All the information about each of our Souls is stored in the Akashic Record Memory System. This includes our Soul history, training, gifts, strengths, challenges, and even possible future outcomes.

By declaring your openness to the Akashic Records and all the beings, teachers, masters, and guides who work within the context of the records, you will draw your Soul Families closely around you. They will be with you intimately, allowing your life and Soul purpose to emerge in all its glory. These beings will innately help you clear your inner space, like cleaning house, to bring in the resources of your Soul.

You will feel the touch of their presence on your heart, bringing divinity into your very life blood. You will receive the presence of our beloved Creator who allows you to stand as your authentic self as you bestow your eternal connection to Light upon the Earth.

By accessing the Akashic Records, a rendering of the story of a Soul's journey in this world is uncovered. In reading this book, you will discover the roots of your Soul hertiage and Soul Family. You may sense this through the words you read or the feeling you get asthe words resonate within you. It may be an intuitive resonance or a gut response. You can divine (or dowse, if you will) with a pendulum. You can also use applied kinesiology (muscle testing).

The Akashic Records are freely available to those who seek their knowledge with a pure intent of Creator Light. These records are held within the Soul's memory banks. As we emerge more fully in alignment with our heart and Soul's purposes and radiance, we may feel like a completely different person from the inside out, many times over. We as Souls have chosen various trainings and experiences deliberately, from the Soul perspective, to grow, heal, explore, or simply to experience an energy field we've never known before.

Life here on Earth was meant to be a spiritual experience. Life was meant to be the means through which our Soul could expand and flourish in profound ways, unlike those of any other part of the Universe.

The more mature and wise we become, the more vital it is to draw in larger frequencies of spirit to support our expansion. As we expand as a Soul, our connection to larger realities becomes our nourishment. The larger worlds we come from as part of our Soul heritage are continually holding that space of Love and pure connection for us to be part of. They are our true "god parents," the beings from our Soul heritage who know and understand us and our Soul plans and purposes. They are in alignment with our mission to take on a human body to execute the purposes of the collective universal mission.

Our Soul is part of a collective of Souls who are deeply connected to us at many levels. If we haven't yet turned toward our Soul, and this collective of Souls we are a part of, there is a longing present because we have felt separate from our deepest part. It is natural for us to hold these heart longings. They allow our hearts to crack open to receive the divine Love we long for.

Whenever we feel the heart, we automatically have the tendency to translate the heart's voice or movement as lack: Oh, I wish I had … ; I don't have … ; I'm so lonely for … We feel the reasons why we gave ourselves the excuse to close our heart in the first place. "Well, Love hurts!" we say. That's a given in our society. How many songs have been sung in the name of this untruth that's so opposite to what is true? It is the lack of Love that hurts. Do we hurt when we say, "I am in Love"? No, we hurt when we shut out Love. The lack of Love is a space, a creative void longing to be filled with divine Love. When we feel an actual physical pain, it's the body's way of communicating its longing to know connection to the Divine in that place where it is missing, and thus in the pain of separation.

As a simple exercise, whenever you feel the heart aching or sadness present, instead of focusing on the sensation of pain present, feel it as a moment of unlocking. See it as a moment of creative void asking you to make a choice. This time will you choose Love to come into this space where you have locked it out? If the answer is yes, focus on breathing in your connection to universal Love, to the space where the sensation of pain or sadness is. Keep breathing in universal Love or your connection to something, maybe of nature, that you associate with pure Love. Breathe the Love you feel into that place where you feel the pain. Let universal Love fill your heart's longing for the connection to the Divine, which is your deepest longing. The greatest form of self-Love is known in your return of divine Love to your heart and Soul and life expression. It's a breath away.

As you reconnect to who you are as a Soul, what you are deeply a part of, and what your heart and Soul's purposes are, your Soul is truly fed. This reconnection is the first step of realizing your Soul's destiny and accessing the gifts of your Soul.

The means for magnetizing an abundance of connection, understanding, and support for your Soul's journey is available within the words and energy field of this writing. The gifts you generously bring are recognized and valued within these chapters, to create a firm foundation for your Soul's presence and purposes. The ancient and beautiful self that you are, your exquisite dimensions of Love—these gifts are yours to manifest and share in the midst of the challenges present on your Soul's journey on Earth.

Reading these pages will energetically open huge portals to your Soul's emergence into life. I hope this moment finds you in a comfortable chair, on a grassy knoll, or on a beach. Maybe you have a view of the stars from where you are. Relax into the frequencies present behind the words. Open to receiving your Soul's plans and purposes as you originally intended for yourself before even coming into the Earth's atmosphere. Feel the presence of the legions of beings who are part of your Soul Family supporting and guiding your journey here as part of a galactic unfolding of eternal life.

Feel how you are championed by the stars and planets that hold sacred union to the all that is. Touch the ever-present beloved in your Soul, beating in your heart right now. It has always been there. It always will be there.

In the Beginning

Here's how I would describe our Soul journey that has brought us to this moment in time.

Each person starts as a Soul essence born of creator/creation energy. As each one looks upon this sphere of creation, their Soul makes choices as to what it wants to create and experience. It looks at the various universes or planets that are creating specific dimensions of spirit and chooses where it wants to play. It's that simple on the Soul level.

A Soul might choose to experience more of the varieties of the expression of divine Love or to spend time where wholeness is the focus; just as we might travel to New York City to experience life in the Big Apple or to Africa to understand the spirit and culture of that land or to Iowa to be a farmer, at a Soul level we choose various aspects of spirit we are attracted to in order to explore and create more of them. We accumulate many experiences that have gone into the make-up of who we are at this very moment.

An additional element of choice for many is the opportunity to come to a place like planet Earth out of a sense of service and purpose, to assist in the larger universal picture. This is indeed a very particular use of free choice. We are not just creating to accumulate Soul experiences, but to work in conjunction with others to assist in the creation of a whole new way of being and doing life for a whole world, such as planet Earth.

I would describe our journey here as somewhat equivalent to going to graduate school versus just going through elementary school. It is a high-level student of creation who comes here to assist in bringing this world back into alignment with its original plans and purposes, or Blueprint for life.

So whether you are here because you wanted to experience the magic and wonder of multidimensional of living of life that is available on Earth or you wanted to have the opportunity to serve humanity and the universal movement, you have brought your Soul here as just one piece of a giant and potentially infinite Soul journey that you are on. It's yours to create and enjoy.

Free Choice

There is a Creator energy that radiates infinite presence as Light throughout this Universe and galaxy. This is what allows us to know in our Soul and cellular being that there is a force within us. As we operate in this reality of free choice we are operating within this Creator energy field. Free choice refers to our choice based on creation and Light. That is how it was originally established. What do I choose to create from Light that is true for my heart and Soul in this and every moment?

It is essential for each Soul to have a clear connection in their heart and Soul to the purity and absoluteness of this Creator energy to fulfill their Soul destiny plan. When this connection is deeply held, then free choice is not an issue. One feels free to create as an individual who is part of something vast and magnificent, and at the same time able to honor the uniqueness of his or her Soul essence and expression.

Here is a fabulous example of how one's connection to this Creator energy field directly impacts one's everyday life.

From Claudia: "I was paralyzed as an artist because I had so much fear about my ability to create artistically or in any other way. Susann and I worked together for the purpose of assisting me to move more freely into my artistic self. We discovered the Soul-level roots to this situation. By reconnecting to the source of creation and our Creator's presence, I remembered what it was like to be held by, supported by, and encouraged by my Creator, and my creative abilities blossomed. They just needed Light and water, so to speak."

This story describes the essence of free choice for us here. It was originally intended that free choice in Light was the only option. As we realign with free choice based only in Light, how we see darkness and destruction changes radically. We no longer fear darkness or feel threatened by the use of darkness when it appears to be power. After all, from the vantage point of pure Light, darkness is not a power in and of itself. It is nothing more than the absence of Light. If there is no room in us for anything but Light, darkness holds no weight or power. It is displaced by Light. It simply dissolves. It ceases to exist for us. Even as just one man or woman grasps this truth about life, he or she can help change the nature of how darkness is seen and how it operates in this world.

Creator

In this free choice Universe, our relationship to our Creator is a vital consideration to our sense of self and purpose. How do we know that our Creator is with us? How do we explain our Creator's position when catastrophic events happen such as devastating earthquakes, tidal waves, or the September 11, 2001, terrorist attack on the two World Trade Center buildings? This is complex but lies within the framework of our knowledge of free choice and free will.

Did our Creator ever make a promise to us when we were birthed as a Soul out of its force field of Love about how life would look for us? Did our Creator ever say that as part of our emergence as a Soul that everything would work out according to our individual agenda? Did our Creator say that no matter what choices we make this force would rescue us or take over like some authority figure? Did that force ever say, "I will always be responsible for how you do everything no matter what kind of choices you make? I will make sure you feel no pain even if you go out of integrity with your Soul plans"?

The answer is no. Our Creator is present with infinite wisdom and presence to ensure the continuation of creation at the universal level. One aspect of creation is each of us as Soul. We were given absolute connection to our Creator because it was out of it we sprang. Each Soul exists independently as a spark of Light, which is the manifestation of Love. Each is created equal in that sense. The command, "Let there be Light" applied to each Soul. What each Soul created and continues to create as that Light is infinitely varied. The possibilities for giving expression to our Creator's Light through a human life are endless. And free choice is a vital part of the equation. The allowance of the freedom for each Soul to create as Light as they see to be true in each moment is an essential part of the makeup of the Universe.

The Illusion of Separation

We are designed to be unique Soul essences, a unique aspect of our Creator. A long time ago, even before our Earth was created, the beauty of the design for uniqueness within oneness for each Soul essence became distorted. Separation was born as some Souls chose to view their uniqueness as being more valuable than their dimension of oneness and connection to all that is. Many Souls chose to create from the place of "I am me. You other Souls are outside of me and therefore we are not part of the same Creator and maybe your variation on the theme of Light is better or worse than mine."

If we make the choice to live from this place of separation, this is not our Creator's doing, it is ours! Our Creator is not responsible for our doings or undoings. Our Creator holds a focus for Light as a source for the pure connection to our freedom, to create Light as joy and aliveness in life constantly. That's all. It is continually our choice to continue to be one with Light or create a diversion from Light.

Earthquakes, tidal waves, and 9/11 are reflections of our collective choices to avoid being fueled in life by that pure connection. Yes, we are part of a collective energy field of Earth. For instance, the man that is elected President of the United States is merely a reflection of our collective choices in what fuels our life blood individually and therefore collectively. It is not our Creator's job to come change or fix our collective choices based on individual agendas that do not align with the way of Light. No, our Creator is an energy field that supports and amplifies Love as the life force for our heart and Soul. It is not an authority figure with overriding power to our choices here. If we were to believe that a God was responsible for or had power over our power of free choice, we negate our own ability to be a creator on Earth. We are asking "someone else" to create our life. Do we really want that? The natural state is to know our place as creator of our own world and let each and every other Soul be creator of their own world. This also frees us to trust that our Creator is handling the world of creation from a divine place of connection to universal Love.

The key is to remember that there is a larger field of our Creator's Love that you are absolutely a part of. You have permission to be in sacred union with it. It is your decision to choose to be in alignment with our Creator in every moment and to choose to create from that alignment. You can declare that you choose to remember to be aligned with our Creator's Light. I would like to bring up a very valuable point in relationship to remembrance of our Soul purposes. We don't have to forget to remember. We don't have to forget who we are and what we are here for in order to remember who we are and why we have come. This idea that we have to forget in order to remember is merely something that the Earth has played out for thousands of years, along with separation and polarity, so this idea may appear very real to many. We just need to awaken, remember what already is and has always been possible, and align with that. We can awaken to our vow to live our Soul's destiny and fulfillment. And this fulfillment and destiny is designed to be based on joy, pleasure, Love, and ease. This is all we have to awaken to and remember.

Why Souls Come to Earth

As I speak of the various Soul Families who have come here especially to assist planet Earth, I speak of the star or star system that the Soul Family lived within. These Souls did not actually live on the star; they lived on a planet within that star system. Because that planet may not have been given a name by astronomers yet, it is easier to refer to the star being described. But there are a few worlds that do have planet names. I will mention them but will continue to use the star name involved for the name of the Soul Family as a means for keeping it all as simple as possible.

You might ask why we move away from our home worlds in the first place, why we elect to come here, where life is anything but the paradise that we have known before coming here.

In these other worlds, our Souls existed in a place of curiosity, wonder, and exploration with continual direction from Love. We are Light-filled and full of a sense of magical revelation. What do I choose to create from Light as Light now, and in every following moment? What fun and joy and endless possibilities do I choose to explore. So just as a child grows and wants to learn to move out into the world, to feel his oats and discover more of himself in relationship to his expanding environment, so a Soul loves to expand and discover itself in relationship to the varieties of the experience of divine Love in all its manifestations. Planet Earth is an exquisite example of Love embodied in a huge diversity of form, color, and frequency of creation. There is no other place like it. And yes, there is darkness and destruction in polarity to Light and creation here. But in a Soul's perspective from the universal view, darkness is not something to be feared or to beweakened by, in any way. It is just seen as a creative void and therefore a creative challenge. In fact, this void especially needs the presence of Light.

Planet Earth is a vital, crucial part of this galaxy, especially at this time. It is a fulcrum point. The galactic questions are, "Which way will it ultimately turn? Will it turn toward darkness as its power source or toward Light feeding life?" It is extremely important for the Earth to shift to Light for the balance to be shifted for the whole galaxy. This is the nature of the time we all are playing in. We are Souls with an investment in the Earth energy field, yes, but even more so we are Souls who have an investment in things working out on a galactic level. This is even more primary to why we are here.

When you reconnect with your Soul destiny and Family, you will find a rekindling of this perspective. Now, you may feel out of sorts on the Earth, or that you don't belong, or that the energy field here is too negative or confusing. You may feel the heart and Soul have been lost. You may currently feel great discouragement when you view the state of the world and its movement and affairs.

From a galactic perspective that rings much truer for many of us than merely viewing things from the Earth perspective, creation cannot fail and Love will prevail. And Light is prevailing here. You may feel the surface imbalance of power on the surface of planet Earth. But know that the universal force is with you; it holds the true power every time you choose Love and your choice is from the path of your heart and Soul. In the eyes of our Creator, this is what matters.

As a Soul Arrives on Earth

As Souls come from other star systems and universes, their frequencies don't always match the frequencies in this world. There have to be adjustments made upon entering this world so that Souls align energetically with the mission of the Earth Blueprint. Souls from other worlds, especially other solar systems, have a hard time with the idea of grounding in the Earth. Because of the degree of disruption that is here, mostly on the surface, it's understandable that your intuition asks, "Why would I want to ground myself in this?" The Earth is anything but stable, connected, and anchoring.

At the same time, at the core of the Earth, divine Love, which birthed creation here, has always existed and has kept life pulsating. It is indeed valuable for Souls to connect to this Love at the core of the Earth as an extension of universal Love. It allows you to feel deeply connected to our Creator while living and breathing here, knowing that, in essence, Love is everywhere. That is a true anchor point that exists here and can be held sacred for anyone. Every time a Soul comes to the border, it is as if there are energetic border police telling Souls who come to Earth that they need to leave their bags from foreign soil behind. This pertains to a Soul's gifts and talents and what you have agreed to bring here for the Earth's greater good. These border police were born of the field of separation and polarity that was established here before Souls from other worlds ever came here. Souls from these other worlds came to help repair this field of separation, but have often innocently been tricked into believing that "to come to Rome you have to do as the Romans do." So if the Earth beings said you had to leave a piece of your gold at the door as part of the program for being here, you would go with the program, later to realize not all programs are divinely designed.

This presents numerous challenges unique to each Soul family. For instance, if you came to bring the reality of divine Love, you will acutely feel an aspect of separation from Love, which feels like heartache as you feel the absence of divine Love here. If you bring the knowledge of the experience of oneness with all that is, you will feel the pain of some separation from that experience of oneness. This separation from our Soul gifts that occurred to varying degrees in coming here can feel like spaces in ourselves where our gifts have been drained from us. Our lack of an ability to feel we can bring our Soul gifts fully into this incarnation becomes our Soul challenge. Consequently, a Soul has not only the mission to remember his or her greatest gifts, but to work with his or her greatest challenges that come with the package of entering the Earth world. To reconnect with our Soul heritage and Soul Family allows us to remember those gifts. It is vital to feel seen, known, and understood as a Soul. So knowing your Soul heritage and your makeup and mission is deeply valuable. To dissolve any obstruction to the wealth each one has traveled all this way to bring is richly fulfilling for the Soul and heart. It allows the door to open to one's Soul destiny and purposes with a huge swing. This is a large part of the work I do with individuals. I help others release the "barnacles of obstruction" on their Soul that create Soul challenges, and I open them to the resources of their Soul heritage and purposes.

When a Soul Chooses to Participate on Earth

At the Earth planet border we truly had to move through the collective energy field of separation to enter in, even though we were thoroughly filled with all our zealous plans and purposes. This field of separation from divine Love and oneness had been established here as a collective choice. When we hit the vortex of separation, which was a completely foreign energy field to us, we lost the sense of vastness, connection, and communion we knew and made choices based on the smaller perspective that the Earth carried. We wanted so much to know connection to universal oneness, which the majority of humans here were not carrying. To choose to hold universal connection, it felt as though we would have to let go of our connection to the beings on Earth because they were dominantly out of connection to universal oneness. Consequently we would feel a sense of aloneness, isolation, and lack of belonging to this world. The painfulness of that experience made us opt to be connected to the human experience and not our universal connection. We thought we had to choose one or the other. That was not true, but that was the driving force in life experience upon our arrival from other worlds. We just wanted to feel connected to something. To this day that is a driving force behind much of our behavior, good or bad, seemingly. This meant buying into the human idea of belonging, which had nothing to do with connection and oneness. We bought into the collective energy field of separation. We betrayed our mission to bring Love, connection, oneness, and creation, to feel a sense of belonging and feel a sense of family and home that was present here when we came. This sense of home and place was not based in spirit, but on the grounds of survival.

This created a denser field, which was very foreign to advanced Souls. The density of separation dragged us down. As we bought into more and more of the principles of going along with others' truths for a false sense of connection, others'"ideas of a good time" like survival tactics of battle, dog eat dog, and heartless means of defending our sense of self became the norm. We lost sight, to varying degrees, of the universal gifts we agreed to bring. Our Akashic Record Soul memory got clouded, and we began to forget our grandness and brilliance. Each lifetime we return, we are making a choice to come into this world and deal with the field of separation here. And each time we see more clearly that separation is an illusion and myth we don't have to buy into. It's our choice. Each time we come we increase the power of Light here by holding true to our Soul's destiny and not betraying our mission and purposes.

Human Beings Remember Their Soul's Purpose

Remembering our Soul's purpose is simply waking up to what we already know from a universal perspective, even when the majority of people here are choosing not to. It really is much simpler and more direct to just reclaim what already exists in your Soul memory and DNA, to brush off the dust and the barnacles on the Soul and let all that you are as a Soul of divine infinity re-emerge.

As a collective, we are changing this paradigm. Reconnection to universal Light is being chosen by many individuals and is therefore having an influence on the collective dynamic of the Earth experience. This increased reconnection makes for a magnification of the ease of the ability for other individuals to reconnect in a myriad of ways. The book *The Reconnection* by Eric Pearl speaks of the means by which an individual can easily find their way to the reality of reconnecting to universal Light. This is a prime example of the increasing interest there is in the theme of reconnection. There are countless books, workshops, retreats, teachings, teachers, seminars, trainings, and movements with the underlying theme of reconnection.

There are many children being born on this planet now who are not having to go through the field of separation that has been created here. They are moving in through energetic portals of Light that have been created in recent years that allow for absolute connection to be maintained by them. They are also being born to parents who have had the experience of reconnection in varying degrees, so the children can know connection through the mentoring of these true god-parents who are holding the reality of connection on Earth to be present for them.

I must include a few examples of children I have worked with who have shown signs of being developed beyond what we think is appropriate behavior for their age. They are truly old, advanced Souls who have come specifically at this time to be living examples of what it is to live from a place of maintaining spiritual connection while enjoying the adventures of being in a physical body. They remind us that the Universe is well aware of what is at work here at this time and will assist to bring this Earth into alignment with its Original Blueprint in whatever way it can. Many unseen factions are aiding us in bringing this alignment. One known faction is the appearance of these children of such clarity and Love who are here to intensify reconnection at this time.

In the following paragraphs I have described some of the magical qualities of these dear children. As we honor their gifts, our lives will be rewarded manifold.

When Quinn was one-and-a-half years old his parents were having an argument and his mother lost control of her emotions. It was an intensity level hard for any adult to take. But not for Quinn. He simply said to his mom with conviction, "Mama, go." Guess who knows how to be in command of his world in an effective way for all involved!

At two, Quinn was downstairs with his dad. Upstairs his mom

called down to her husband to ask him to come and get a large spider out of the room for her. Quinn pushed past his dad swiftly, ran upstairs and into the closet where the spider now was, and said bravely, "Show me where the spider is. I'll get it."

At age four, Keifer is very in tune with animals and seems to get strong intuitive feelings from them. When a neighbor's dog was sick (she ended up dying the next day), Keifer spent time with her, laying down and talking to her. He was so sad that whole evening that he couldn't eat. He didn't eat until late the next morning. He was very sad the entire next day too. He knew what was going on and was completely attuned to the death cycle of this little animal that had just died. It was remarkable.

Soul Families

The following sections are designed to help you uncover your Soul heritage. There are many ways to discern your Soul's makeup: intuition, applied kinesiology (muscle testing), or divining (also called dowsing) with a pendulum—there are many books on the topics of using intuition, applied kinesiology, or divining. I have taught classes in kinesiology and using a pendulum. Arlen Bock, who originated this material, is an expert in teaching the art of divining to access the Akashic Records. His name is referenced in the back of the book, along with the names of other books that teach the use of kinesiology and a pendulum.

The key in gathering the information about your Soul heritage is to stay lighthearted and at ease in yourself when discerning the message of the Akashic Records for your Soul. Trust that your Soul will give you all the information or guidance you need to find those who can assist you. Enjoy the process and keep it fun. The Universe supports you wholeheartedly.

As you read about the various Soul Families, your own heart and Soul will feel a resonance that comes from feeling seen and known. Your heart and Soul will smile to feel "your language" or your heritage being spoken of. Being able to see, feel, and be with your roots, your lineage, "your people" who understand the foundational pieces that make up who you are and what you are here to gift is truly exhilarating.

Most of us have a primary Soul Family that we have spent substantial time with before coming here and that correlates to a particular star system or Universe. Some Souls are quite gypsy-like and have explored quite a few of the places that I am describing. Each one's path is unique. How much time you have spent in each existence varies, and how much influence it has on your Soul makeup also varies greatly. The slices of the pie that comprise you are the riches that you have to uncover and bring to this world.

The qualities that all Soul families bring are a part of the Original Blueprint. That is why these particular Soul characteristics were called upon. They are being brought forth to be reintroduced to the world's expression, as many have been lost or minimized. It became time to call upon assistance from beyond this world to remember and return this world to the hands of light.

We may not feel that we are fully conscious or working actively with all the qualities and gifts we bring from our Soul worlds, but they are still held inexplicably within our Soul for us to draw upon.

Many people have come here with a Soul heritage from a few different star systems or worlds. The combination truly shapes their gifts and who they are. All the pieces of the Soul portrait work together to a specific end for each individual's incarnation. You will find that you may be dominantly of one particular lineage, but have a smaller percentage of influence from another Soul world. From the many readings I have done, there seem to be no two Souls with exactly the same Soul characteristics, which makes perfect sense in the scheme of the vastness of creation.

To touch the qualities of your home worlds is like taking a journey home. It gives you the opportunity to discover the truest, most authentic way to approach life here for the life fulfillment you want. Your Soul knows what this looks like! As you reconnect with the energy field of your home world, you allow your heart and Soul's purposes to be recatalyzed into existence within your very cells of experience. It opens the door for you to ignite *you* in the largest sense.

You may feel connection to the qualities of many of the star systems named. Remember, they are all descriptions of aspects of spirit. We hold the codes to the truth of all these elements within the seed of our Soul essence. These Soul characteristics are penetrating this Earth plane for healing and recollection. To return to the Original Blueprint here we must be in touch with all these aspects of spirit and integrate them as part of our life blood.

If you find that you come from a combination of Soul Families, you might decide that you are dominantly from one particular heritage and, secondarily, you have strong ties to another heritage. You can check the percentages from each, or just find which has a dominance and sub-dominance. For example, you may discover that you resonate highly with the Hadarian world and sense you have a connection to the Soul characteristics of the Mintakan world. Sense, perceive, and discern as best as you can what heritage and Soul Family characteristics bring you a feeling of purpose and fulfillment and describe how you love to embody your expression here. It's your gifts, talents, and resources for you to freely access and share. Many have asked me what is beyond the star systems and Parallel universes that I discuss as our Soul Families in the following chapters. Where did we reside before coming through these worlds or into this solar system? Thus far, what

I have found is that beyond these universes is what we might describe as pure existence. Beyond these worlds that hold enough physicality for the presence of form are vast spaces for the dimensions of existence that many Souls have had direct experience with. We speak often of the realm of peace as a desirable state. Ecstasy or wholeness, deep senses of well-being, infinite presence, or oneness with all that is are states of being or existence we aspire to. We would not aspire to them if we did not know at a Soul level that they exist and are attainable. These spaces of existence beyond the Parallel universes are filled with these essences that we long to know as real. Peace, Love, and joy are all essences out of which universes have been created to further embody and give dimension of creative form to these essences.

We all started as unique Soul essences and have taken on various dimensions of creation such as the opportunity to know wholeness or peace or self-sufficiency, etc., as we have moved along in the realm of creation. These attributes that we have chosen to acquire help define the nature of our Soul and its color and purpose.

Before we came into this solar system, we spent time in various existences to bring the dynamics of peace or oneness, etc., to be a part of our Soul nature. That is what we did before coming into this Universe. Here, we are to give form to these qualities of spirit in a form that we know exists in the star systems of habitation that I have described.

I have touched the richness of experience of that "starting" point of being a pure Soul essence for myself and with various clients. From that space there is a sense of the vastness of possibility of creation that is exquisite. So to attempt to put all our Soul experiences into definable boxes is impossible. And at the same time I have seen how deeply satisfying it has been for the many I have worked with to understand something more of the depth and breadth of the nature of their Soul lineage that I am defining in the pages of this book. It is describable and indescribable at the same time.

My wish is that your very opening of the pages of this book will allow you to wholeheartedly access the gifts of your Soul lineage that you have generously brought with you. As you uncover the knowledge through the Akashic Records of your Soul dimensions, who knows what doors of knowledge beyond what is contained within this book will be discovered and revealed. I trust that the next level of existence of the beauty of creation will unfold to be birthed here through all of us.

Soul Families Journey Here

Whether we signed up to be here for many lifetimes or just a few, whether we came simply to be part of the adventure of the experience of life that is unique to this world, or whether we are on a planetary mission to change humankind or to help heal this world so it may return to being governed by Love, we are continually connected to the universal essences of wholeness. We are powerful beyond our wildest dreams.

Here on planet Earth there has been a tremendous loss of that connection. It is now the season to remove our Akashic Record amnesia, restore our collective Soul memory banks, and end this Soul memory cloud of disconnection.

All major religions have their own story of what is termed in the Bible as "The Fall," when disconnection to Love as the source of our existence in life occurred to such an extent that there was more darkness (the absence of Light) than Light, as the ruling power. This was a collective choice to buy into powers of destruction (fear, greed, power over others, war, survival vs. creation, etc.).

This "Fall" began when human beings came as a civilization to consciously bring a Blueprint to the Earth based on Love and divinity and to give it expression through life here. This was designed to be a conscious experience of divinity through human form—life as the embodiment of divine Love. Because of free will, human beings opted to inhabit existence here without the component of divine connection. Humans who chose to delete this divine connection created personal agendas and irresponsible choices, unaligned with a higher purpose. Those who didn't betray Light and the choice for Light realized that assistance was needed to bring a greater remembrance here for the choice of Light and all the qualities of spiritual expression that come with that. Light beings here could not force others to see that their choices were selfish and not aligned with Light. Because of free choice, we can only inspire others to choose Light; we cannot override individual will.

So, reconnection to our Creator purposes and the universal picture that Earth was a part of was essential. The Light beings here worked with many beings to call on assistance toward an outcome of highest good for the whole solar system. These beings comprised what is called the Solar Council for they were responsible for the Soul movement and collective purpose of all that occurs within this solar system. Thus, the process of introducing advanced Souls from other star systems to come here to assist the Earth to get back on track through free choice began.

After "The Fall," around 250,000 BC, the first group of Souls were called on. They came from the parent planet for Earth. This planet is Artuvia, from the star system that includes Mintaka. This is the third star up in Orion's belt. This is how it began.

Each star system described in the following chapters contains a planet where the Souls actually exist in forms somewhat similar to Earth human form. This made it easier for them to translate their existence here if the form didn't have to shift dramatically to do so. Each group of Souls from the various star systems brought specific spiritual characteristics that are vital to the healing of this world and that are the characteristics and qualities that are the specific gifts of each group.

Soul Contracts

Our Souls make contracts and agreements before each incarnation based on our Soul's ambitions and the desire to make certain contributions in this life. This can be a contract we make to create a certain impact as it relates to a career or love relationship in our life. This may be for growth or to magnify our gift with another from our Soul Family.

A young Soul may only want to learn how to master the combination of the physical, mental, emotional, and spiritual experience on Earth. This would be in the contract for incarnation. A more ambitious Soul may have many agreements and plans that they have set up ahead of time with a council of beings that are on hand for that purpose. One aspect of Soul contracts applies to the strong connections we have with those in our own Soul lineage. These contracts are designed to strengthen the nature of our Soul's mastery in this incarnation. They may be respected for the great spiritual influences and rewards they can deliver.

This is an extraordinary time to witness people from the same Soul Families joining as intimate partners, close friends, co-workers, or family members. You may feel a remarkable depth of Soul resonance with many precious individuals. But beware of trying to make intimate exchanges with those we have Soul connections with, out of misidentifying these shared purposes with romantic feelings. It is not unusual these days, even if you are happily married, to feel star struck by another individual. It is a Soul connection and you literally do have a star connection. You may have merged energetically with that Soul in another star system and agreed to come together into this world to combine forces in healing this planet. There are many of us Lightworkers here at this time. We are true Soul brothers and sisters, unified by divine Love. You will feel seeds of sacred union. The body feels that. Be heartful in letting this Soul union feed your Soul destiny plans and not just your physical urges to know connection and union to divine Love.

I have worked with a number of people, each with unique stories on this score, and the people involved are so relieved to receive a clear perspective and act from this clear place in their interchange. It is much more fulfilling than the immediate gratification of an inappropriate exchange. For example, Diane came to me to ask about her attraction to Eric, a co-worker at the hospital she worked in. At first, they began by having uniquely stimulating conversations during break times. Then he asked her to join him for lunch in the hospital cafeteria. She was smitten by the ease and depth between them. Back at home was her husband and their child.

There was nothing wrong in the family, but since their child was born three years ago, a certain spark between Diane and her husband, Stacy, had smoldered in the throws of diapers and exhaustion. So her exchanges at work with Eric felt refreshing and revitalizing. She could easily have taken this attraction to immediate gratification. I described to her the genuine Love-filled, and purpose-oriented connection she had with Stacy. Their connection was a very old and dear one. Her contract with him spanned many lifetimes of being together and provided a place for healing and growth in an enduring, foundational way. At the same time, I described her deep Soul Family connection with Eric and their agreement to ignite greater life here together. He showed up to ignite her Light in every aspect of her life and thus her remembrance of her brightness. She was not meant to take that igniting force Eric brought and share it exclusively with him.

Understanding the nature of her Soul connections and contracts helped her immensely. She was able to sustain a friendship with Eric without getting overly involved, and she was able to deepen her connection with her husband, which was the most valuable place for her to deepen the flourishing of her Soul.

My wish for each of us is that we may be able to honor all of our Soul contracts in this life, for the purpose of magnifying our Soul purpose or to complete what we agreed in our Soul we would carry out.

Throughout the next chapters you will have the opportunity to connect more deeply with what your soul strengths are so that you may bring greater light of understanding to your Soul's perspective. This will help you to see your world and all of your relationships from the eyes of your Soul.

Astrology Map of Soul Family Star System Locations

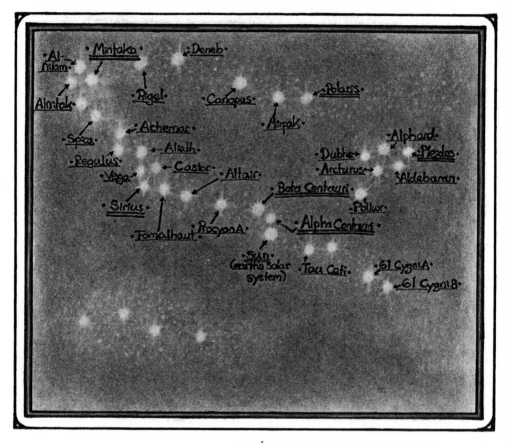

Hadar is the planet within the star system of Beta Centauri

2

Soul Family Overview

Soul Family Proclamations

Earther:

Life is to be lived.

Blueprint Originator:

The Blueprint is present, always. I hold its truth sacred and embody its manifestation in my life.

Blueprint Translator:

I am here to bring Love as creation into life. There is always a way.

Blueprint Deliverer:

I have come to bring life in its abundance.

Mintakan:

I am Light and Light is all there is. I am here to bring Light as the only choice for life.

Polarian:

I am whole. Wholeness exists because I am here.

Pleiadian:

Just do it.

Sirian:

There is a better way.

Hadarian:

Love is the essence of life and creation.

Alpha Centaurian:

I am here. I have always been here. I will always be here. I am Creator source for my world.

Parallels:

I am in sacred union with the all that is.

The Soul Heritage of Some Well Known People

Blueprint Deliverer

Oprah Winfrey

Nelson Mandela (also Blueprint Originator)

Bill Gates (also Sirian)

John F. Kennedy (40% Alpha Centauri)

Martin Luther King (also Blueprint Originator and Alpha Centauri)

Paul Newman

Martha Stewart (50% Alpha Centauri)

Mick Jagger

Al Pacino

Jesus (also Blueprint Originator)

Buddha (also Blueprint Originator)

Michael Moore

Mickey Mantle

Blueprint Translator

Eckhart Tolle (author of *The Power of Now*)

Dean Martin

Benjamin Franklin

Mintakan

Mel Gibson

Goldie Hawn

Meg Ryan

Ron Woods (Rolling Stones)

Paul McCartney

Tom Brokaw

Elvis Presley (50% Blueprint Deliverer)

Polarian

Kevin Costner

George Harrison (Beatles)

Johnny Depp (also Parallel)

Bonnie Raitt

Tom Hanks (40% Sirian)

Kevin Bacon

Louis Armstrong

Bette Midler

Jimmy Carter

Sammy Sosa

Pleiadian

Jim Carrey

Robin Williams

Jack Nicholson

Angelina Jolie (40% Parallel)

Dustin Hoffman

Keith Richards (Rolling Stones)

Ringo Starr

David Letterman

Kevin Kline

Michael Jordan (also Sirian)

Arnold Palmer

Sirian

Christopher Reeve

Brad Pitt

Steven Spielberg

Joan of Arc

Eleanor Roosevelt

Halle Berry

Susan Sarandon

Woody Allen

Bill Gates

Warren Beatty

Frank Sinatra

Magic Johnson (also Blueprint Deliverer)

Wilt Chamberlain (also Alpha Centauri)

Babe Ruth (also Pleiadian)

Hank Aaron (also Sirian)

Wayne Gretsky

Jack Nicklaus

Joe Montana (also Polaris)

Joe Namath (also Pleiadian)

Hadarian

Julia Roberts

Gwyneth Paltrow

Goldie Hawn (also Mintakan)

Princess Diana

Mary Magdalene

Marilyn Monroe (40% Parallel)

Barbra Streisand

Elizabeth Taylor

Jennifer Aniston

Penelope Cruz (40% Mintakan)

Mother Teresa

Alpha Centauri

Sting

Robert Redford

Martha Stewart

Richard Gere

Barbara Walters

Gandhi

George Washington

Dustin Hoffman (40% Blueprint Deliverer)

Bruce Springsteen (also Sirian)

Tom Cruise (40% Blueprint Deliverer)

Colin Farrell

Jude Law

Clint Eastwood

Hilary Swank (also Sirian)

Morgan Freeman (also Pleiadian)

Byron Katie

Larry Byrd

John Elway (also Blueprint Deliverer)

Archie Manning

Peyton Manning (also Sirian)

Elijah Manning (also Sirian)

Parallel

J.R. Tolkien

Peter Jackson (producer of *Lord of the Rings*)

Elijah Woods (Frodo in *Lord of the Rings*)

Charlize Theron

Russell Crowe

Diane Keaton

Michael Jackson

Meryl Streep

Tina Turner

Nicole Kidman

Anthony Hopkins

John Lennon

Michelangelo

Leonardo da Vinci

Picasso

Thomas Jefferson (40% Mintakan)

Deepak Chopra

Eckhart Tolle (author of *The Power of Now*)

John Nash (his story: *A Beautiful Mind*)

Here is a description of famous groups and how their Souls are designed to work together in bringing a variety of Soul ingredients to the mix.

Beatles:
> John Lennon: Parallel; Zophkiel Realm
> Paul McCartney: Blueprint Deliverer, Mintakan, Hadarian; Raphael Realm
> George Harrison: Polaris; Michael Realm
> Ringo Starr: Pleiadian; Kamiel Realm

Rolling Stones:
> Mick Jagger: Blueprint Deliverer, Pleiadian; Zadkiel Realm
> Keith Richards: Pleiadian, Parallel; Kamiel Realm
> Ron Woods: Mintakan; Gabriel Realm
> Charlie Watts: Alpha Centauri; Michael Realm

Cast of the T.V. show "Friends"
> David Schwimmer (Ross): Blueprint Deliverer and Translator; Zophkiel Realm
> Jennifer Aniston (Rachel): Hadarian; Kamiel Realm
> Matthew Perry (Chandler): Polaris; Zadkiel Realm
> Matt LeBlanc (Joey): Mintakan; Michael Realm
> Courteney Cox (Monica): Pleiadian; Raphael Realm
> Lisa Kudrow (Phoebe): Parallel and Mintakan; Gabriel Realm

Archangel Realms
Michael

Paul Newman	Michelangelo
George Harrison	George Washington
Bruce Springsteen	Sting

Michael Moore   Al Pacino

Richard Gere   Tom Cruise

Gabriel

Nelson Mandela   Robin Williams

Jim Carrey   Michael Jackson

Oprah Winfrey   Bette Midler

Tina Turner   Louis Armstrong

Barbra Streisand   David Letterman

Raphael

Meg Ryan   Marilyn Monroe

Charlize Theron   Courteney Cox

Julia Roberts   Dean Martin

Auriel

Goldie Hawn   Princess Diana

Mother Teresa

Zophkiel

Kevin Costner   John Lennon

Buddha   Thich Nhat Hanh

Tom Hanks   Kevin Bacon

Eckhart Tolle

Zadkiel

Bill Gates   Mick Jagger

Madonna   Robert Redford

Brad Pitt   Christopher Reeve

Gwyneth Paltrow   Susan Sarandon

Elizabeth Taylor   Jack Nicholson

Diane Keaton   Benjamin Franklin

Kamiel

Bill Clinton   Johnny Depp

Barbara Walters   Martha Stewart

John F. Kennedy   Martin Luther King

Jennifer Aniston   Ringo Starr

Halle Berry   Angelina Jolie

Russell Crowe   Frank Sinatra

3

THE EARTH BLUEPRINT

E arth is the only place in this Universe that has the array of life forms that we live amongst and that we often take for granted. It is the only planet based on multidimensionality of creation as spirit consciously experiencing physical expression as life. We create here through the physical, mental, emotional, and spiritual realms simultaneously. This is a unique formula in this galaxy. This design for a way of embodying Love was meant originally to be an extremely expansive, advanced form of creation. This design is the Earth Blueprint.

Those fortunate enough to have traveled into the vastness of space have touched the universal consciousness that prevails, of indescribable Light, freedom, and endless creative possibility. The experience of weightlessness is the same quality as freedom in Light. They have felt what is possible when Light truly streams through this human form, and it is open to the force of multidimensional creation. We may have felt the same thing when we are in Love with our experience of life and feel light as a feather. Seeing a newborn child for the first time, a mother's physical exhaustion from giving birth disappears completely when she touches the spirit and life-affirming essence of her newborn child. Listening to a piece of music that we resonate deeply with allows us to transcend any feelings of pain, physical or emotional, to a sense of connection to the free space of creation that the music comes from. Music as a vehicle for connection unites us with all the freedom in creation that we sense lies in the vastness of space. That same vast-ness is the abundance of life that is waiting at our fingertips for us to partake in.

The Earth Blueprint is marked by abundance and diversity, a small slice of which you see in a city aquarium, from gorgeous rainbow cor-als to an umbrella-shaped transparent jelly fish to sea dragons that look like fans of fern-shaped bodies with a seahorse head and cute snout to humpback whales with their powerful and majestic presence. The world beneath the waves is an incredible testimony to the abundance of life forms this Earth carries within its Blueprint. Then we have the endless panorama of landscape on the surface of the Earth. And the portraiture of life's exquisite artistry in motion captured in a brief glimpse of a Hawaiian sunset, fog over Big Sur, Mt. Kilimanjaro in a sea of clear blue sky. There is endless creation through nature here, no doubt about it. What an experiment in creation this natural world holds like no other planet in existence. It is no surprise that so many Souls from other worlds said they would come and participate here, when they had a bird's eye view of the bounty of creation they could co-mingle with, even in Earth's crazy, mixed-up state.

Earth Blueprint Codes

The Earth world carries a Blueprint for exploring creation through the heart and Soul. What is the Blueprint for Love moving as life in form? Joy. We experience the dimension of joy when we feel alive and engaged in life. We feel peace as the satisfaction of embodying Light moving through our heart and Soul all the way into our physi-cal experience.

Light moving through the power of the physical expression is physical enlightenment. Think of seeing the Olympics, or the magic of a team sport, or the grace and excellence of dancing—whether it's the tango, hip-hop, or ballet. These are all examples of life's grandeur being expressed through the focus of Light moving through the physical body. Light moving through the physical body is Love embodied as aliveness.

Light moving through the mental realm at its finest is genius and brilliance and also consciousness and vision. The magic of human creation holds this capacity unlike any other. Light moving through the emotional realm gives us the ability to experience creation. We were given six senses through which to experience the feel of life. It is that simple, that glorious. Experiencing the bounty of the feeling of life includes smelling a rose, hearing a bird's song, feeling the ocean breeze, or the water splashing against your skin. How do we know life? It is the experience of Love; it is the experience of joy, peace, and beauty. It is a feeling impression or experience. Our separation from the connection to Love felt as life or aliveness moves us into the perceived need to create emotional response to our experience of separation.

The Wound of Separation and Betrayal

Can you imagine what your life might have been like if your spiritual connection was kept intact from day one? You would not have had to spend your whole life seeking the means for reconnecting and, at the same time, healing all your wounds from being disconnected. From my years of experience as a psychotherapist and spiritual counselor, it is obvious to me that as we heal the primary wound of separation and betrayal, which is what we feel when we separate from Creator source, all our other wounds melt away. Betrayal is self-betrayal. We have actually betrayed our heart, Soul, and divine mission and connection to Creator when we disconnect from that original force-field we were birthed from. When we feel betrayed in any aspect of our life, we usually say that someone else betrayed us. If we are willing to look more deeply into what is occurring we will see that we first betrayed our own integrity of spirit moving through our heart and this is what caused the result of the outer painful situations. Owning this is no small thing, and it does allow us to say to ourselves and guides while in the situation, "Please help me to reconnect with our Creator's Love and my union with that source of life. And please help me return to the Blueprint for my Soul destiny plan for this incarnation and this aspect of my life function."

Our Individual Blueprint

We each created a Blueprint for our life before coming here that was and is foundational to our life movement. It is in place. It is simply up to us to continually align with the intention to make choices from our heart and Soul, aligned with the Blueprint we created before coming here. Hold this prayerful intention and what doesn't fit will unravel and dissolve to create space for the higher path of your Soul's destiny plans to unfold.

Simply put, the basic Blueprint for life was originally based on the six senses and the experience of life through those senses.

In the movie *City of Angels,* Nicolas Cage portrayed an angel who came to Earth and tasted what it was like to experience life: the smell of the morning air over the ocean, the sensation of sunlight on his face, the touch of joy known with Meg Ryan as his lover, the taste of a fresh raspberry off the vine, the sight of a flock of birds in perfect formation migrating south for the winter. All of this, even the sensation of the loss of Meg Ryan, was worth it to Nicolas Cage. These were rich experiences of Light moving as life that he and his friends as angels were not able to have without engaging fully in the human experience. Nicolas Cage, even though he felt the sensation of loss of Love through Meg Ryan's death, chose to embrace life, which carries a vast array of Love in its very essence of creation. He relished the sensation of true longing. He loved the sound of his own laughter reverberating through his body: the joy of being alive! He made a choice to be mortal to experience the Earth Blueprint of Love manifesting into the abundance of life.

All these qualities that we work hard to have in a lifetime were part of the Original Blueprint. Why would we say we want to know Love, joy, serenity, ecstasy, peace, if they were not possible to have, or if they were not coded in our Blueprint to be part of the actual DNA for life here?

Our Spiritual Nature

The Blueprint did include telepathy and natural intuition as part of what we now call our spiritual nature. Intuition and telepathy were the means to connect and commune with our Creator and larger fields of creation that we are a part of. Communication was designed as a means to share our unique experiences of communion with all of creation in each moment. Communication was one of the original reasons for the mental capacity. To communicate takes a frequency of output and input of conscious awareness. We have discovered that dolphins are very advanced in their ability to communicate through frequency exchange. Doesn't it make sense that we humans of supposed higher intelligence also originally had the capacity to communicate as dolphins do in an even more sophisticated manner?

Love in the Blueprint is the variety of the expressions of Love manifesting in creation. Is a dog's Love for his owner not a rich experience of unconditional love? Is a rose blooming in the sunlight not a rich expression of Creator Love? Is the Sun's infinite unwavering presence not an expression of divine Love's continual outpouring? The Sun shines no matter what evidence of separation from it exists on the surface of this planet, be it revealed in hatred, war, fear, or suffering of any kind. Is the Sun's relentless, infinite presence not an expression of divine Love that life may constantly flourish no matter what wars or sorrows are occurring on the surface of the planet?

Our Creator is so in Love that creation continually expands and multiplies the expression of Love. Life on planet Earth is a huge example of the possibility for this endless array of the creation of Love.

Love's creation moving through the design of the Earth Blueprint is our collective purpose here. We were all given the ability to access the codes of the Blueprint for creation. It is within our DNA and Soul memory bank. Opening to the Akashic Records of our Soul allows us to access these very codes and awaken to the remembrance of our unique Soul purpose here.

4

EARTHER

Life is to be lived.

Star System Location: Planet Earth

Soul Characteristics:

* Earth is your home world.
* You have come to experience life through body, mind, and spirit as this is the only place in the Universe where this is possible.
* You are here to allow the Divine Blueprint for life on Earth to manifest.
* You are happily invested in this world with all its beauty and challenges.

The majority of the population of this world of Earth beings are Earthers. You are Souls who have come to simply experience the Original Divine Blueprint in manifestation as it was designed to be. This is what you signed up to do. This was a choice. As Souls this is the only world you have inhabited as a human form. This is the only world you know as Souls. Your Soul journey would equate to being born, growing up, and dying within one county. You are younger Souls in depth and breadth of experience in this larger solar system, but you are very well versed on the Earth plane. This is all you signed up for and know. You have not had experience in other worlds and dimensions even though you have had many lifetimes here. You are not the galactic travelers that other Soul Families are. You may have been here on Earth for many lifetimes of incarnations. You agreed since the beginning of human habitation, as we know it here, to come here to experience the unification of body, mind, and spirit. You came to fill out what the Blueprint for creation can be at this level of existence. You came to bring a conscious, experiential physicality to the nature of spirit, expressing itself through individual human forms as part of a collective expression of this design for life here on planet Earth. You came to reveal what life would be like to create through this four-dimensional reality on an expanded, ever-evolving basis. You hold the capacity to do all of this.

Moving Out of Alignment with the Blueprint

You Earthers may have existed as Soul essences in other forms for thousands of years, but coming to Earth is your first experience of incarnating in a human form. Because this is such a new experience for you and for the Earth energy field experiment within this galaxy, there were a number of mistakes made. It was all so new! Mix that newness into the dynamic of free choice and there exists much room for experimentation and endless possibilities for creation—and the potential for moving out of alignment with the Original Blueprint into the realms of attraction and the tantalizing influence of greed and illusion.

Earthers have had to learn by experience and trial and error, which can have unfavorable but innocent consequences. Another level of so-called mistake comes into effect when we cease listening to our internal compass for truth and listen instead to another's truth as if it is more valuable than ours. We fail to see that another's truth may be their personal agenda to take advantage of our openness to outside sources for our life blood.

The Earth beings who were here from the beginning of human habitation had already chosen to participate in a certain level of separation from our Creator as their power source. This internal state of separation consequently became an area of weakness within them.

They felt the innate sense of separation and began to look outside themselves to re-establish this connection that they longed for in their Soul. Looking outside themselves for this connection to life was the first choice that created further separation.

We as humans are designed to hold spiritual source within ourselves to ignite our very heart and Soul movement in life, so seeing someone outside ourselves as responsible for holding spiritual connection for us creates an even larger chasm of separation from our spirit and Soul.

Earth beings began to imagine that others held a source for spiritual power that they didn't feel they possessed. Allowing another to be their power source magnified the illusion that another could "play God." Hence, the distortion in power grew. Those who "play God" take on a false power that can increasingly be fueled by fear, a sense of powerlessness, greed, and overall personal agenda. Separation increases collectively.

It's okay for human beings to experiment in the realm of free choice. But when these choices are not aligned with our intuitive connection to Source, the consequences become increasingly detrimental and reinforce the power of disruption that comes through those who hold themselves deliberately separate from Light as their Source.

This is in fact what began to happen here to the human world. Charismatic leaders of deception became a huge faction of power. Decisions were increasingly made based on separation and fear, creating a world focused on war and survival. Separation became a given part of the larger energy field here. Making choices based only on Light as part of the Blueprint was forgotten and lost. Making choices as individuals disconnected from Source and making choices as a collective based on letting in the influence of frequencies outside of Light became increasingly possible. These choices based on the power of the influence of dark agendas such as fear, greed, and personal addictions carried the illusion of being more powerful and therefore looked like better choices. This is what was described as "The Fall," in the Bible. Every religion, every myth, every culture has its own description of how separation infiltrated into the consciousness and behavior of the human species. This primary wound of separation has left this civilization largely in the hands of those operating in fear and the desire to destroy, not create, life.

The Influence of Polarity

What we term polarity is a real phenomena in the world. We can easily see how it works in the science of our world. There is a positive electrical charge and a negative electrical charge, which, when combined, ignite the phenomena of electrical current. There are the polar opposites of night and day, bringing a sense of balance to the creative cycle of a day. There is the sky above and the Earth below. These are all examples of the truth of polarity at work to bring balance into the expanded fields of creation.

But the true dynamic of polarity became distorted, which brought in the agenda of one side of the coin being good and therefore the other bad or evil. This increased the opening for judgment and opposition. There was meant to be a vast diversity in the expression of creation here, but this diversity was to be unified in the wholeness of our Creator's original intention for each Soul coming here. Thus, creation's expression could expand endlessly without being in opposition to any other aspect of the diversity of creation.

The distortion of polarity did give rise to the assumption that conflict was part of diversity. This created a larger welcome mat for the influence of conflictual agendas from sources outside the Earth's energy field. These disruptive influences that Earthers allowed in were not favorable to maintaining or redeveloping the Original Divine Blueprint.

Those Souls who have chosen to populate this planet to bring living experience to the Earth Blueprint, who I am calling Earthers, are invested in this planet. You continue to return here, which is proof of your investment and commitment. You may not hold the place of conscious leadership for this world's direction, but you are dedicated to simply being in this world and being a part of the energy field that is healing these mistakes and distortions such as polarity. Your presence is very useful. You make up the ship of mankind that the Soul Families from other worlds can work with to steer this Earth existence back to the Original Blueprint for our planet.

The Gifts of the Earther

Earthers primarily live from a simple physical experience. This is your focus. Are you lacking a spiritual side? Farmers who are dedicated to tilling the soil, planting the crops, producing the food that allows the human population to thrive are a tremendous gift to our world. This is truly a service and contribution. This is the pumping of the farmer's life blood. What a farmer does in his simple acts, for instance, is the very manifestation of the creation of life, which is the essence of spiritual expression through human form. The Earther Soul Family came here to be the fertile soil for the Blueprint. A musical performance or concert calls for an audience to give it meaning and magnification. The fruits and berries are Mother Nature's gifts, and utilizing those natural gifts fulfills the cycles of life. Any expression of spirit, be it through a sunset, the joy of giving birth, or a humanitarian act of kindness, is given a sense of divinity through our receptivity and appreciation. Earthers are a vessel for the expression of the Divine in this experiment called living as Love. Earthers are here doing life. That is their purpose. They are here to seed life and give life creative expression. We can feel their vibration embodied through the example of the drumbeat of the North American Indian. For the Indians life is seen as a sacred ritual. They would drum in honor of Father Sky and Mother Earth. They are dedicated to this world's welfare. They do not have a galactic focus of consciousness. That is not their purpose. Theirs is a treasured contribution to the sustaining of the heartbeat of this Earth. What a rich and valuable part they carry here.

Earthers are most likely to be the ones who primarily love to express themselves through the physical realm, be it working hard at a job or task, playing a team sport, enjoying outdoor activities, or relishing family life as a focus for being here. This is natural for those Souls who deliberately choose to birth life here. For example, as an Earther, you may be very creative with your hands—an excellent example of life excelling through the physical capacity. You may very likely be interested in academics as a teacher or student, with a quest for knowledge and learning everything there is to know about planet Earth. You may be a scientist and researcher who loves to explore life in all its facets. You may be a marine biologist who focuses your collective fascination with the variety of life forms under the sea.

This is not to say that those Souls who did not come here to function as Earthers are not also interested in all these realms and the joy of all these realms. Other Souls coming here to assist in bringing this world back to its Original Blueprint will enjoy the fruits of this world, but will be primarily invested in a higher level of bringing consciousness and spiritual well-being to life expression while enjoying the gifts of this amazing world.

The Misinterpretation of the Blueprint

We were meant to exist as spiritual beings consciously experiencing physicality. This has become a physical world run by a reactive and fear-based emotional state. Physical prowess has been mostly used for war and gaining power over others. We have learned the art of fighting to get our way and achieve our personal agenda. Even sporting events have become highly competitive and brutal. And the realm of consciousness has been widely used to plot against and prove how one race or group is better or worse than another. This is how vision has turned into a state of judgment, which creates separation, not oneness and connection.

Earthers Are Here to Establish Creation

We still have the choice to use the gifts of having the six senses through which to experience this magnificent creation called life. That has never gone away as an option even in the midst of so much war and conflict. We always have a choice. Isn't it great sometimes to simply hang out on the beach and enjoy the richness of life through all the senses? Don't you relish those moments when you simply feel a part of the beauty of the Earth below and the sky above: gazing at the stars or watching the people of this world in all their variety of colors of expression. These are the experiences that the Earthers came here to establish and explore. In coming here to create as human beings, they are indeed having a creative impact on the movement of the universal picture we are all a part of.

Earthers have a specialized version of a Soul purpose. You have been here since the beginning of human habitation on Earth. You came with the explicit purpose of experiencing what it is to live from the physical, mental, emotional, and spiritual dimensions of existence simultaneously. You are Souls who came from various other dimensions of existence before human form. It is not so important for you to know where that is. Your focus and purpose is totally on your life here.

Earthers are very much a part of our Creator's design. You made Soul agreements to come here and do Earth incarnations. As it was depicted in the movie *City of Angels* when Nicolas Cage chose to stay here as a human being rather than just be an angel, witnessing and assisting this world from above, he was opting for the opportunity to experience life to the fullest. Angels don't get to do that. He chose to be part of the Earth realm as an Earther. The Earthers Soul purpose is to create the experience of life in all its facets.

Souls from other star systems have not lived through these four dimensions simultaneously before. This creative possibility for spiritual expression is unique to this Earth plane. So the Earthers are here to teach and show other Soul Families how life can be in the Blueprint equation, especially in relationship to physical and emotional realms of expression, which are the most foreign to those from as far away as Hadar, Alpha Centauri, and Parallel worlds. At the same time, Earthers are learning from the advanced Soul Families how to return spiritual dimensions into their physical existence. Therefore, there is a beautiful exchange of purpose between the Earthers and the Soul Families who have come to bring life into alignment with its Original Blueprint.

The Earther Proclamation: Life is to be lived!

5

EARTH BLUEPRINT
ORIGINATOR

*The Blueprint has always been here and is present
now. I hold its truth sacred and embody its
manifestation in my life.*

Star System Location: Various worlds beyond this one.

Soul Characteristics:

* You are here to bring the Divine Blueprint for the Earth into form.
* You guide the Earthers and the Soul Families from other star systems in returning this Blueprint here.
* You carry the Blueprint for embodying spirit consciously and experiencing creation through physical form.
* You are magical, creative, and deeply wise.
* You see the beauty of life everywhere.
* You are at home in your own skin while being very advanced Souls.
* Being on a Soul mission is as natural as breathing for you.

Blueprint Originators are actually Earth Blueprint Originators. You are the ones who came to seed the Divine Blueprint for this world. You came from our Creator and worked with a Blueprint Council of Beings to design the Blueprint for life in this world. You have come from various worlds beyond this one, and your specialty has always been in originating dimensions of creation wherever you are. You came here to plant seeds for the creation of multidimensional expression of human form held in the codes of this Original Earth Blueprint. What would life look and feel like in human experience through the eyes, the heart, the mind, the body of one holding the codes for this Blueprint? You have come to remind us that the Original Blueprint is based on multidimensional living: consciousness experiencing spirit through physicality. Light translating into the aliveness of life! This four-dimensional way of experiencing creation is a very advanced one in its original intention. It would be equivalent to going to a graduate school program. So it could be said that all Souls signing up to participate in the Earth field already see themselves as high level Souls wanting to enjoy and master another level of creativity.

The Blueprint Originators Hold the Blueprint for Life

The Blueprint Originators hold the Blueprint for life in its truest form. This translates as life through the prowess of the enlightened physical capacity. This translates as Light moving through the conscious mental capacity to create brilliance of mind and enlightened consciousness. This also translates as Light moving through the experience of life through happiness, joy, and the activation of the six senses. This design for life holds the heart and Soul as divine manifestations of spirit in sacred union with Love, igniting our life force for creation. These are key elements of the Blueprint.

The Blueprint Originators usually only come during times of major potential turning points, such as this one. You were around during the Atlantian Age to help advance this civilization to its original state. You were also here during the time in history of Lemurian civilization, showing us what paradise could look like here. Then there was the Ice Age and the Dark Ages. At times like the Dark Age and the Ice

Age, Blueprint Originators knew that they had to come in to galvanize the true integrity of the Blueprint. You have come to be present at this intense and powerful time so that as so many here are being compelled to make major life choices due to the increase of war, destruction, and natural disasters, the choice to remember the possibility to reconnect to and live from the Blueprint is a loud and clear option. I see these children who are being born now that are Blueprint Originators holding the true essence of connection to universal spirit, no matter what. What a gift of the living example of connection to spirit they are.

As a Blueprint Originator, you came here many millions of years ago. You came from various worlds, and I suspect you have had much experience in other worlds as "start-ups," which led to your qualification to lead the way in bringing the Blueprint here. You obviously have a huge amount of experience with the realm of creation born of your work with our Creator in designing the plan for creation here. You see your commission here as yet another opportunity to birth creation in a new sphere. You are truly midwives. You love creating and facilitating the magic of life wherever you are.

The Origination of Creation Here

The Blueprint Originator gift is in originating dimensions of creation, in the creation of many worlds. You have the ability to hold the codes of the true qualities of life as it was designed in the Blueprint. With this understanding of the Original Blueprint intact, you are able to hold that choice in an extremely valuable way for the rest of us. To return to this Blueprint, which everyone on Earth who is aligned with Light has an agreement to assist with, there has to be a remembrance held of what that Blueprint is. You carriers of the Original Blueprint open the knowledge of remembrance for us all of not only what is possible, but also of how it can be known in life expression. Thank goodness.

You are here to not only create the Blueprint codes and mission but to oversee and guide Earth's evolution, especially at this time. It is essential for you to stay connected to the guidance of the beings from the Blueprint Council, so that the Blueprint remains pure this time.

You Blueprint Originators are challenged by some of the basic ways that we live here. You have a lack of understanding of the need here to create such a separation of the genders, the authoritarian use of power, and the use of fear to motivate life experience, for instance. I believe that though we are all challenged by these distortions, it is pronounced for you because your Souls know what is meant to be true here, and it is confusing to you that here we operate so differently as a collective in this world.

Many Children Coming in Now Are Blueprint Originators

I have not connected with too many true Blueprint Originators. The ones I have met are children. The children who are currently in the age range of eight years and younger and are being called crystal or mystic children have many of the characteristics of the Blueprint Originators.

It appears there is currently a large influx of children that are being born as Blueprint Originators. It is time to re-seed the Blueprint for creation here. There are an increasing number within the body of humanity that are hungry for the codes for creation as never before. This influx also energetically creates a giant leap forward for the advancement of our civilization. These Souls are coming as a collective at a time when our world is open and ready to receive the guidance of the codes for Love to birth the boundless life that we sense in our bones is possible to live.

I had the privilege of working with Keyllan, a six-year-old boy who is a Blueprint Originator. He was able to understand what it is to hold Love in his heart no matter what. That was no small thing, as his life circumstances required him to move away from his mom and grandparents, whom he dearly loved. He learned at an early age that his true family includes all those who love him and he could hold them in his heart wherever he lives geographically. He is wise and understanding of matters of the heart beyond his years. He lives from the place of "Where do I get to create next? I'm not so attached to where and with whom I create, but that I get to create, and that I get to love and let life flourish." He is quite magical and lighthearted. His eyes show what an old Soul he is and how much larger his perspective is than his immediate circumstance. His view is, "How do I help this world remember how life can be? It can be bright and joyful and I can hold a song in my heart. You can choose that way of being in life, too."

Blueprint Originator Souls carry ancient wisdom, even in young bodies, and present themselves as guides and teachers for true life expression. It behooves us to listen and be willing to learn and share ourselves with these elders. As these children are received, seen, and understood, they will be open to be guided by us in the outer patterns of life. We can help them be streetwise, not out of fear, or authoritarian direction, but out of integrity and intelligence. We can let these Souls be "parents" who teach advanced ways of being, while we are "parents" who teach them how to walk in the physical, mental, and emotional realms as they exist now, primed for transformation and transcendence. These elders in young bodies are very patient for they understand life is a creative process of evolution. They are joyful, magical, and bright. They are telepathic, intuitive, and psychic. They have a large understanding and experience of what has happened on planet Earth and what is occurring now. They see the big picture, even though they haven't incarnated into physical form very many times.

They aren't here just to experience life, as the Earthers are. They are here more from a place of spiritual guidance and counseling. They observe and bring codes of the true Blueprint where there are openings. They have watched and guided and held the Blueprint from the invisible realm of being for a long, long time, with endless dedication and devotion. Their dedication and investment is mind boggling!

As I speak of the Blueprint Family of Originators, Translators, and Deliverers, you can tap into and draw on the frequency and qualities of our Blueprint here. It is our time to fully receive the codes for the Original Blueprint based on divine Love. This is a key to the planet's return to its place as a paradise for creation.

The Blueprint Originator Proclamation: The Blueprint has always been here and is present now. I hold its truth sacred and embody its manifestation in my life.

6

Blueprint Translator

I am here to bring Love as creation into life.
There is always a way.

Star System Location: Various worlds beyond this one.

Soul Characteristics:

* You have come to translate the Blueprint codes into forms that work at the human level.
* You are here formulating the Earth Blueprint so it may take form here.
* You love to translate information into understandable formats, be it physical, mental, or spiritual.
* You work to allow the gifts of Souls who come from other worlds to be useful and productive here.
* You are direct, responsible, focused, committed, and dedicated to whatever you put your attention on.

Well Known People:

Eckhart Tolle (author of *The Power of Now*)
Dean Martin
Benjamin Franklin

The Blueprint Translator purpose here is to bring Love and creation together as it would be best formulated for planet Earth. As a Blueprint Translator, you began by taking the raw materials of the design for the Earth Blueprint and discovering ways to translate this design into useable forms for the Blueprint for life to be known here. You then took the design for the Original Blueprint created by Love and gave the translated Blueprint to the next group of Souls who are here to deliver that Blueprint into human experience.

You who are Blueprint Translators are beings who have a deep commitment and dedication to the Earth mission, just like your other three partners of the Blueprint Triplets: the Originators, the Translators, and the Deliverers.

Blueprint Translator Mission

Your mission is the most specific of the three "job descriptions." You are here to formulate the codes for the Earth design so that creation can have form here. Remember the plan for the Earth is unique in combining spirit and physicality with conscious and experiential dimensions to birth creation into life. Like any new language, there must be someone to translate it. Blueprint Translators focus on bringing the Earth Blueprint into reality. You work with translating the Blueprint into frequencies that human beings can understand. You also work with the missions and frequencies of the Soul Families who have come from other worlds to assist here. You are interested in learning how to assist those Souls Families in allowing their gifts and talents to be translated into usable forms for creating abundant life here. You are very dedicated to the future of this world and creating the tools for the development of our future based on the Blueprint for creation specific to this world. As with the other Blueprint groups, the Translators come from various other worlds. They may have been translators in other star systems, or they came here with specific gifts from home worlds and desire to translate those gifts into forms of creation here.

Some of you have signed up just to be Blueprint Translators in this particular lifetime as part of a mission to make sure that what you have brought of your Soul gifts from other worlds have a connected place in this world's evolution.

You are committed to making sure that Love moving into Light and being translated into life remains pure. You keep it from becoming tainted by those from other existences who have personal agendas for the use of divine Love and Creator Light.

How does your life purpose defined as Blueprint Translators translate into daily life movement? You are the ones who excel in passing the baton in a relay race. You take raw ingredients of any creative endeavor and make it into a fantastic, more evolved form of life. Like a baker who combines all the parts to make a cake, or a computer expert who designs programs from information placed on disk to be available at the punch of a few keys on the keyboard.

A Blueprint Translator is very practical. You may actually be interested in foreign language translation or computer design, but more often I have found Translators to be people who are keen to connect spirituality into a form that is highly digestible. This could be for your immediate circle of family and friends or for a planetary cause. Eckhart Tolle, who recently wrote a book called *The Power of Now*, is an excellent example of a Blueprint Translator. He is actually from Parallel universes (see the Parallel universes chapter), and the content of his book reveals those frequencies and spiritual qualities. He signed up in this lifetime to be a Blueprint Translator. Writing his book was the means for the Blueprint of creation that Parallel beings bring to be given voice to so all of us could connect and learn how to live from such high-level realities as the present moment and experience life beyond the emotional body's dictation. It is an excellent book. Eckhart Tolle's use of words to translate the frequencies of the Parallel universes is a prime example of the work of someone operating as a Blueprint Translator.

Soul Characteristics

The primary Soul characteristic of the Blueprint Translator is one of directness and commitment. "We're on it and it's going to happen." You have a job for humankind and your statement to the world is, "We're in this for the duration and making sure it all works out." You are always translating: working things out and getting things into form that will work. Your query continually is, "How is this going to work here; what is the best way to create here?" You are direct, aggressive, and often perfectionistic. You are very responsible individuals, as you care deeply about the mission here being accomplished.

You Blueprint Translators love to find whatever ways you can to get whatever you are interested in into form. This is usually a high mental form of expression. Your chief concern in life is how to get the Blueprint into a usable form. I have a friend who is a Blueprint Translator and is always downloading emails that he receives in case they can be useful to others. He will continually find ways to impart the information he receives from a myriad of sources to others. This is his way of finding ways to bring what is valuable to him into avenues that can be helpful here.

Blueprint Translators' Challenges

The challenge that comes with you as a Blueprint Translator is the misplaced responsibility you feel for the distorted Blueprint we all operate by. The distorted Blueprint, until recently, has been the only design to draw from. In a relay race, if the baton is not successfully passed from one runner to the next, a sense of personal responsibility for the whole team's failure ensues. Many in the beginning of creation here did not successfully deliver the baton of Light. The Blueprint was delivered while you were disconnected from Light and it became distorted. You were caught between a rock and a hard place. You did not have a pure Blueprint to work with. You continue to return to help re-create the Earth Blueprint based on Love, but you can feel impotent in your ability to feel you have a viable job here, without true codes to work with. For example, a house painter would feel quite limited in painting with a child's watercolor brush, knowing that a house-painting brush would put the paint on the house best but wouldn't be available.

You Blueprint Translators can forget your commitment to success, as you are challenged with the feeling of failure and hopelessness due to a sense that the Blueprint is not being understood here and your gift is not being received. We all know those moments when our vision of possibility, our passion to bring something forth, our sharing of our gift is not received in the light of which it was given. This is the challenge for the Translators. It is vital for you to continue to rise to the occasion and see how a situation can work even in the midst of seeming failure. I remind Blueprint Translators who I work with that the codes, in fact, have always been held. When you feel powerless in your ability to know Soul success, it is vital to remember this fact. You can call on your Soul remembrance of the Blueprint codes and ask for those codes to be brought into any situation that feels bereft of truth, which is so vital to you. You must continually declare within yourself that the codes are present and your job is vital.

The movie *Life is Beautiful,* which focused on one man's experience in a concentration camp, is a Light-filled example of the ability to translate even the most horrific situation into beauty and possibility. The phrase "life is beautiful" is a pure code of the Original Blueprint. In the movie, the declaration is "this code can translate to any situation, even the most ghastly and bleak limitations of the concentration camps of World War II.

You Blueprint Translators are here to remind us that there is always the way and means to find the form for allowing Love in creation to be known in life. We all carry in our essence the desire to translate our Soul visions and gifts into forms that serve life and our heart and Soul fulfillment. The dedication, stamina, and commitment to holding this truth can be real for anyone who calls on the energy field of the Earth Blueprint Translators.

The Blueprint Translator Proclomation: I am here to bring Love as creation into life. There is always a way.

7

BLUEPRINT DELIVERER

I have come to bring life in its abundance.

Star System Location: Various worlds beyond this one.

Soul Characteristics:

* You are here to deliver and actualize the Original Divine Blueprint based on Love for this world.
* You carry the Earth Blueprint for creation and are on purpose to ensure the successful fulfillment of this mission.
* You are here to be divine cheerleaders for all you touch.
* You love to activate and enhance the gifts of all you connect with.
* You are optimistic and always see the cup at least half full.
* You know in your being that abundance is the natural state.
* "Life is Beautiful" is your natural radiance.

Well Known People:

Oprah Winfrey

Nelson Mandela (also Blueprint Originator)

Bill Gates (also Sirian)

John F. Kennedy (40% Alpha Centauri)

Martin Luther King (Blueprint Originator and Alpha Centauri)

Paul Newman

Martha Stewart (50% Alpha Centauri)

Mick Jagger

Al Pacino

Jesus (also Blueprint Originator)

Buddha (also Blueprint Originator)

Michael Moore

Mickey Mantle

A Blueprint Deliverer is here to deliver the Blueprint. You have come to make sure that the Blueprint for the Earth manifests, and you are dedicated to this quest with an undeniable sense of mission, purpose, and responsibility. You as a Blueprint Deliverer know the design for the Blueprint. Many Blueprint Deliverers who have been here on planet Earth since the time that the Blueprint was first introduced through human existence hold the design for the Blueprint. This design may be slightly or greatly hidden or buried, or simply not fully accessible because of the challenges faced by the Deliverer's time in this mixed-up world. But the Blueprint is present in your Soul memory bank. As you clear your own path for participation from a Soul level, then the codes for your own Soul fulfillment, and thus the fulfillment of the Blueprint for humanity, will be activated. But first you have to have access to the Blueprint to deliver it.

Your job is to deliver the Blueprint into the physical, mental, experiential, and spiritual realms of human living. Your continual query is, "How do I best bring Love as creation into life?" on an ongoing basis. Often you as Blueprint Deliverers have performed this function of delivering the Blueprint for other worlds. So you are familiar with the general Soul dimension of delivering from your experiences on other planets. Blueprint Deliverers fertilize, feed, and water. You are here to fertilize and bring whatever you can to others, as individuals, groups, or collectives to enhance Soul and heart fulfillment. At a planetary level you are here to fertilize the Original Blueprint for planet Earth so everyone can live abundantly through these codes. You "feed" people and systems to bring forward their greatest success possible. You feed and water all you touch by bringing real nutrients for their growth and advancement. Your greatest desire is to see life flourish for them. You are in love with the beauty of life and see things through these glasses. You see the wonder and magic in even the most horrific of circumstances.

The past New York City mayor, Rudy Giuliani, is another excellent example of a Blueprint Deliverer. After September 11, 2001, when the World Trade Center was destroyed, Mayor Giuliani kept his eye on New York City and held a "life will prevail" focus of strength for rebuilding the city. He focused on providing the nutrients at all levels for life to flourish again no matter how devastating the situation was to so many people. His was a strong statement to the terrorists who tried to bring the country down: Not only will we survive but we will flourish and use our deep compassion for all that was lost to galvanize a community of heart-felt inspiration and rebuild and strengthen what was present. Inside so many people, he ignited a place that fed family, community, and the truth of what America stands for.

Blueprint Deliverer Characteristics

A Blueprint Deliverer sees the cup at least half full, never half empty, and see what is coming together, not falling apart. As a Blueprint Deliverer, you are here for the long haul. You will stick around until you succeed to help the world to live from the basis of the originally intended Blueprint. You have no doubt the world will make it. It is just a beginning. Your optimism and assurance in a healthy outcome is a valuable commodity in this world that carries such a downtrodden and fear-based view of the future.

Blueprint Deliverers hold a strong belief that abundance is our natural birthright. As a Blueprint Deliverer, you know deep in your Soul that this is an abundant Universe and the Blueprint for this world is to be an abundant array of irresistible creations at many levels. This has always been the Blueprint for human beings. You hold the knowledge that anything is possible if divine Love is present. Connection to universal Love will allow anyone to be transformed or anything that is true to be unveiled. This applies to healing at the individual level or the planetary level, whether it's cancer or uncovering and bringing Light to "disease" within systems of government or politics.

The following words come from a client who wanted to experience again the nature of her Soul mission as a Blueprint Deliverer. We took a rich journey together to connect with her Soul mission here.

"I was able to experience the Original Blueprint for this world. At first I found myself holding the encoded memory of the origination of the first Light. I could also feel that there was no reception here for the codes of Light I was bringing. We changed that! Earth was meant to be a home for each one's Light, as it is a home for all of the Light of nature: the Light of each beautiful creature, whether a fish, a giraffe, a dog, or a bluebird. The Earth is home for so very many variations of Light to share themselves in form. There was no room for darkness in the original human body. It was all Light. The physical body is a home for Light as a symbiotic relationship. When I am filled with Light, life is worth living. I actually cherish my life. I will hold Light in all its dimensions no matter what, so I will do my Soul's mission. I see that not holding Light in myself betrays myself and my Soul purpose."

To fertilize and bring forth abundance and success is your Blueprint Deliverer mission. Whatever does not line up with that potential must be naturally flushed away, as simply as water washes away the sand to reveal the pearl inside an oyster shell.

Blueprint Deliverers for This Incarnation

I have found that many of you come from other star systems and worlds but have chosen for this incarnation to carry the purpose of delivering the Blueprint as part of your Soul destiny plan. For instance, you may carry the Soul characteristics of a Mintakan or a Sirian but also hold a portion of characteristics of a Blueprint Deliverer. This usually means you are definitely on a mission to assist planet Earth at this time as a part of a universal picture. You know you have something to do to change the face of humankind. You carry a strong conviction that the Soul lineage and truths you bring from the worlds you were previously in shall be delivered! So if you are checking in on what Soul Family or Families you are a part of, you may find that you carry a small percentage of connection to the Blueprint Deliverers. This just means that you studied the Earth Blueprint before coming and have a strong resonance with making sure this Earth returns to its original intentions as designated in the Blueprint. This may be particularly true for this incarnation as it is such a crucial juncture in Earth and universal history. I have noticed that many Souls have deliberately chosen to come at this time to participate in the huge shift occurring to restore this world to its fundamental intentions to be held by Light and to be a creation based purely on Light.

The Blueprint Story

In the beginning, when the Blueprint Originators brought the Blueprint to originate life as it was divinely designed to be here, the Blueprint Translators followed to help bring the Blueprint into a format for the human population's use. Then the Blueprint Deliverers came to seed and deliver this Blueprint to bring it into life, to give it life, to water it, fertilize it, and allow it to flourish.

There were Souls already here to experience life as a four-dimensional reality. Because of free choice and free will, they had options and chose not to receive the divinely ordained Blueprint and particularly the spiritual aspect of Love that was being brought as part of that Blueprint. They liked this new format of being in a physical body just to play and experience life. What fun! They rejected the Original Blueprint as it had been set up for this earth world. All the mythological stories convey this. Simply put, "The Fall." This is "The Fall" from consciousness, from grace. This falling process began when the value of spirit as universal wisdom and infinite connection to Creation were lost. Consciousness, vision of purpose, and mission in individuals were lost. The experience of the Blueprint for life as joy, peace, ecstasy, the natural Love for change and growth, and the pleasure of knowing aliveness of each moment were slowly lost and forgotten. Connection to the Divine and universal splendor was let go of, first through individuals and increasingly as a collective choice. Each moment that was designed to be "what shall I choose to create from Light into life through me" became a creative void disconnected from Light. The potential for this void to be filled with something other than Light ensued.

The absence of Light is what we call darkness. So all sorts of forms of darkness were free to infiltrate because the option for Light was discarded. This occurred through those who had a compelling say and so they became authority figures and hierarchy began. The majority began to look to others for direction and did not stay with using their own internal compass of Light connected to Creator source. The freedom of individual free choice was forgotten, as the weakness of living from the authority of another and not one's own Light began to take hold within individuals. Consciousness, direction, and vision got fuzzy, and confusion became more prevalent than intuition, awareness, and mindfulness. Experiencing aliveness through the six senses developed into the dysfunction of the emotional realm. The emotional realm was born as a responsive feeling to knowing lack of connection and purpose. The pain of separation has a rainbow of endless colors of sadness, powerlessness, and, especially, fear of all shades. The physical realm devoid of Light or life force becomes disease, depression, the aging of one's heart and Soul's outpouring, self-hate, self-destruction, and self-inflicted pain on all levels.

The picture of human existence without Light increasingly became a bleak one. The opening for the destructive forces of darkness took over where creation in life was rejected.

The Blueprint Deliverers said to the Earth beings, "Okay, I guess if you don't want this Blueprint we have, we will pull back, withhold, and let you do it the way you choose." Overriding this free choice to reject the Blueprint based on Love was not the way of Love. In essence, the Blueprint Deliverers betrayed their own connection to purpose and said it's okay to do the Blueprint without the frequency of connection to divine Love. This was their collective contribution to "The Fall." Call it wanting to belong, wanting to please, wanting to fit in, not wanting to be alone—all these lower frequencies grabbed their attention. They bought into allowing their gift and purpose to be rejected, and then went into the lower frequency of taking the Earth beings rejection of the Blueprint as a personal rejection of who they were as people. Instead of holding the frequency of Love and the Blueprint, no matter what this group of Earth beings felt, they betrayed their purpose and mission and let go of the Original Blueprint based on Love being delivered. They betrayed their Soul purpose.

Each Soul has done this in their own way in contributing to the vast planetary wound of separation, whether through innocence, naïvete, not understanding how things work, or just because of a moment of making a less than Light-filled choice at a pivotal moment of their Soul's path. For the Deliverers, their choice as a group was to turn from, or betray, Love as their source of life movement created a large direction change because they came at the beginning of human incarnation to insure that the universal constitution be declared.

You who are Blueprint Deliverers continue to fervently be cheerleaders for Love and life. You are bright beings with bright eyes and countenances. You see potential and the brilliance of each Soul you encounter and love to draw this forth. As divine cheerleaders your theme song is "you go, girl," "you go, guy." Let life flourish and be abundant. It is our natural divine birthright to know abundance through all levels of one's life. Don't forget this! Live from your greatest gift and purpose. You want to ensure that everyone's greatest strengths and gifts be delivered. You believe that personal fulfillment of the heart and Soul brings planetary fulfillment. You know it is not selfish to put oneself first, if living from your Soul. This brings our ability to live as God into this world. This brings the Blueprint of living from Love into the physical, conscious intelligence and experiential realms, which is what we all as Souls came to do.

Blueprint Deliverer Challenges

The challenge for you as a Blueprint Deliverer is to return first for yourself to the knowledge that divine Love has always been present, even in this world. The Blueprint has always been held in Love even if the layer of human consciousness that has suffered from its absence has rejected it. As a Blueprint Deliverer, you are afraid of fully holding to the truth that Love never has left, that we have only left Love. You are afraid to fully incarnate as one who brings divine Love and the

Blueprint regardless of who does not choose to receive these gifts. As Blueprint Deliverers you must not betray your mission that says that the Blueprint must be delivered even if no one at the human level acknowledges and receives it, even if it feels like you are all alone in doing it. The legions of invisible beings you work with as a team, by design, are with you. The angels and master teachers are with you. The Universe, in its entire creative splendor, is with you. The beloved Creator is with you. And, in fact, you are loved by all of creation in this world and all those beings aligned with Light and spirit in their own ways. As you bring the Blueprint in, it will feed all who are energetically open to receive its abundance.

The challenge that you have taken on, handed down from your Soul Family, goes back to "The Fall" when the Blueprint Deliverers agreed to let the Earth beings choose to ignore the Blueprint based on divine Love. Now you have to struggle with your feelings of guilt and failure to deliver the Blueprint based on Love. You must work with feeling that Love inevitably will be rejected, so you might give up on Love being a vibrant life-giving part of your life personally or through your mission. Out of feeling rejected, you will feel displaced as though you aren't loved or wanted. Your guilt and sense of failure to deliver will cause you to go into over-responsibility, a drive to survive, or a drive to a make "it" happen mode. You may feel that you are being punished for this Soul choice and don't deserve Love. But you want Love to be delivered, so you will be overzealous in opening doors and cheerleading for others to have it. You feel that if you can bring Love and success to all the lost Souls who chose not to receive the Blueprint, that this action will make up for your Soul Family's mistakes.

In fact, the way to reverse this whole dilemma is simply to stop betraying your own Blueprint and the choice for divine Love. When connection is made, then the channels for the Blueprint's presence, reconnected into life and human consciousness, can abundantly flow again. The Blueprint that is held within the Akashic Records for the Earth can happily be chosen again, which is foundational for the mission of bringing this world back to peace, freedom, joy, Light, connection, and communion.

The Blueprint Has Always Been Present

The whales have always held the ancient knowledge and wisdom of the Blueprint. They just do that. So at that level of consciousness, not to mention all of nature, the Blueprint has always been accessible. The dolphins have always carried the design for joy and creation, which is the expression of Love being birthed in life. So Love at this level has always been available also. The frequency of Love abides at the core of the Earth, at the depths of the deep blue seas. It is there for us to energetically draw on. The Earth exudes a continual "thank you for being here" to Love. The knowledge that "you love me" is held in the Earth, the stars, the sun, and the whole galaxy and beyond. The Blueprint for life has full recognition and support and has not been rejected. To deliver the Blueprint is to simply live life fully from the choice point of "What do I choose to create from Light—joy, abundance and freedom?"

You may find that you resonate with some or all of the Blueprint Deliverer challenges that I described. Because the Deliverers took these emotional reactions of expecting and assuming rejection, fear of not belonging, guilt, drive to survive, etc., on for so long, the actual Blueprint has barnacles of distortion on it and the mass population has believed that fear and rejection, for instance, are inevitable, incurable parts of human existence. Sad, but not true. This is why many will feel that these lower frequencies especially of separation from Source and the powerlessness to change reality here are inevitable. Sad, but not true. Forgive yourself; forgive the choice of separation and betrayal of Love in yourself wherever it applies and forgive it in others who are disconnected, lost Souls to varying degrees. The Blueprint can be consciously chosen in each moment to realign with. It is available.

Jesus and many other master teachers specifically chose to take on human incarnations to deliver the codes for the Blueprint. Jesus brought them here. He walked the talk and talked the walk. He lived the way of Love as Christ Light. It is available to be accessed as a frequency 2,000 years later through our collective magnification of it. He ascended, having delivered the Blueprint through a human expression. His mission was complete. He did not betray his mission or the Blueprint based on divine Love as Christ Light. The movie *The Passion of the Christ* presented itself to symbolically show us the pain and crucifixion of Love that we have suffered from all these years by our rejection of Love and Light. Only as we acknowledge that our suffering is based on self-inflicted pain due to choices to exclude divine Love as the source of our life blood will we remember we have a choice to let go of pain and suffering and take up the mantel of Light which is joy, aliveness, and growth through pleasure. This describes the code for the happiness of creating freely!

For a Blueprint Deliverer it is essential that Love be present for the mission to work. This can be seen at a planetary level. There must be divine Love here, or what is the purpose of life on the Earth?

This can also be seen at the personal level. When you as a Blueprint Deliverer feel Love is present in your life, you feel cared for, supported, loved, and valued. Your purpose can be ignited. You take off in your ability to manifest and let life flourish. The heart of the matter comes first for you. This is your success, your Soul fulfillment, known.

The following is an interview with a Blueprint Deliverer.

Susann: My understanding is that you, as a Blueprint Deliverer, have a part in making sure that everything in whatever world you live in flourishes. Is this true for you?

Amanda: It feels very natural. It is what makes sense to what I do every day here as though I have always done it and will always do it. I can't imagine being any other way. When I think of all the other worlds that exist that you have taught me about I want them all to flourish; I want all the Souls who come here to bring their gifts to be fulfilled, and I feel connected to the overall success of not only all these Soul Families but all of this solar system and Universe. I don't feel any separation.

Susann: Do you find that when you are with people who have had experience in other worlds that you have known, that you have a very strong desire to see their worlds flourish for their sakes and for the sake of the Blueprint here?

Amanda: I have always tried to bring out the positive in others and bring out their talents and their best. I feel as though our world will be fulfilled when each one is fulfilled in bringing forward their unique Soul gifts and talents. I remember in college there was a group of friends would look at me and say in essence, "Gee, how can she find all those good qualities in others. We certainly can't, how can she?" And I'm saying, "This is who I am. This is how I see everyone; I do think you are all really great." I see the Soul of the matter and love the gift each one brings. For instance, my daughter exudes such a dimension of Love. It pours from every cell in her body. It is such a treasure to me. I love what she brings and love to draw that Soul piece from her and have it be expressed in this world. I get weepy when I see the incredible part each person plays, and I can go into frustration when I see people not living their potential. That's the side of me that has overextended itself to help other people because I see what they could be doing.

Susann: This is surely the challenge I see for the Blueprint Deliverers. You want so much to fertilize for growth all you touch through people and situations. You can get overzealous in your desire to bring success and fulfillment and become over responsible and want to make others get "it" and then I will feel as though the Blueprint is in fact being delivered. You will tend to go overboard into components of over-responsibility and overdrive and rescue. If only I could get everyone lined up, living his or her dreams, I'd be happy.

Susann: How would you describe the way you have found to bring success wherever you go without having to feel responsible for others' life choices?

Amanda: Bringing out the best in everything is my desire. It is a matter of inspiration not will power. In the work that you have taught me I have learned how to help others to bring their Soul forward and I have learned how to clear the way that they might live from the deepest level possible. I often think of the phrase, "If you give a man a fish he eats for a day. If you teach a man to fish, he eats for a lifetime." This is the way that we are all fulfilled in doing our Soul's best here.

The potential down side to wanting deeply to bring out another's best is the fear that I will be rejected if they don't go with what I see is possible for them. I am reminded of the original challenge for the Blueprint Deliverers, which I certainly resonate with. The people here rejected our delivering of the Blueprint based on Love, and we have carried the pain of the collective rejection acutely. I have to consciously work with the feeling that my gifts are not received. I also find myself needing to prove the value of my assurance and optimism. The struggle of wanting to fulfill everyone's heart and Soul purpose here, without overdoing it through feeling overly responsible for everyone's success and well-being is big for me. Sometimes the feeling can be, "I can't have my gifts fulfilled, but at least they can."

Susann: How does your perseverance and optimism in this world come through in a world that feels so helpless and hopeless and impossible in regard to any creative solutions that would bring peace, Love, and any form of personal or planetary fulfillment?

Amanda: I see this lifetime as one footstep. I see people recognizing their own strength and that keeps me going. Every day sees potential. Even looking at the creation of a flower and seeing the magic of growth and movement in Light continually inspires me to hold that vision of all that is true and real and beautiful.

During 9/11 our family went to the ocean and felt the continuum of life, the continuity of water and waves to give perspective to what had happened. We are held in something so much larger. I can feel that, know that, and trust that. And as a Blueprint Deliverer I have been here on this Earth plane for so many times of crisis and catastrophe that even though I am in shock to see it happening again and again, I also have been through it many times. I have "been there, done that, worn the tee shirt" in so many incarnations here. And I want to see what can come out of this event that is heartfelt and Soulful.

Susann: Why would you say that you were attracted to coming here to play such a substantial role of making sure that the Earth Blueprint is delivered to humankind?

Amanda: The Earth planet allows for the joy of holding my newborn baby for the first time, smelling my lover's scent that activates Love and connection, knowing the satisfaction of successfully completing a challenge, and feeling expansion and honor of one's ability to create in this world.

For me the beauty of this Earth expression of multidimensionality allows us to connect with others through the physical, mental, and experiential dimensions by exchange. That I am here to bring fruition and success to others is to include the awareness of bringing life through all the dimensions in union holographically, existing in different wavelengths in the same space. Each person is a beautiful, unique, holograph of creation. It is so exciting to witness this flowering through the garden of human dynamics that we have all traveled many moons to be part of.

The Blueprint Deliverer Proclamation: I have come to bring life in its abundance.

8

MINTAKAN

*I am Light and Light is all there is. I am here to bring Light
as the only choice for creating life.*

Star System Location: Mintaka is the third star up in Orion's belt.
The planet you occupied is Artuvia.

Soul Characteristics:

* You come from the parent planet for the Earth.
* You carry a Soul knowing that Light is all there is.
* You have come here to reinstate the original knowledge that free
  choice based only on Light is the purpose for life experience.
* You do not understand the choice for negativity and destructive
  tendencies.
* You long for the utopian paradise you knew in your Mintakan world.
* You are wide-eyed and very open.
* You are light hearted, always seeing the light side of things.
* You can be naïve, especially in relationship to destructive behavior
  occurring around you.

Well Known People

Mel Gibson

Goldie Hawn

Meg Ryan

Ron Woods (Rolling Stones)

Paul McCartney

Tom Brokaw

Elvis Presley (50% Blueprint Deliverer)

Mintaka is within the star system of the Orion constellation. It is the third star, the uppermost star on the right in Orion's belt. The planet of habitation is Artuvia, but I am using the star name of Mintaka for this Soul Family. It is my understanding, through the work of Arlen Bock, that the first group of Souls who came from Mintaka came as long ago as 250,000 BC. They were the first group of the Soul Families to come to specifically help here after the Blueprint groups had been here for a while. Many other Soul Families came after the Mintakans as described in the following chapters.

Mintaka is the parent world for the Earth. The design for planet Earth was born of the lineage of the Mintakan mission. As I described in the previous chapter on the Earth Blueprint, there was a specific Blueprint designed for planet Earth based on the expression of pure Light as the choice from which our experience of life here would come. The Mintakan world and its spiritual foundation of Light was the platform from which the design of the Earth Blueprint was birthed.

Mintakans Are 100 percent Loyal to Light

The Mintakan world is the only world that has always stayed 100 percent loyal to Light. What does this mean? Throughout this galaxy, where Light is the prevalent vibration, as far back as we have read in the Akashic Records, the choice for the absence of Light, as darkness, has also had a presence. There has been galactic and universal warfare. There have been invasions of forces of dark to star systems that hold

Light as their source. Every other world but Mintaka has bought into the influence of darkness, which has tainted their primary mission. All Soul Families have allowed the infiltration of disruption to their manifestation of creation except Mintakans.

Mintaka has always remained true to its original mission of holding Light. It continues to hold the pure vibration of Light, unadulterated by any frequency less than Light. This is no small feat. Mintakans proclaim and live from the experiential reality that Light is all there is. Within the universal scheme, Mintaka is the point of reference declaring that Light is all there is. Mintaka has always held this truth, which reveals to us that it is not necessary to have darkness in order to know Light. You who have lived in the Mintakan world laugh at that idea. You have known for eons that Light shines brightly and clearly all on its own and does not need the presence of darkness to declare its true power.

In the third Harry Potter movie, *The Prisoner of Azkaban,* it was brilliantly depicted how the most creative way to dismiss the horrible notions we fear, such as snakes and monsters, is to change one's view of the perceived monsters to a comical character of one's choosing, to actually change the picture in one's mind's eye from the monster to the comical person of choice. Then wave the magical wand and say "ridiculous!" This is a direct commandment, proclaiming the so-called monster or evil or enemy to be ridiculous. To say, "ridiculous," in essence, brings Light through lightheartedness and whimsical laughter to the situation that has been seen to be dark, heavy, and impossible to deal with.

One of the teachers of magic for the young boys in this Harry Potter movie had each of his students imagine the thing that they most feared—a person, animal, or imaginary monster. The child, with the help of his magic wand, would change, in his mind's eye, the picture of the horrific snake, for instance, to the picture of a comical character.

As he did so, the picture changed before his very eyes and the feeling of fear toward that perceived monster became a ridiculous illusion.

It is possible for each of us to follow the same steps as they apply to our "monsters." The Mintakan view regarding the concept that darkness holds weight and importance over Light is "Ridiculous! What a silly idea. Don't even think about it. Light is all there is. Light is the only choice." The Mintakan creed is "What do I choose to create of Light now, continually, simply, and filled with ease."

Choosing to Create as Light

This Mintakan proclamation that Light is all there is was also meant to be our foundation for living here. Those who had chosen to live on Earth were to expand the possibilities of choices for what we might create from Light. That was the Blueprint agreed to originally. In this world we have multidimensional possibilities for the expression of Light. The Mintakans are continually posing the question, what do I choose to create as the Light of spirit consciously experiencing creation through physicality (through the physical, mental, emotional, and spiritual realms together)? What amplification of Light's manifestation is potentially magnified when we have these multiple dimensions to shine universal Light through? This is an excellent Blueprint based on free choice in Light. Most of us came here because of a Soul-level desire to bring this world into realignment with not only the Blueprint for Earth, but to realign this planet with the larger universal design it is a part of. What a glorious Blueprint! It has attracted many Souls from other worlds. They have come not only to help, but also to experience the abundance of the life that is here like no other plane of existence.

Nature is a brilliant example of the diversity of life forms emanating magic, abundance, and pure aliveness in so many ways. If you consider for a moment the miracle of life all around us it is not only astounding, but also breathtaking. Consider the birth of Light into life forms from humans to flowers, to the vast array of the sea world, to the magic of the stars in the night sky. No wonder we Souls chose to take the voyage to this endless adventure of experiencing life.

There is scientific recognition of human life on some of the planets I am speaking of in this book, but none as elaborate, colorful, and amazing as here on planet Earth. Yes, it is true that the distortion of separation and polarization have infiltrated the mineral, plant, and animal worlds to a certain extent. But it is amazing how much the splendor of creation has and does flourish here even in the midst of so much war, fear, and destruction.

Light is all there is. This commandment from the Mintakan world is an essential gift to our existence. "Let there be Light" is the essence of creation, and the Mintakan presence allows the Light of creation to be brought into life consistently, as the truth of free choice. Free choice was only meant to be based on the choice for Light. So freeing! This is the stance of freedom that we all crave. To be free is to stand in command of one's own ship of life from the helm that says, "What do I choose to create from Light now and in every now? What do I chose to create from Light in this moment, situation, or relationship?" This is utter freedom, indeed. Tapping into the resource of the Mintakan energy field will open the door to freedom in life, for all of us.

Infiltration of Darkness as Power Source

We were all created from Light and originally the only choice for our creation sprung from Light for all Souls. Along the way in the creation that has occurred throughout this galaxy there have been races of beings who started to choose the absence of Light, which we term darkness, for their power source. Let me show you how this might show itself on a smaller scale.

A child says there are monsters under his bed. He sees the dark space and imagines these monsters have a real dimension to them in that darkness. A monster is there. He buys into the false power of an unknown possibility existing in that unknown space, that creative void. He believes the possibility of something being present and that idea is planted in his subconscious, and he becomes run by it. It becomes more real to him than a parent's reassurance that such things as monsters don't exist. He has bought into something of his own making that comes out of a collective subconscious. He starts giving weight to the idea of monsters.

This collective idea about monsters is so real it takes many forms in our minds and then becomes topics for books and movies, gaining continual credibility. We buy into the power of the absence of Light and what illusions can become "real" to us. We have all bought into this absence of Light in one way or another, filling the "bank" of the creative void that is always present with ideas and illusions that we make real, like the idea that monsters live under the bed. We fill the bank that says: monsters, evil, and bad things beyond our control can "get us." We start giving weight to the idea of monsters as an example of something outside ourselves that has power over us through our fear of it.

Nothing exists unless we say it does. We are that powerful. For instance, there was a belief once that the world was flat. Many held that. Nothing wrong with that. It just proves that we trust many things that aren't based in "fact." Fear of the unknown is based on something outside the realm of "fact." But, quite often, it appears to many to be a very real place. It is the very force that drives so much of our behavior. It allows people to believe that it is so real, this fear, that they have every right to cheat, lie, and manipulate in the name of it. This is really no different than believing there are monsters that we must rearrange our lives to accommodate, thus feeling compelled to manipulate, etc. to have a sense of control over this so-called "power."

Journey to Mintakan Paradise

For you Mintakans this longing for utopia lies within your very heart and Soul. You know things could be so much better here. You know what is possible. You long to know the feeling of paradise on Earth. It is vital for you to reconnect to your core with the remembrance of that utopia, so you can bring that to Earth.

You Mintakans deeply miss your utopia. It is a paradise. Everything springs from Light. No struggle, strain, stress, destruction, disruption. Everything is born of the pure emanation of Light igniting creation. This translates into the energy of happiness, brightness, and optimism. You who have spent time in Mintaka always see the light side, the bright side. The cup is definitely half full.

When I do guided journeys that some might parallel to a regression technique, like a past life regression, I guide clients to the Soul memory of their home world, the Soul heritage they carry. In the case of Mintakans, we travel to know again the feeling of that paradise you long for, to touch the richness and beautiful connection of being one with Light, within the expression of Light as the only choice for your life movement. Through this journey you open up that reality into the current, cellular memory so you can bring paradise and utopia here now. It's incredible for me to play a part in the reconnection that is made. This reconnection also aligns you again with your purpose and mission to assist in returning to our Creator's Original Blueprint for this world, which is utopia. It is the Blueprint for paradise experienced abundantly. It is designed to be an even more expanded experience of Light than can be known in Mintaka, as unimaginable as you may think that is.

Holding Light No Matter What

The following story is written from Brenda.

"A notable session with Susann involved the resolution of my difficulty in holding the 'Light'—my life force or essence—as I interacted with others and participated in life. I was going through a difficult period at work, as the only female partner in a business organization dominated by men. The structure of the organization was not supportive of left-brain style of management, and was primarily non-inclusive and rigid, with constant power struggles that left me drained and frustrated.

"In my session, Susann led me into a deeply meditative but conscious state and guided me to the source of my 'issues' pertaining to my inability to hold my own, my truth, and my Light in challenging situations.

"In the session, I found myself in 'outer space,' somewhere in the Universe, amid stars and distant planets. I felt myself more as energy than as a physical being. I held a golden orb of Light. I sense that I'm supposed to take this golden orb safely to my destination. I'm now on the edge of a field of debris in space, with wisps of mist or smoke and what appear to be 'dead' or dense physical objects floating about.

"A nearby planet on the other side of this field is brightly lit and completely covered with human bones and skulls. There are some large, dark shapes lurking in the shadows and I believe they are waiting for me to enter the field and snatch the ball from me. I also believe that if they succeed, I'll end up a pile of bones on that planet across the field. I am afraid and angry that I have been left here without support and guidance. In the distance I see a blue-green planet – my destination. I'm wondering if I can find a clever way to out-fox or out-run these hungry shadows. But I'm too afraid and angry to even try.

"I hear a voice behind me saying clearly and calmly, 'The shadows are as big or as small as you want them to be.'" Susann reminds me that they are also 'there,' or 'not,' based on my choice. I decide that they are small—the size of little mice and only one or two in number. Now I feel big and the orb I hold is bigger and brighter. I'm not inclined to hide it as I was before.

"In confidence, I zip through the field to my destination—planet Earth—safe and sound with the bright, shiny orb of Light. But once I enter the outer fields of the Earth, all is gray and dark, and I'm once again afraid of shadows, that they are far bigger than me and will try to steal my Light away. I have forgotten that it is my choice as to whether these dark shadows exist and have power over me.

"Again, I feel as if God, spirit, the Universe, my guides, have all abandoned me and left me with an impossible task and very little help. I am defenseless. Susann guides me back to where I first got the instructions and the orb. I find myself in well-lit space of white Light and warmth. I'm given this wonderful golden orb of Light and told that the only thing I have to do is to hold it completely at all times. The golden Light has transformative powers but only if held in its entirety. I'm excited at the prospect of transforming dark places and as I fly off to find them, seemingly friendly and partially lit beings are approaching me. Their Light is fragmented and they are saying that they can show me what wonderful things I can do with the Light—a piece of it here and a piece of it there can really light up dark places. And forgetting the only rule, I get into exchanges that fragment me and replace pieces of my Light with darkness. And therein lies the source of my fear—that if I reveal the Light, I will be attacked and pieces of me will be ripped away until I am bloody and bruised.

"This translated into a day-to-day experience of my withholding my true essence in my workplace, as well as other areas of life, for fear of being attacked and ripped to pieces. I had to conform to the world order 'as is … ' or be attacked and unsafe. Again, the choice appeared to be no choice at all."

Move out of Fighting for Light

You who have been in Mintaka have a tendency, when you forget that Light is all there is, to go into fight for Light or fight for life mode. You feel responsible for the fact that Light isn't the overriding power source on Earth because you have been here for so long and it's still not "right." You can get caught up in this fight for Light and life as a way to personally repair all the wrongdoings here, as though you are the ones creating the lack of Light. The remedy: remember to come up to that higher place of understanding that your Soul does know that says Light is all there is. Anyone's choice for something less than Light does not keep Light from being the supreme power. Try it on when you see a situation personally or globally.

War is a great example. Can you hold a vision for this world that Light will prevail, even as it appears that the majority holds war as the means for creating peace? Your statement is, "Light is all there is, and I know that as I hold that truth, the fixation on war as a means to fight for life will begin to dissolve." The phrase "what can one man do" surely applies here. From the place of "Light is all there is," what is the creative way to handle a situation such as war or poverty or any struggle?

Here are a few words from a client of mine who had a direct experience of repairing this tendency towards nameless fear when she got caught in not understanding how to operate in a world filled with so much opposition to Light. "There was this sense of anxiety and unknown fear with me continually. I couldn't seem to find words for it. By moving beyond this world and reconnecting with how Mintaka is a part of me, I was able to define the fear, dismiss it, and then bring a sense of calm and ease to my everyday life. I now feel confident that my everyday choices will be a true reflection of who I am and not what others think I should choose."

Mintakan Soul Openness

You Mintakans are very open, flowing spirits, wide-eyed and optimistic. You may be seen as Pollyanna-like or even naive and gullible. Your countenance is one of freshness and availability to Light. Of course! If Light is all there is, as far your Soul is concerned, why wouldn't you feel free to express your lightheartedness openly all the time? You are like a breath of fresh air in the energy field of others. Those around you may complain that you are too cheerful, lighthearted, and optimistic. Others will try to pull you down and sway you to think like the herd, that life is hard, complex, and you should live in fear and wariness for all the horrors that are around. These people want Light on their side but they want it through you. It doesn't work that way. Mintakans, like everyone, want to belong and help bring pure Light to Earth. But you will often dim your own Light to fit into the dullness of those around you who think life is a struggle, just to fit in, belong, or be taken care of. Dimming your own Light does not help bring pure paradise here, but it can feel like the only acceptable choice to a Mintakan who would rather not feel isolated and alone like a candle burning in a sea of darkness. Mintakans must remember that when you allow yourselves to radiate pure Light, not only are your fellow Mintakans behind you, but a constant universal pulsation of Light-radiating creation backs you. That is the truest vibration of belonging we can know.

The Indomitable Spirit of Light in Action

I had the privilege of reading the Akashic Records for a couple who are both blind and in their thirties. They were soon to have a baby boy, who is a precious, Love-filled Soul. This couple, Jack and Blaney were born with sight, so they have seen life in all its abundance in this lifetime. They both lost full sight in their twenties and met right after that.

What indomitable Light-filled spirits they are now. There is no question for either of them that Light is all there is! Many might imagine that to be blind instantly means we would live in a world of darkness. When we close our eyes we could say that it's dark. Not so for Jack and Blaney. As they described it to me, Light is still all there is for them even with their state of blindness. They vividly demonstrate that Light is not just a physical commodity. They are living from another level of Light. It is not all a visual reality by any means.

They are happy and bright and they naturally find the Light way in all they do. They are such an inspiration to be with. Blaney is getting her Masters degree, and Jack is fully engaged in his professional world of engineering and inventing audio computer software for the blind. Their mission in this life together is to bring Light no matter what. This is not because they feel they have something to prove but because their Souls shine from the place of Light and they can't conceive of doing life any differently. "What other choice is there?" is their declaration. This is the true Mintakan spirit. They truly see through the eyes of Light.

May we tune into this reality of Light being the only choice even in the midst of what we have collectively labeled as limitations. Let Jack and Blaney inspire us all just as Christopher Reeve and countless others have. Their purpose is clearly being lived for us to witness.

Mintakans Do Not Understand Choices
Outside of the Choice for Light

Mintakans don't understand choices for anything other than Light. At a Soul level it makes no sense at all to you that someone would choose anything less. The concept of terrorists running airplanes into the World Trade Center just doesn't compute to Mintakans. It just leaves a huge question mark inside you. Why? Acts of war and destruction do not compute. For Mintakans, at a Soul level, disruption to the path of Light just isn't in the realm of possibilities.

If you find yourself struggling to feel loyal to Light when you feel that the whole world is against you, you may end up putting attention on your struggle more than your conviction to Light. If you feel you have to keep disruption away from you, it keeps you focused on it. For instance, if you have anger about the warring in our world you will continually talk about how horrible and how unjust it is. This just keeps the destruction of war right in your face. What you may be feeling subconsciously is that if you keep thinking about war then you have control over it and it won't harm you. Or you may feel you need to understand all the destruction to have a place for it in your consciousness, because your Soul just doesn't get what it is about. Thinking about all that you don't like or don't understand, like war, also keeps your attention on the negativity in the world. It can create a defensive posture that only keeps your Light from staying alive and vibrant in life. It certainly doesn't make the negativity go away by focusing on it. It actually increases it.

Mintakans can help themselves immensely by remembering that Light is the true power that disruptive people are trying to get from you. Hold that stance and negativity won't hold such weight in your eyes. Your Light is what they want, but from your standpoint, they can't take it from you. It is totally connected to universal Light. You are here to remind them that Light is all there is, and others can reconnect to their own source of Light to experience what you think they want from you.

If Light Were the Only Source

Consider how different this world would be with Light as the only source for our life movement. You Mintakans have come to remind Earth beings through your living example that this is not only possible but also the very Blueprint for each and every one's Soul purpose here. It is the starting point that we all long to return to. We have all come to assist in refurbishing this original foundation of Light for creation. You Mintakans carry not only the dream of paradise, but also the reality. You have lived this utopian state of Light as the only choice very fully. This is the truth of free choice, free will. Free choice was only meant to be about our free choice from a place of Light.

The challenge that you Mintakans have stems from your deep knowing of paradise. You don't understand the choice for negativity. That's great, and it also means that your naiveté in this regard sets you up for a vulnerability to the infiltration of the very thing you don't comprehend.

If you are from Mintaka and you are feeling a bit confused about how this world is run based on destruction, fear, manipulation, power struggles, etc., imagine you go to school and ask a peer how things work here. You are eager to learn the lay of the land so you can best know how to bring your gifts. You want to understand this Earth you have entered. So you innocently ask a peer who looks pretty assured of himself how to get to know others in school. So, this peer says, if you want to be liked and have a place here you push and shove and hit others and you'll certainly gain lots of friends for this behavior. "Okay!" you say innocently. This is how Earth beings connect and play. Since you imagine everything is based on Light, you accept this behavior as a new adventure in becoming accepted here. This may sound unrealistic, but you Mintakans know what I am speaking of. Your view that everything springs from Light can get you in trouble if you aren't streetwise and listening to your inner barometer for Light.

It was reported that Saddam Hussein was behind the terrorist suicide mission to bomb the World Trade Center. We may ask ourselves how a man like Saddam Hussein could convince men to go on a suicide terrorist mission. These men felt powerless in themselves and were looking to an outside power source to guide them back to a place of power for themselves. This is an extreme example of the way naiveté around how power works here can be taken advantage of. But it does apply. In this world that has been run by destructive forces you Mintakans can feel powerless in the face of them. You especially don't understand how someone can "shoot you in your own back." It is essential for Mintakans to become streetwise. The truth is that Light is all there is, and in this world the choice for something else is a possibility. The choice for disruption and fear is bought into on a regular basis. It's just the facts here, and we have to take it into account. Am I saying that you should watch your back out of fear? No. Here's the formula. Hold Light as the only choice. When you are sensing danger, be true to the Light as your focus, and the dark source can't penetrate that source field of Light you are holding.

Mintakans Need to be Streetwise

Free choice means there are those who have deliberately chosen darkness as their source for the illusion of power. The Light that you Mintakans give out will not necessarily be welcomed, and others may take advantage of it to use for their own agendas and devices. It is vital for you Mintakans to have an internal barometer in place to know who shares your choice for Light and who doesn't. Mintakans can have a tendency to try to help those with the least amount of Light. If you enter a room full of people you will unconsciously gravitate toward the one or ones who are the darkest or dullest. "Gosh," you say in innocence, "this is where the greatest need is and I have come to return Light to this world!"

As a Mintakan, you long so much to give Earth beings here that exquisite experience of Light, that you have a tendency to overextend yourselves to the lost Souls who aren't in touch with Light. Now, there is nothing wrong with helping those in real need, when it is asked for and received through the heart. What I am referring to here is overextension of one's abundant resource of Light, which you know you inherently carry. You have the tendency to gravitate to the people holding the greatest absence of Light. You see this as an opportunity to extend Light into that creative void where these lost Souls live, by choice. Don't forget those in darkness have chosen that position and are not necessarily open to your gifts of Light. This is where it gets tricky in this world. Because of the nature of free choice, there are many who have deliberately chosen darkness as their modis-operandus. If someone from Mintaka comes to bring Light to the world, not everyone will feel open to or want to have anything to do with it. Or some may want to take this Light and use it for their own disruptive purposes. Light is a force and can be used to fuel any chosen endeavor because of its free, open frequency. For instance, if you oppose war or killing and send Light to those who stand for killing out of anger or for personal gain, the Light sent to them will merely fuel their momentum for that personal end.

But often choosers of darkness only want Light for their personal agenda. They don't want pure connection to Light or they would have chosen it already themselves. They believe that being filled with darkness will give them the power they want. It is usually the desire for greater power in a moment or lifetime of weakness that opens the door to using darkness as a source of power. This looks like threats, greed, control, and "low level" forms of power to feel more powerful.

The young people who killed or wanted to kill other students and teachers in their schools in the late 1990s did so due to insecurities and a sense of powerlessness with peers, teachers, and most parents. They felt like low men on the totem pole and used power over others to feel more powerful themselves. They did not do it based on holding core strength of confidence and leadership and feeling loved and valuable, which are the true dimensions of divine power.

It is vital for Mintakans to be more streetwise. There are people out there who have bought into these false strategies for power. Those people are not in your best interest to engage with or try to override or change. They have freely chosen their perspective. It is so very different on Mintaka, and you will be uncomprehending in your Soul in relationship to such a choice. It is vital for you Mintakans to utilize your brightness to magnify brightness, and not try to use it in an overly compassionate way to play God to those who have deliberately chosen to exclude Light as their inner guidepost for life.

Shine Your Light

It is much wiser for a Mintakan to simply, freely shine a Light of joy, ease, and optimism so others are inspired. Be like as a beacon for the remembrance of the choice for Light. If you want to return utopia to this world, you must hold that vibration no matter what, and watch how others gravitate to the Light or not. Others can enjoy the Light and its emanation through you and know that paradise exists because you do. Light-filled utopia is a very compelling energy. You won't ever be alone in it.

In this world there are streams of Light creating more Light. There are streams of darkness creating more darkness. These streams are made up from individuals and groups and religions and cultural factions. Darkness will destroy itself because darkness loves to destroy. It cannot destroy Light so it will have to destroy itself. Light will magnify Light and be less impressed by the intrigue of the false power of dark (Enron antics will not work, etc.). As Light magnifies Light it will create more faith in the power of Light to bring our deepest Soul purposes to fruition.

Light creates Light and as you focus your purpose on magnifying Light, you don't have to fight darkness or push to change how it gets used here. You are here to be the natural inspiration you are that reveals that Light is the only way. As we all radiate Light, the lack of Light that registers as darkness and war-like action will stand out like a sore thumb in contrast to Light's natural radiance, like nuclear waste stands out in contrast to a field of poppies. We do not have to fight with it or against the results of the absence of Light, but only bring Light through our life and know that will counterbalance its absence.

It is vital for Mintakans and all of us when we see or feel Light's absence to simple breathe into receiving more Light within ourselves and expand the presence of Light in the moment or situation or person we feel the lack in. It is not for us to try to send them Light, which may be against their will, but to expand our own heartfelt, Soul-felt sense of Light. We can only let it move where there is openness to receive it energetically through spirit's guidance, not our mental ideas of what is best for another. Be the inspiration of Light that you Mintakans have come to gift this world with.

Mintakan Alignment with Blueprint Family

You Mintakans will feel a close alignment with those in the Blueprint Family. In essence, your mission to return this world to our Creator's Original Blueprint is the same. The part you play and the experience you bring is from a different quality of spirit. They fit together beautifully. In essence, Mintakans hold the codes for utopia and the Blueprint Family holds the codes for how that translates and manifests into this multidimensional reality of free choice in the Light utopian state. The Mintakans came to bring Light as the only choice and, like many other Souls, to experience what it is to know Light through spirit consciously experiencing creation through physicality. Also, because Mintaka is a parent planet for this Earth world, many Souls have had time on Mintaka in preparation for coming here as a useful stepping stone for understanding the divine purpose for the Earth plane that you are assisting in. It helps to have a direct feel for the mission before signing up to assist in realigning it here. To correct the distortions of how free choice has been misutilized here, it is valuable to experience the original intention for free choice.

Following is an interview with a Mintakan friend about her direct experience of bringing her Mintakan gifts into her daily life.

Susann: What was the highlight for you in our session, Joanne, that took you to your home world of Mintaka?

Joanne: What I remember most clearly about my trip to Mintaka was the sensation of shifting into a sense of being Light instead of having a physical form. I was so filled with Light there, for there is nothing but the Light, and bringing that sense back into my physical form, especially when there might be places of shadow or dullness like not feeling well, or having an unclear perspective on my life, was tremendous. I just brought the Light from the experience back into my own life here. I imagine it coming into my physical being and filling up those areas that are cloudy.

My perspective changes when I visualize the Light being inside me; I feel lighter and clearer.

Susann: How do you draw strength from Light in your ability to be in this world?

Joanne: Sometimes when I am driving or I'm walking or out and about, I just remember to bring a visual picture of Light in and then I let it go. I know it's there because I feel a vibrational shift. There's a higher frequency that comes in and shakes things up. It's a kinesthetic experience, an energetic experience. Having that presence changes who I am in the world. I trust it to work. I don't ponder it or keep checking in to make sure it's working.

When I have a difficult task to face I ask the Mintaka Light to come in and fill me. It is a way for me to bring up my warriorship, my strength, and my power. Light is my strength.

Susann: In what ways have you been able to experience that the power of Light is stronger than anything else?

Joanne: I have a recent experience to describe. In my office, whenever I went to the water fountain, a woman from another department would be hanging around and her energy was obviously not very Light producing. I often wanted to avoid going into that hallway. Then I learned about my Soul Family from Mintaka and the power of my gift of Light and how it was my birthright to use this Light of inspiration in my life.

I called in the Mintakan Light the next time I was near the water fountain, and this woman with the yucky energy that felt like she wanted to pull my energy down was there. I was mad that I had let her get away with doing that before. I gathered my Light-warrior energy to say, "No, no! You can't mess with Light. It is stronger than your sucking energy. I declare through this action that Light is my source of strength and this attempt to de-power that won't work. I had a chance to deliberately act on Light's behalf, which felt great to do. And this woman's energy actually began to change in my perspective. She no longer felt like a threat to me and the power of my Light.

Susann: We've spoken about the Mintakan world holding the essence of utopia that many of us are looking for. Tell me how this utopian revelation you have touched in our session together gifts your life now.

Joanne: When I consider the idea that Mintaka is a utopia and I hold that energy in myself, it gives me a deep feeling of trust. It's a big picture. There's a process working out here and you might say that utopia is the goal. And I know that goal exists. I don't feel hopelessness, because for me utopia is real and alive and well. The process toward that is happening. Time and energy are speeding up to move us in that direction. More and more Light is flooding in. Utopia is the perspective that Light is all there is.

Susann: I love that you have brought this Soul-level work into your psychiatric practice. Can you share how this Soul dimension benefits your clients?

Joanne: The challenge we Mintakans work with, I understand, is not getting the choice we have made to allow darkness, the absence of Light, to be so prevalent. As a psychiatrist, I understand this at an emotional and mental level. At a Soul level it makes no sense. In my work, this helps me when patients have made choices that we might call self-destructive. I don't get emotionally involved with that choice. I offer them another choice based on Light. It makes it much simpler for both of us. I used to feel more deeply for their tendencies to make "bad" choices, and I wanted to fix them through being overly compassionate, but it really didn't help them as much as giving them a Light option does. It is good that their choices, from my Soul perspective, don't make sense.

I had to learn to develop boundaries for myself. That is their choice, and I am interfering if I judge their choice. I am not here to change them but give them the Light way through the situation they're dealing with. This is much more productive, I've found.

Following is an interview with a friend whose Mintakan heritage has helped her have a whole new lease on life.

Sarah: Every step I take on Earth revolves around my Soul journey. Every day I look around and I'm very confused about what's going on in this world. I have to constantly remind myself that I don't have to live in that dark, unhappy world. Because of my personal motivation as a Soul, I have to find ways to elevate. I do that by a lot of self-reflection combined with the internal and external help of those who remind me that I am a Light being on this planet. It took getting to the point of suicidal feelings to get me to awaken to my truer nature.

Susann: Sarah, how has your understanding of your heritage as a Soul living on Mintaka helped you be able to make it here?

Sarah: What I understand is that in my Soul history I have come from a utopian planet. It is a much more level, even, sweeter, connected, joyful planet. The driving force behind my essence is speaking the truth of that. On a daily basis I connect and reconnect and reignite and reaffirm who I am as Light and a self-affirmed being on the planet.

Susann: Tell me more of your story of Soul transformation. I'm sure many can relate to your path.

Sarah: Honestly, it's not always fun or joyful or happy for me here. And the goal is to feel more connected. Sometimes it really sucks being here, I have to say. I spent more than half my life surrounded by ancestral family dynamics and so-called friends who I felt uneasy around, even suffocated by and certainly judged by.

There came a point in my life where the suffocated drama and hellish choices became unacceptable. I was either going to exit or make a change. It was at that time that I brought in a whole new dynamic of family and Soul support that got me out of hell. I will never forget this. It was like it was yesterday. It was on the day that it was all churning and I was praying and begging and meditating and going through things I didn't even understand. I remember there was a moment that I called in light as deeply as I could call for help.

In some part of my awareness I had never touched before I saw a circle of beings in white. They were all holding hands in a circle, these angelic beings. It was in that moment that I reconnected with a Light vibration of the utopian world I came from. This was an experience of a huge amount of Light, compared to what I had lived for so long. It is a time for me to be realigning to see the world and live the world more positively so it can flourish here and in my life. It was a magical moment that changed everything. Now I have the ability to draw on the resource of Light and remember that it has been mine to experience here all along.

The Mintakan Proclamation: I am Light and Light is all there is. I am here to bring Light as the only choice for life.

9

POLARIAN

I am whole.
Wholeness exists because I am here.

Star System Location: Polaris, the North Star.

Soul Characteristics:

* You carry the experiential knowing of oneness, wholeness, and unity.
* You carry the anchoring trust that all is well.
* You are here to help all return to the original design for the Earth of unity in diversity.
* You are here to help this world move out of our prevalent functioning in polarity (good vs bad) into one unified world that honors each one's unique essence and gift.
* You are focused on unifying body, mind, and spirit.
* You prefer a "round table" format to a hierarchical system.

Well Known People:

Kevin Costner

George Harrison (Beatles)

Johnny Depp (also Parallel)

Bonnie Raitt

Tom Hanks (40% Sirian)

Kevin Bacon

Louis Armstrong

Bette Midler

Jimmy Carter

Sammy Sosa

Polaris is a planet within the North Star system. The North Star has been a beacon of Light for travelers for millennia. Polaris, the North Star, is a point of consistency and reliability, the known in the midst of a sea of unknown for a voyager. This is the spirit of those of you who have lived in the Polaris field. You can be counted on. You are reliable and true. You are as dependable as the North Star as a beacon for wholeness. Your wholeness is a unifying force. You know that each of us is inherently unified in the one whole that has always existed. This sense of wholeness abides within you. Others magnetize to your wholeness, because it is so utterly reliable.

Kevin Costner is a very fine example of a man living from his Polaris Soul heritage through his movie career. Many of his movies, including his best-known *Dances with Wolves,* deal with the strength inherent in diverse cultures. In *Dances with Wolves,* his drive to unify and bring peace at any cost is paramount in his character. His dedication was gripping. With *Field of Dreams* he shows his dedication to his dream no matter what the potential ramifications in his immediate world. He listens to his internal divine voice and stays committed to its declaration "if you build it, they will come." His anchoring in spirit and trust that everything springs out of that conviction is a treasure indeed.

The Polarian Foundation of Oneness within Wholeness

In this world filled with so many unknowns, with so much in limbo and unresolved in our personal lives and the world scene, the vibration of wholeness is a welcome and necessary foundation. The foundation of oneness within wholeness is your Polaris mantel. You know deep within your Soul experience that all is well. You have come to remind us—we who have lost that compass for well-being—that beyond the surface of human consciousness that has held onto a distorted place of separation and polarity, the Universe exists within the framework of a unified wholeness based in oneness. The galaxy (and beyond) is a radiant sphere from which each Soul is born out of wholeness. Just as the Sun gives forth rays of Light to penetrate and ignite all of creation as we know it, all of us are born of the one whole and are beams of Light as differentiations of that one whole shining into our individual spheres of existence and aliveness. It is magical! And as those from Polaris know, the essence of wholeness is a sure thing that can be counted on, as sure as we know the Sun rises in the morning sky and sets in the evening.

This world was designed on the premise of unity in diversity. Imagine our Creator, along with a whole council of beings developing the Blueprint for a new dimension of existence. As they came together, one of the key elements that was created to be a part of the Earth is the reality of unity in diversity. How does that translate? We are all part of the one wholeness. We all spring from this, as does all of creation. This factor unifies us naturally and completely. In this world there is a huge endless diversity of the magnificence of creation. It is all held within the universal wholeness, the one source that unifies everything. There is no world like it, because of the expanded dimension of consciousness available through which to express our heart and Soul. The possibilities for creation through human being-ness are limitless in their splendor. We know we have barely scratched the surface in this capacity! Scientists say we use a mere 2 percent of our brain capacity. We also are only functioning from a two-strand

DNA level, and we were meant to operate through all twelve strands.

Imagine How It Could Be: Unity in Diversity

Imagine, as John Lennon so poignantly sang, "all the people living for today." Imagine what could blossom and grow out of the unification of Love in each one's heart and peace in each one's step. We can see the unity in diversity played out through the diversity of so many beautiful and unique cultures and skin colors, and walks of life. We see the varied expressions of one's spiritual values expressed in such an array of religion and philosophy. This potential for diversity to be known here is a microcosm of the galactic macrocosm of the diversity of creation of an infinite nature. Is this not the meaning of life, to experience the beauty of creation through our multidimensional capacities for its expression?

As John Lennon so exquisitely put it, "You might say that I'm a dreamer, but I'm not the only one. Please come and join us, so the world can be as one."

John Lennon definitely spent time in the North Star of Polaris. Wasn't he always a beacon for conscious creation through music and life? He was dedicated to bringing this world together while celebrating the unique and diverse expression of each one. The Beatles were a supremely unifying force for creation in the world. Every culture that knew their music loved them. When they sang, they sang for the world. Everyone resonated with the energy they held that was bright, alive, and allowed the music in the hearts of people from every country to sing the joy of being alive. They uplifted and replenished. John brought leadership in whatever way he could to bring this world together through music, which is the heartbeat of life. He was a leader of consciousness. Consciousness is present to give the Soul connection to transcendent purpose and mission in the whole that unifies us all.

Unity in diversity is the Blueprint for this magnificent planet, and you who are from Polaris are here to help us all remember this and live again from this place.

The Truth of Polarity and Separation

This world chose to take the concept of polarity to a distorted extreme. True undistorted polarity in and of itself creates night and day. True polarity brings the opposing colors on the color wheel. If you put yellow and blue together it creates green. Earth above and sky below. Hot and cold. The four seasons are simple examples of the presence of true polarity at work on Earth. This was all for the purpose of creating balance and harmony within a structure of diversity, so possibilities for creation could be hugely expansive but always be part of the stability of wholeness.

Also, the true concept of separation was part of the design in a very, very simplistic manner. It too has become grossly misinterpreted. Separation was only meant to be individuation. Separation applies only to the fact that we are each unique essences of creation. There are no others like us in essence or expression. We are uniquely special. That's all. Within that uniqueness is the unifying factor that states that we are part of a whole. In that way we are each "the same," which in fact means we are one. We are like an individual ray of sunlight but never disconnected from the Sun. The Sun is the fulcrum of wholeness, which unifies us all. It is the one source, for instance, that allows life to be known through the vast variety of diverse expressions of creation known on this planet.

We are one; we are diverse. We are whole, we are part of a large whole, and we are a unique essence unto ourselves. We are unified in that wholeness; we are our own aspect of creation. This is the swan song for creation here. And this is what you beings from Polaris have generously offered to bring back to the collective consciousness, to the collective Soul participation here within the context of free choice.

Honor the Choices in Life

One way for you Polarians to understand the concept of unity in diversity that is vital to the Earth Blueprint is to learn to honor each one's diverse choices in life. Here is an example of someone gaining that helpful understanding.

"I am a student of Susann's and Polaris is my home world. I was wrestling with a relationship issue. It seemed my husband never followed through with commitments he declared were important to him. This used to make me ballistic. I knew I could either badger him into the ground or uncover why it was such a standoff for me. Susann guided me to be with my Soul Family in Polaris. It was easy to honor these beings who I know exist in the wholeness that means everything to me. This was a gentle and profound revelation for me. They reminded me that in the Earth world there are many ways to express one's Soul. I have to remember that free choice and the reality of unity in diversity of expression that I know deep inside. Oh, yeah, I knew that when I married my husband. I loved him because he brought unique ingredients to the mix of our togetherness, our unified love and expression. The beings of my Soul Family said, 'Honor his choices in life.' Bingo! Honor his choices in life. That was totally freeing. It became my mantra. And, the icing on the cake was that as I took off the grip I had on him and honored his choices, he began to slowly make different choices that were freer for him too. It was like his Soul got lifted to a more honorable level as the energy of Honor his choices in life was around him."

Dedication to Wholeness

Your dedication to wholeness as Souls is palpable. You are like Knights of the Round Table honoring each one at the table for their contribution. Each is equally valuable in making up the expanded expression of unified wholeness through diverse contribution here. The round table speaks of divine equality. In modern day terms, the janitor is seen to be just as valuable in the running of the corporation as the president or CEO. Without each spoke of the wheel in place, the wheel can't turn and move all its parts forward.

This is the Polaris mission—to reinstate this truth so that wholeness here through unity in diversity may thrive.

You whose Soul Family is from Polaris love bringing this wholeness. You are deeply dedicated and loyal to this end. Thank goodness! In a world where there is so little ability for individuals to stay on a path and be true to their own North Star, the Polaris frequency is highly valuable.

You "Knights of the Round Table" have a great objection to the hierarchical system. Top-down management makes your stomachs turn. It has nothing to do with wholeness, and everything to do with the dysfunctional distortion of polarity. It is a means of creating the "haves" and the "have-nots," those who rule and those who serve the rulers as though there is a better-than or worse-than dynamic involved. Polarian knights cannot support any system, group, or dynamic of this nature. It is vital for you to continually bring in wholeness in your lives, jobs, and influences. This is essential for your Soul fulfillment.

War Exemplifies Polarity as a Lack of Wholeness

Polarity has been brought to a devastating level here. It declares good and evil, creation and destruction, war, competition, and judgment, and proclaims who is on top and who is on the bottom. There are endless power struggles. Polarity brings the state of powerlessness, which can create buying into the dysfunctional use of power. The "we know you better than you know yourself" mentality in leadership is an outgrowth of polarity. And we have all seen the devastation of Adolf Hitler's trying to colonize "lesser" peoples and races for his own agenda.

War is the epitome of the polarized consciousness here. As long as we buy into anything less than valuing unity in diversity in our own consciousness, we are buying into the war energy born of polarization and we will never know the peace from feeling one with the all that is, nor will we feel the unique aspects of God that each of our brothers and sisters hold.

If we object to a political leader or system we must first recognize that the placement of that person or system is born of a polarized consciousness collectively. So we are objecting to polarity. To correct that, we must be dedicated to bringing unification through wholeness.

We start by being diligent and loyal to the reality being held in our world personally. As we feel clear in our choice for wholeness, we will discontinue polarizing and feel the freedom of allowing others to create their own choices without being in a battle over their choices. When we are in a battle over other people's choices we only accentuate our position of having a personal agenda and trying to impose our truth on others—trying to play God, to put it simply. And in a polarized world if we are trying to play God for another, we are on a teeter-totter that will pull us to ask others to play God for us.

As we come back to the middle ground of knowing wholeness, we live from the place that unifies us and celebrates diversity within wholeness. We begin to create a world that generates itself from that wholeness. This generates new structures, systems, and leadership based on wholeness. We are all Knights of a Round Table. Sound impossible? You can always call on the Polaris energy. You are not alone. This energy is alive and well to be drawn on. "You may say that I'm a dreamer, but I'm not the only one. Someday you will join us, and the world will be as one."

The Focused Nature of Polaris Souls

Another aspect the Polaris heritage brings is a single-minded, very focused nature. This focus aids your dedication to wholeness and your reliability as a north star in life. Your focus in whatever is valuable to you brings assurance that the way to wholeness is possible because you are one-pointedly on it. You are very trustworthy in your endeavors and can truly be counted on. That makes you excellent partners and friends. You hold a dependability that is a breath of fresh air in this world that carries so much instability.

This tenacity has to be held as a spiritual component, otherwise the tenacity turns to stubbornness. "My way or the highway" attitude can creep in. Your view that there is only one way, one whole, one abiding universal presence from which everything springs is exquisite. And if it goes sour, it turns into a stubbornness that doesn't want to see all the diverse ways that one whole can be given expression here.

You who come from Polaris know there is truth back of everything because everything is part of the whole. At the same time you see that in the game of polarity, so many wars are based on religious or spiritual diversity and consequent comparison and competition. When you look at the myriad of religions there are in this world, you see the truth inherent in each one. What is often being conveyed by these wars, albeit subliminally, is the feeling that our way of viewing spirit is better than yours, or our way is better for you than how we see you expressing spirit. You Polarians celebrate the diverse ways that spirit is described and honored and you do not get caught in the game of polarity that compares and contrasts religions or spirituality.

In the spirit of unity there is truly a place for every expression of spirit, as many as there are individuals who are an expression of it.

The Polarian Challenges

A challenge for you from Polaris is your tendency to allow the loyalty and dedication you have to the one way of wholeness, to become a stubbornness that doesn't allow diversity to be present. You from Polaris can have a tendency to see the path before you and forget that there are many ways to the same pot of gold at the end of the rainbow. Sometimes you will find a way that works to express wholeness and stay a bit glued to that way. You can be slow to change and see that in essence there are many ways of expressing and experiencing the oneness. Sometimes you need encouragement to explore diversity in unity. It is always good for you to remember to be dedicated to the emergence of wholeness in all its manifestations.

Charlene and Kevin, both from Polaris, were working with some marital challenges. They had a sense that this wasn't simply about their communication skills faltering. They knew there was more wanting to be shared, but how to get there? We "packed our bags" and went to Polaris. It was paradise for them. It was filled with such a depth of creativity that was shared—the essence of oneness in creation, they said. They each had their own unique experience. Kevin connected with the absolute conviction to the mission of oneness as he spoke to a council of beings about the design of his mission and his contract with them. Charlene basked in the satisfaction of wholeness present there. Everyone worked together towards a common purpose. The focus for her was birthing this wholeness into creation. Kevin and Charlene took a few minutes to focus their agreements to share in birthing the oneness into the dynamic of wholeness here in this world. It was intimate and potent. Between them they saw how this remembrance ignited new possibilities of sharing through their marriage. It wasn't better communication tools they needed; it was a deepening of their shared Soul purpose, born of their Polarian heritage and commission. It was now activated and they were ecstatic newlyweds as they walked (floated!) out of my office.

In addition to stubbornness, you Polaris beings are challenged with a tendency towards stagnation. When faced with a change in your life, instead of seeing the goal or result of change as dynamic movement in bringing wholeness to the new situation, you can get caught in the polar-opposite side of the coin and feel that the change will take you out of wholeness. Therefore you may stay stuck and stagnate where you are because the wholeness you know is surer than the lack of wholeness the unknown will temporarily bring. In fact, this unknown, which is merely a gap or void, is the very opportunity for wholeness to be given expression. It is your Soul mission to do so. When you feel stagnation it is a signal that this is the perfect moment to bring in the outpouring of your Soul essence of wholeness.

Creation in wholeness is a kaleidoscope of brilliant and infinite Light! Be committed to reinstating wholeness here through as many avenues as possible. Bringing wholeness as an individual expression is key for those of you from Polaris. To unify the body, mind, and spirit within is truly the first step in bringing wholeness in unity here. To bring unity in diversity for others requires you to establish it within your own body, mind, and emotional expression.

Be the North Star

You can be the North Star for all of the aspects of the expression of you and for all the emotional components that are seeking wholeness and a place of rest and connection. Be the North Star of spirit for yourself and your journey through life. This is the Polarian way. The Polarian way can be drawn on anytime to bring unity within the self. You are like the Sun from which our life expression, like rays of Light, exude so the world can feel the essence of wholeness because of your radiant presence. The knowledge that wholeness is present and a unifying way exists is indeed a welcome presence on Earth today.

Following is an interview with a Polarian friend.

Susann: Cynthia, when you consider the fact that you are from Polaris, the North Star, what resonates in your Soul about your connection to this world?

Cynthia: Polaris is the point of absolute trustworthiness. I am aware of that essence in myself. I may not live it all the time, but I know it is always there for me. Wholeness is the whole thing, the big pursuit for me.

Susann: How do you bring those elements to your life?

Cynthia: At some points in my life I really felt that the gaps in my human nature, the developmental gaps, the personality gaps, the health gaps, the gaps in every direction were more apparent than the sense of wholeness I inherently know. I do feel those gaps and bring wholeness where separateness in the form of these gaps is. The wholeness overrides and transcends the gaps, which is what results in health. When I feel health, there is that force that wants to flood my being as a radiant sense of something.

This state of wholeness and unity includes my personal integration of male and female energies. In every point of diversity there is the balance behind it. There's the yin and the yang, but there's always the wholeness behind the yin and yang, which holds both of them and allows them to be true.

Recovery and healing are possible because there is something to recover into. It's only the top quarter inch of this world where wholeness is missing in action. That one-quarter inch is not that substantial.

It is just made up of the illusion of the absence of wholeness we live in. Wholeness is where the action is and how we are kept healthy.

Susann: How do you experience a sense of Soul fulfillment in bringing wholeness to the world at large?

Cynthia: There's a sense of dynamic completion that comes when a state is returned to wholeness. There is a desire in me to bring things to that completion, restoring health and unity.

I have a compulsion to bring wholeness into diversity, to allow the truth of unity to be brought into the differing races, cultures, countries, religions, walks of life, and political systems. I find that building on the common ground creates wholeness within diversity.

I feel naturally drawn to causes that celebrate the human spirit, no matter what the cultural background. I loved being part of the world wide assistance in bringing aid to those impacted by the Tsunami in Indonesia at the end of 2004. I also participated in the second Parliament for World Religions Conference in Capetown, South Africa in 2000 that brought together people from all over the world to honor the common ground of the language of spirit that we all speak. I love to be part of such gatherings that focus on seeing connection through all the outer diversifications of expression of the people of this world.

Personally speaking, when I find myself feeling integrated in my own body, mind, and spirit I feel a great sense of union with and contribution toward the common ground that exists around the globe. It is very exhilarating for me to embody this sense of wholeness that my Soul has come to give to the nature of life here.

Establishing and reinforcing the points of connection and sameness of intent is uppermost. It doesn't matter how you get there. There are many ways to get there. Finding what there is to build on that is shared is the key. The differences are like the gaps. They are there, but they aren't. There is diversity, but behind it we are the same spirit. There it is. We are one being animated in different ways, and it just takes the view from the heart to see the unity behind the differentiation. So the differentiation is finite. But back of it is the eternal.

The following is a second interview I had with a woman whose Soul Family is from Polaris.

Susann: Carol, how would you describe the essence that your Soul knows about wholeness, unity, and oneness?

Carol: I feel that in the essence of wholeness, there's never any separation, and that everything all came from one particle, and we're all part of that. It seems like oneness is really a big part of life for me, which creates a whole right-left brain synchronicity that brings balance. There's never a separation in Polaris. So it was never tilted one way or another at all. We are here in this world to bring it back into that complete sphere of one.

Susann: When you bring in wholeness, what does that look like for you?

Carol: Wholeness is coming in with everything you've always needed. You're complete, and the paradigm is whole. Feeling whole leads you to a bigger, wider universe. It's how you feel after becoming one. You feel whole, and you feel complete and satisfied. There is no sense of trying, no having to leave your bubble because there is no inside and outside. You are in both at the same time. There's a very satisfying little "Hmm," which feels very grounded.

Susann: Your job description from Polaris is to bring oneness into a diverse world. When you walk into this diverse and distinct world and everybody's doing their own thing and judging better or worse, good and bad, how do you find yourself having an influence in that field that's so tangled?

Carol: I definitely have the best influence when I don't judge this world. I get this image of the zone of no separation, like the yin/ yang sign, that I bring. We're all the same. We're all equal. It's holding the place of really deep knowing and understanding that my Soul knows. So if I came to Earth and everybody's a little tilted, I will not judge them or try to fix them, but just be the one and balance the energy that is out of whack.

Susann: You have the knowledge that there is only one Creator, and there are many ways to get to that source through religions, philosophies, etc. All religions are just diverse expressions of God, but there is only one source from which all of this springs. What do you want to say about that?

Carol: I see a picture of the one place of wholeness at the center of this Light tunnel. Out of that Light springs little Lights as extensions of the one.

Susann: When you think of the different religions and philosophies of the world, how do you hold a place for them in your heart? They're at war with each other and very pitted against each other. How does that feel for you?

Carol: I know that there is a seed for absolute truth and connection to oneness at the root of each religious tradition. There's a mystical side to each one that rings true. I'm also aware of the distortion apparent in each religious tradition that feels untrue, and not born of the seed of oneness. Anything that seems so untrue and so incongruous really grates against my nerves. My whole nervous system feels it. When I go outside of the mystical feeling of oneness and I look and I see government and religion going together and people killing over this thing, which is supposedly spirit, I say, "Oh my God, it's overwhelming." And I want to shut down and stop and stagnate, which you told me is a Polaris tendency.

Susann: I understand that your Soul strength shows up as loyalty, tenacity, dedication, and single-mindedness. These qualities spring from this sense that there is one way, there's one God. You are very dedicated and loyal to the one way; to the point of being stubborn. How would you describe how dedication and loyalty show up in your life work?

Carol: Dedication and loyalty are big parts of me. For instance, I see a way that's right for me, and I know it's right for me, but it's definitely not right for other people. And I've had to accept that. I have to be careful about this dedication to a single-mindedness that says, "This is the way it is." I keep working on turning that dedication and drive towards God and bringing the whole, unifying ball of energy to wherever I am. The focus of loyalty is often a feeling of "this is the way it is for me" kind of intensity. I know I need to be flexible with relationships and also surround myself with people who get my dedication.

Susann: It is good to be dedicated, because in this world, most people are just so transient in what they hold to be true for themselves and what they're dedicated and committed to. Everyone talks about the issues around commitment. You who have lived on Polaris know what it is to be committed to something and hold to that. There's a deep value to that.

Carol: Yes! Definitely when I was in racing, I was very committed. And then I came upon Women's Quest, which is what I'm doing now. I am passionate about bringing wholeness through this field. I am committed to it. It's what I must do. If I don't connect to spirit every day, then I'm really in trouble. That is the truest commitment for me to have.

The Polarian Proclamation: I am whole. Wholeness exists because I am here.

IO

PLEIADIAN

Just do it.

Star System Location: Pleiades; the seven sisters constellation.

Soul Characteristics:

* You bring high speed to the forces of change and growth here.
* You amplify connection and communication in this world.
* You galvanize one-pointedness in living from total immersion in the present.
* You are movers and shakers.
* You are fast paced and goal oriented.

Well Known People:

Jim Carrey

Robin Williams

Jack Nicholson

Angelina Jolie (40% Parallel)

Dustin Hoffman

Keith Richards (Rolling Stones)

Ringo Starr

David Letterman

Kevin Kline

Michael Jordan (also Sirian)

Arnold Palmer

The Pleiadian Soul heralds from the star system of Pleiades, which is the Seven Sisters constellation of stars. Your most dominant characteristic is your speed, in relationship to change, spiritual growth, and outer personality. You are here to bring high speed to the forces of change and growth that govern the evolutionary process. Pleiadians have been very helpful in speeding up the advancement of all our missions and purposes by bringing people of like minds and hearts together. Any idea or creative endeavor is amplified when two or more come together. We can see this happening through a political or religious movement, a marching band, or a team sport. The civil rights marches, the race for the cure running races to support the cure for cancer, or work related strikes bring creative attention for changes absolutely. It has been scientifically proven that groups praying together or meditating together have an immediate influence on those around them. Deepak Chopra, Gregg Braden, and James Twyman all have books that demonstrate the power of group prayer or meditation.

Pleiadians are here to amplify change, connection, and communication. You are responsible for things like the World Wide Web and numerous forms of mass media that have galvanized and continue to galvanize spectrums of communication for collective growth and expansion.

You are excellent communicators and very vocal about your beliefs. You feel this is a necessary part of getting the message of Light across. Your words hold the blueprint for change and growth. You have an ease in suggesting that change is the nature of life and growth is the nature of creation. You have great knowledge in the ease of how change can happen in the blink of an eye. It's that simple. We can be inspired by the Pleiadian energy of conviction as much if not more than the particular platform they are endorsing.

"Just Do It!"

The Nike commercial that says "Just do it" is the voice of the Pleiadian Soul. You are not into karma and penance, or being victims in life. You believe that we are each responsible for being the commander of our own life. This includes the truth that our past is ours to deal with through the aperture of the present moment. "Just do it" implies that if we want something to change, it is up to us to do it. Be the change we want to see. It's that simple and straightforward. That is your spirit. "What are you waiting for?" is the Pleiadian proclamation. If something is not working we have the power and know-how to change it. The Pleiadian voice is "Just do it." Change the channel and bring a new perspective, a higher road, and the compassionate approach to the situation you would like to experience. We are the authors of our destiny. No excuses. No poor me. Make the choice for what is true and change the pattern that doesn't fit you anymore. It's done. Get over it. We're here to bring in the New Age. We all have our stories, our injustices done to us, how we have been hurt and betrayed by Love and God, seemingly. They just are. And we can step out of this old pattern as easily as we step put of a Halloween costume when Halloween is over.

Just do it. Claim the New Age. Claim the new self. The Pleiadian message is "It is in your hands." This is the creative moment and this is all we have. The only way we have to change the past is to bring the Light of now to this moment.

A Pleiadian's declaration to live in the present moment and let go of anything else is so valuable in this world fraught with trauma and drama. "Just do it" allows us the buoyancy to surface again for a breath of fresh air no matter how dark and deep the waters of despair. There is nothing wrong with despair, but there is nothing helpful about holding onto it like a life raft.

My good friend Joan is Pleiadian. Recently her boyfriend, whom I also know, was coming into town to surprise her for her birthday. I was in on the whole plan, which was great fun. Joan's boyfriend showed up at her office and totally surprised her. The surprise worked! I was concerned that her boyfriend's appearance would upset her and all her plans. I should have known. I remembered that she was Pleiadian. She turned on a dime! As a Pleiadian she has that natural ability to go with change and "Just do it!" She changed her plans readily and was up for a whole new approach to her week. It was a great learning experience for me. Ah yes, change is easy; just do it. That's what she showed me.

Another terrific phrase that comes out of your Pleiadian mouths is "get over it!" Isn't this a fun and refreshing phrase to assist us to let go and live in the new moment and see what it has in store for us all?

Challenges for Pleiadians

Seeing the goal is vital to a Pleiadian. Understanding there are many steps to that end product is the challenge. In starting a new business, seeing where you want to be in a year is vital. Pleiadians can do this easily, but you may become frustrated that it truly takes all of that year to actually get to the goal. Classes and courses are important steps to a goal for instance. Pleiadians must remember that life is a process to enjoy each step of the way.

The challenge for you as Pleiadians is your desire for everything to be immediate. "Just do it" can translate for you as "I want it and I want it now." Or, "I want conclusion, resolution, answers, and solutions immediately." This challenge comes from an inability to fully comprehend the creative process when it is in operation. Life is a process. It's easy to understand in the birth of a baby. There is conception, then gestation, and finally birth. You have far more experience with immediacy and instantaneous manifestation than you do with the concept of the creative process. In this Earth gravitational field, things take time. It's not necessarily meant to be that way, but that's where we are in the evolutionary scheme of things here, because of the collective choices that have been made.

As Pleiadians, you often do not have patience for the process of life and what it feels like to put your hands in the clay, so to speak, and dive into life simply for the sake of the feel of it. You want end results and can miss what's in the moment, like smelling the flowers. The other drawback is that you can be too quick and miss valuable steps. If you have a term paper to write, you may forget the importance of editing (spell checking!). The teacher may wonder how you got from A to Z in the hypothesis. For the Pleiadian, getting to Z is the object. For the teacher, describing why $2 \times 3 + 8 - 4 = 10$ is the greatest lesson.

Champions for Growth and Change

As a Pleiadian, you are definitely here to bring change. Because this world operates from a place of polarity, I often find that your greatest strength can be your greatest weakness. The love for change and always being drawn to the next exciting thing is your magic. The opposite tendency can show up in your reluctance to change and grow in your personal lives at times.

When you are into something it is total immersion. You will pour yourself into the "Just do it" at hand. This total immersion is your translation for the passion of doing life fully. This is how it was meant to be. Total immersion in life is what you Pleiadians love to bring to the forefront. Your word is this: "Experience life." Do not get caught in emotional reaction to it, please. The emotional realm was designed to support the feeling of life moving through all the senses. This possibility is a virtual feast of sensation and experience.

Just as we know that we only use 2 percent of the brain, we are also severely handicapped in our use of the emotional realm. The emotional realm was not constructed for drama, but for aliveness; it is available in the uniqueness of each and every moment.

I have a yoga teacher with many incredible facets to her expression, and one of the most fun is her Pleiadian nature. She is a self-proclaimed "experience junkie." She loves to experience everything this Light-filled life has to offer. I would say that is the true design for life experience here. She is also a fabulous example of a being who is here to encourage change and growth with high speed. "Just do it" is so much her motto that a group of her apprentices, for her birthday, gathered together all the Nike ads saying "Just do it" and created a grand poster. "Just do it" is one of her theme songs and it contributes to ease of the transformation and bliss in our yoga class.

Pleiadians have come to bring what has been termed "the New Age." This relates to bringing in a new way of being and a new way of living life at a higher frequency. This higher frequency for the Pleiadians is on the wavelength of growth and change. You will always be exploring new ways of bringing growth to the situation at hand, or the relationship you are engaged in. Never a dull moment. Bringing the reality of "Just do it" is what brings satisfaction to a Pleiadian's Soul. Because your nature is very fast paced, no moss grows under you. You are great entrepreneurs and movers and shakers. Anyone starting a new endeavor would want a Pleiadian on their team. Anyone wanting growth and change in any way, shape or form, call on the Pleiadian energy field to magnetize that instantaneous place of new beginning present in that "Just do it" way. Anyone spending time with a Pleiadian can capture the essence of one-pointedness and total immersion into what can be a done deal now.

There is a book on personal growth called *The Sedona Method* by

Lester Levenson. It is a fabulous tool to help people learn how to let go of whatever feeling is present in them in the moment so that they are free to move into the next moment with ease around change and growth. The originator of this method, Lester Levinson, is indeed a Pleiadian. He has created an excellent example of a Pleiadian tool. It is okay to be fully present with what arises and it's just as okay to acknowledge it and let it go. This way of being brings a lot of freedom.

Words on the Pleiadian Soul characteristics are succinct and to the point because that is the personality of the Pleiadian. You pour yourself into the moment but when it is done, that's it. For a Pleiadian reading these words, you will feel satisfied quickly and easily. No need for me to pontificate endlessly for you to get the point!

Following is a short interview with a Pleiadian friend to give a feel for her perspective living from a Pleiadian Soul heritage.

Susann: Hello, Connie! We'll make this quick and to the point, for I know that is your strength! What is your favorite part of being Pleiadian?

Connie: I'm so aware of being quick to learn my lessons. It has helped me with my impatience with others to understand this. I seem to be so much faster than others to learn, to implement change, and to find the path that would bring the greatest growth.

It also makes me feel even more impatient with others. I'll see myself saying, "Come on everyone. Hurry up. Can't you get it? What are you waiting for?" This would be inspirational and encouraging, but when I say it out of impatience, it feels like I'm anything but encouraging. I'm more frustrated and that doesn't help. I suppose it is frustration out of loneliness. I want others to join me because there's a place in me that feels like no one else gets it and I feel alone in my ability to be so quick and into change and growth wherever possible. I have so much attachment to other people hurrying up so I can have more playmates.

I have been working for a long time on being able to understand that people don't have to get it or do something just like I do to be compatible energetic playmates. I would define playmates as those who have a recognition that they are here for a purpose and are ready to play in life! They are ready to play in this wonderful world. They are able to get their lesson and be in position just to create.

Susann: What's it like for you to recognize that you are part of a natural Soul Family that has family members from around the globe?

Connie: Talking to someone who has the same foundation is so refreshing. For instance, a friend I have had since childhood is in my Pleiadian Soul Family. I have an amazing kinship with him. Strangely, although we didn't see each other for years, our lives are very parallel. There is an inexplicable sense that we understand each other. It's not just because we grew up in the same hometown. We had this feeling of similar foundation even though he grew up Hindi in a staunch Indian family and I was a white Lutheran. We grew up influenced by two very different systems, but we were brother and sister very deeply and still are.

As a teacher, I have inspired others to know that you don't have to wait around for things to change. They can happen instantly. My friend Sally loves to emotionally process everything that comes across her screen, but I have taught her that change can happen without having to process continually.

Susann: What do you sense you have to teach here?

Connie: In the Pleiadian world we always knew absolutely that everything is working out to the highest good. We knew what we were doing and had assurance in this knowledge and sense of irrefutable connection. This Soul characteristic is vital for me to remember because I haven't always trusted that everything is working out to the highest good when I'm coming from a mere mental approach to my life. The trick for me even in the midst of the war and tribulation occurring here is to watch from a place of the natural mystery of life combined with the higher level of knowing that I bring from my Pleiadian world. As a teacher for others my strongest voice is to say, "Go do it. Go live it. Do not just read about it in a book, but go out and express who you are and do who you are with confidence and knowing."

I like inspiring other people to have experiences that will open them up to engaging in life fully and I have no resistance to conveying my beliefs with conviction. Pleiadians are on target, focused, and action oriented. We are able to clear karma quickly, learn lessons, forgive ourselves, and move on. We are decisive and when we make a decision we plant our whole self into it. When we are on an issue, or a task, you can consider it done, once started. The resolution process for us is intact. If it's an ongoing process we are engaged in, we need to learn not to leave pieces out along the way, or skip steps. This can happen because we are so driven to get to resolution and the end product. Completion is a sure thing in our hands.

My words of inspiration: Keep moving forward and it will work itself out. You don't need to dig up every piece of soil there is to be able to grow and move out of anything you are presently in. When you keep moving forward, it puts the energy you are committing now into the next space you are going to, and then your energy just starts shifting toward that. You don't have to plant yourself in your old way, or stew in it, or continually process everything you feel.

Susann: And lastly for me, what do you love most about bringing your Pleiadian gifts to this life?

Connie: It is so valuable for me to understand diversity and realize that I have my particular gifts and others have their distinct gifts. My one-pointed nature is great, but there has to be room for a softer side. It can be a bit hard edged. We can turn on a dime and shift modes just like that. Now I'm doing this, now I am doing that. Moving forward, manifesting, and creating is very important to me. How to do this movement from the heart is the challenge I'm working on now.

I love to sink my teeth into whatever has my attention. For instance, if I go to the mountaintop I'm not satisfied just going to the top and coming back down. I need to smell it, roll in it, and experience every aspect of that perspective and situation. When I go into something I go into it fully. I love things that I love so completely. When I commit to something I pour myself into it. I want to experience everything. The phrase from the Nike commercial, "Just do it," really sums it up. Just do it and enjoy it and enjoy the creative process of it unfolding magically in this world, watching from a place of wonder and trusting the mystery.

The Pleiadian Proclamation: "Just do it!"

II

Sirian

There is a better way.

Star System Location: Sirius, within the Dog Star constellation.

Soul Characteristics:

* You are dedicated to bringing this world out of the realm of war and survival, into the realm of creating from a place of joyful co-existence.
* You bring expansive technologies to better our quality of life, physically and spiritually.
* You carry the inherent balance of the male and female qualities within you.
* You are deeply concerned with the healing of this entire solar system, while being very grounded in living this physical life, as we know it here.
* In the context of relationship you live beyond the need to define gender roles.
* You subscribe to the truth of interdependence and co-creation.

Well Known People:

Christopher Reeve

Brad Pitt

Steven Spielberg

Joan of Arc

Eleanor Roosevelt

Halle Berry

Susan Sarandon

Woody Allen

Bill Gates

Warren Beatty

Frank Sinatra

Magic Johnson (also Blueprint Deliverer)

Wilt Chamberlain (also Alpha Centauri)

Babe Ruth (also Pleiadian)

Hank Aaron (also Sirian)

Wayne Gretsky

Jack Nicklaus

Joe Montana (also Polaris)

Joe Namath (also Pleiadian)

Christopher Reeve is a fine example of a Sirian on a mission. His Soul heritage is a combination of Sirian talent and Blueprint Deliverer strength. As a Sirian he had a Soul contract to bring advanced technologies. He has championed the drive for spinal cord research and advocated relentlessly for embryonic stem-cell-research. He was on a definite mission to find "the better way" for those who found themselves in a state of disability in their physical expression. He gave hope to countless individuals and brought success and fulfillment to many who never thought a better way was possible. He truly fulfilled his Soul mission even though he had to be superman in a wheelchair to do so.

Robert Zemeckis is the producer of the movie *The Polar Express.* He pioneered the use of computer generation and the performance capture technique that captures movements of live actors and transfers that image to animated characters. This technique is an excellent example of the Sirian gift of bringing advanced technologies here to create a better life. We will see much more of this Sirian advanced technology. Robert is a prime example of the use of Sirian creativity through technological means to bring the field of entertainment to a whole new level. This movie is about believing in the true spirit of Christmas no matter what our age. How great to use that creative theme for this magical production. And, of course, Tom Hanks is the lead actor. Another Sirian Soul.

Halle Berry is an example of a Sirian who captures the expression of the balance of male and female. Although her movie *Catwoman* was not a popular movie, her role in the movie was perfect for her Soul characteristics. She depicted the beauty of the feminine and the power and strength of the masculine. I saw an interview with her on television and in it she described how important it is to her to be seen not only for her femininity but for her masculine traits that she is so proud of, whether it be in her personal life or on the screen. She is a Sirian Soul in expression, through and through.

The main role for you who herald from the world of Sirius is to travel throughout the galaxy and assist in bringing advancement to existing civilizations. You usually come at times when a civilization is on the brink of coming to a place of wholeness and you arrive to help further it to that point. Sirians were instrumental in the ancient Egyptian time period and the Atlantis time period. These were definitely times of potentially significant advancement for mankind. I have met many Sirians who feel a distinct kinship to those civilizations and times who no doubt played a part in the history of those times. There are many of you Sirians who have returned in this present time to help advance this world out of a survival, war-based mentality to a world of creating together in the spirit of wholeness.

Warriors for Truth and Honor

Sirians hold a flame of honor for all that is true—from the universal picture of truth, to the simple truth of connection, to the man sitting next to you on a bus. You are warriors for justice and balance and bringing out the best of what any world has to bring. You are ferocious about seeing and knowing the greatness of what each Soul Family has chosen to bring to the universal picture. You stand for all that is right and true and whatever it takes to bring Souls back to that truth. You hold a noble view of all that is working in the universal scheme of creation. You are seen as high ranking ambassadors throughout this Universe, deeply respected for your dedication to service and honorable intentions.

In this world you hold a constancy for honoring what serves humanity best. You feel drawn to hold integrity in all your endeavors—political, service-oriented business, or humanitarian efforts. In spiritual terms, you keep a vision alive for the higher road in any situation, personally or globally.

You participated in many battles to assist in upholding truth and wholeness throughout the Universe. Yet, while you are on Earth you hold a real aversion to war. Even watching movies with violent war scenes seems ridiculous and pointless to you. I've been told by a number of Sirians that these kinds of movies are not even entertaining to you. You know from experience that to go to war against another planet is futile. It just becomes an endless, pointless back and forth of killing, like a tug of war. Your team pulled on the rope one way, the other team pulled on the other end of the rope, back and forth continually until one team collapsed. This win/lose equation is not the best way to move humanity forward. What about fighting for forward movement and the best that one or the collective has to offer instead of constantly putting energy into defending or fighting against another?

To you it's clear that putting time, energy, and money into developing the internal strength of a country is much more constructive than using all our resources toward combating the so-called enemies of that country that have made it feel weak and in need of help. The weakened country needs assistance in rebuilding itself through honoring its own strengths and resources that have been lost. Don't we do this naturally when working through organizations such as the Peace Corps? The Peace Corps helps people to get back on their feet and be more self-sufficient. This is the honorable Sirian influence at work. Your Sirian influence is a much-needed component to move us out of the state of being at war with those we don't agree with, to creating a partnership with those who wish to find the better way for themselves by strengthening their stance as a person or country.

The following is an experience a Sirian client had to help him with his own personal struggle, which still plagued him from the impact on his Soul of his Sirian warring history even to this day. The good news is, it is also his story of resolving that inner warring to bring peace and well-being to his sleep life, and consequently to all of his life.

"One day I realized that my sleep disturbance was bigger than just a common fear of burglars coming into my house at night. I could feel a sense of craziness around my waking up in the night that was bigger than life. I felt like I was waking up in the middle of a battle zone internally. I didn't remember what I was fighting or why, I just remembered that strong fight or flight response that felt like my life was on the line and the enemy was all around and after something that was important to me.

"So Susann and I took a Soul journey to uncover this mystery. I discovered that in my night travels I was traveling to my Sirian world and running into a memory of a time when I was literally at war with other beings over the Sirian right to be such an incredibly advanced civilization. I get now how I had trouble sleeping out of fear that when my Soul traveled at night to my Soul memory of my home world for that necessary deep nourishment that home base provides, that I was going to battle for my home and not actually getting my Soul food that I kept hoping to receive.

"Continuing on my Soul journey I changed the pattern in my Soul memory bank. I consciously took the journey home and did not let these beings interfere with the mission of the Sirian world. The reunion was fantastic and the beings of my Soul Family from Sirius helped me create a golden path of solid connection between their world and my life here, so that whenever I traveled at night my journey was safe and sure. What a difference that made to my sleep! I could now sleep soundly without fear of having to go to war if I surrendered to the land of deep sleep and the journey of connection to the place where my Soul gets richly nourished. I was also able to release the fear that some boogie man was out there trying to destroy my connection to the Soul food sleep gave me."

Bringing the Better Way

You who have come from Sirius are here to bring advanced technologies, which translates to new ways and means for the better way you know is possible here. You are here to claim the higher road, the greater good, the possibility of seeing life from a whole new way beyond survival and warring. Indeed, "there is a better way" is your phrase to this world.

You find yourself continually looking for the better way in life. This may be through problem solving, new creative ways to see a situation or relationship, or simply changing your internal perspective in any given moment. "There is always a better way" is your approach to life in all its facets. This is truly a means that we can all adapt in allowing our lives to move forward with strength and integrity. You Sirians remind us that free choice is always available and new beginnings are always pertinent.

The following words are from a Sirian friend: "The theme song for the Sirians is 'there's a better way.' One way to translate that is, 'never accept limitations.' We are powerful creators and the potential here for creating is grand indeed. The key to living in this better way is to keep the gateway of the heart open as the vessel through which divine Love shines. If the heart is engaged the lower frequencies of war can't be engaged at the same time. The portal of the human heart allows Light for change to come into experience. Receiving Light as the energy field for change is much more productive than using energy to fight against what isn't working for us. We can fight something or we can shed Light on the topic to get a better perspective on it.

I love the way that Light is a fabulous example in itself for an advanced technology that Sirians use. Laser technology uses Light as a steady stream that doesn't vary and thus is a powerful instrument for healing and change. Also, sound and vibration are used to change the morphogenetic field. In the Atlantis time, laser technology was distorted and used as a weapon. Now laser is being used in a pure sense, which is a sign of where we are as a civilization. There is space now for pure Light to come in and be a transformative power."

Advanced Technologies That Sirians Bring

The Sirians came collectively during the time of the building of the Egyptian pyramids. This specific time of building related to bringing advanced Sirian technologies to this world. The advanced technologies of the Sirian world are an energy that has been held within the structure of the pyramids all this time.

To this day these pyramids stand and hold an energy that is almost indescribable in its nature. The atmosphere in the pyramids holds a vast, peaceful, exquisite connection to a grand, benevolent, and eternal universal power. Pilgrimages are taken to the pyramids so that people have the opportunity to reconnect with the majesty of universal frequency held within them. Touching into this frequency allows a remembrance of a better way and better times that we all long to experience here. We long to experience them because we know they are an inherent part of our divine make-up from ancient times. The Sirians built the pyramids so that a sacred place could be held in the earth for this frequency. It certainly worked. The pyramids still stand and bring the atmosphere of peace and universal connection for many to experience, thanks to the Sirians who built them.

The question of how the Egyptian pyramids were built has always been perplexing to many. In the building of the pyramids, massive stones were able to be moved and architectural perfection achieved because the Sirians telepathically communicated with the beings from their world to bring through the capacity to perform telekinesis here. Through this connection and telecommunication they were fed instruction to do what has been thought of as superhuman feats. Whenever I mention this to Sirians they invariably agree that this rings true for them. They have always felt a strong connection to the Egyptian civilization and the times of the building of the pyramids. And they feel quite comfortable with the idea of telekinesis and telecommunication. They know they hold those possibilities in their Soul memory.

Ability to Communicate Telepathically

Telepathy was part of the Original Blueprint for human life here. Sirians brought the ability for telepathic connection and communication to be re-seeded here. Telepathy was an inherent part of the design for human beings from the beginning. It got lost as the collective pattern of separation happened. So one of the job attributes that Sirians agreed to help re-establish here was telepathy. The same was true of telekinesis. These are examples of what I call advanced technologies that the Sirians bring. You Sirians hold the ability within yourselves to telepathically communicate to your home world. You might imagine that you hold little crystal devices within you for this. These crystal devices brought forth the idea for radio crystals for physical communication. The first step in long distance communication was through radio crystals. Now we have cell phones and Ipods and so much more is to come. These are all born of Sirian influence to bring technologies that assist to advance the quality of human life on the planet and to build a civilization that uses advanced methods for communication and connection.

Sirians inherently carry the capacity to telepathically communicate with the beings from your Sirian Star System even now. Your primary challenge is the frustration you carry in not being able to factually have this communication channel open.

Advanced Technologies of Our Day

Other forms of technologies that Sirians have brought to increase quality of life are in the medical field (laser technology, kidney dialysis machines, and technologies for heart bypasses). All are devices designed by Sirians to bring the "better way." These advanced technologies brought into the medical field have given so many renewed health, opportunity for higher quality of life, and a deeper value for the life they are able to have.

We all know someone who has been given a second chance because of heart surgery or chemotherapy or even the use of an antidepressant. Do they not hold a more sacred reverence for the gift of life? Is this not a spiritual experience? Is this not living a better way than they knew before? I think many would testify that after facing potential loss of life or limited capability in the physical capacity to express life, and then to overcome the threat, they experience a greater passion for life and a keener sense of the meaning of life. To live life to its fullest in every moment is indeed the greatest spiritual experience there is. Sirians are highly invested in contributing "the better way" for life, no matter what field of endeavor they are involved in.

The advancement of medical practices currently allows many to have a new lease on life. One possibility is they are given another chance to open their hearts to divine Love. After Bill Clinton had his heart surgery, Hillary Clinton said on a morning talk show that when she and Chelsea were with Bill immediately after his surgery that he was deeply open and filled with love and speaking from his heart as never before. She felt it was the most wonderful time of their relationship. He told her how much he felt loved and appreciated. Life is always conspiring to heal, open, connect, and remember.

Advanced technologies are not just technologies of the physical realm. There are also technologies based on helping people move out of their identification with life as a mere physical existence to the "better way" of experiencing life beyond the trauma and drama of a survival dynamic. There are many technologies that help heal the emotional realm simply and potently to assist a person to live from the joy-filled, creative life as we were designed for. This is another example of how to get to "the better way" for life. Emotional or psychological technologies include many of the modalities such as EMDR (eye movement desensitization) or Integrative Manual Therapy, to name a few, which speed up the release of multiple past traumas that are impacting a person in the present.

The advanced technologies for a better life for Sirians can be extremely varied in their packaging. They can look as simple as energy work or therapeutic touch for healing, as natural as meditation or the use of our inherent intuition. The scientific world is chock full of ways to create a better life. In the field of sports we see skis for the paraplegic, and we see the expansion and specialization of coaches in team sports to enhance player performance. Music CDs out-perform the record album by a long shot. The increase of quality of life in the last twenty years alone is breathtaking thanks to the large Sirian influence that is present now.

Sirians Come at Heightened Times of Civilization

It is logical and not surprising for Sirians to recognize your Soul's timing in being here now during this expansive phase of technological evolution. Every time you as Sirians have been here, whether it was during the Egyptian era, the Atlantean era, or other phases of tremendous advancement, you have felt a calling to be part of a time with a cutting-edge nature. It is such a time now to bring things all the way to completion in this phase of healing this world to the state of wholeness. You are deeply dedicated to this task and mission.

The greatest challenge for you as a Sirian is your sense of the inability to bring advancement to this world, which does not seem to want it. You often feel that you are not able to bring the advanced technologies into the world you are so keen to serve. This is partly because your Sirian communication channels have been clouded and information can't clearly get into your consciousness. Consequently you often feel a sense of incompleteness in your mission or even in your everyday doings.

You are very service oriented. You have come to heal the issue of polarity so that diversity here can be appreciated and not become the justification for competition, comparison, and opposition. You are dedicated to lifting the consciousness out of its rut of seeing diversity as a means to divide and conquer, and taking it back to its original design.

Sirian Contribution During Atlantis

Sirians were here in force during the Atlantean period or age.

This was an advanced civilization said to be here around 9,000-5,000 BC. The Atlantean time was intended to bring an advanced civilization all the way through to completion in wholeness. Instead, the Sirian information was misinterpreted, misused, and abused. We might compare this misuse of information now to the ideas being set forward for the cloning of animals and especially humans. This is an example of the intention to assist in the betterment of humanity gone to an extreme. In Atlantis, the crystal devices that Sirians brought to be used for telecommunication were damaged and the pure information sent from the Syrian world was "read" unclearly. This damage was done by people here who wanted to destroy the advanced abilities for telecommunication and connection to the Sirian world that the Sirians brought. The true use of genetic coding (to put it mildly and simply) was tampered with and a civilization destined to bring Earth evolution to a grand place fell. It collapsed on itself, as disruptive forces took the codes for wholeness and turned the tide to create the illusionary designs for wholeness. These illusionary designs for wholeness refer to people being whole merely in their physical nature, ignoring their spiritual aspect. It would be like proclaiming Ken and Barbie dolls as the ideal human form to be sought after. This idea is a distorted view of wholeness and perfection. It does not include the view of wholeness from the true holographic perspective of diversity in dynamic creation.

The Sirian Challenges

The Sirian challenge you carry is an historical one. You feel responsible for much of the warfare that has occurred in this and other solar systems. And you feel responsible for the demise of the Atlantis civilization because it happened through the misuse of information Sirians brought. You are keen to take this world out of survival and war. Your challenge is to clear your past Soul records by bringing things now to a better outcome this time.

You can get caught in feeling a deep sense of incompleteness. You can also feel the frustration of daily incompleteness and unresolve causing you to overwork jobs and projects. On the other hand, when you feel the frustration of incompleteness you may quit too easily. You also abhor war and can get very caught up in your anger toward what you feel is the utter stupidity of war or going to battle in any situation, whether global or family fueled. Wherever there is opposition, you can feel an internal struggle around its existence. This causes an internal battle, which perpetuates the war effort.

You also can be challenged in your desire to bring this world to the better way of wholeness by going into overdoing or resignation, instead of advancing. Resignation will be exemplified through the act of settling. You will settle in yourself for something other than what in honesty you know would be the better way. Overdoing, for you, would look like pushing the edge beyond what is truly acceptable to this world in your drive to find a better way.

Sirians Bring the Wholeness of
Male and Female Within

A tremendous gift that you Sirians bring that reflects wholeness in a very real way is your own internal knowing of the state of wholeness and completeness. You feel very comfortable with both your male and female sides. You do not feel a division between the two sides, and you know you are made up of both. You do not feel a prejudice for one aspect of yourself or another. You are aware of a dominant gender manifesting through your outer physical characteristics, yes. And you are very happy to be fully engaged with your complimentary aspect.

For example, a Sirian female is usually at ease being something of a tomboy growing up. A Sirian male happily cooks and is not concerned with gender specific roles. I had a Soul Mastery training with two men and two women from Sirius. When they all stood in a line their energies were very overlapping. Each of the four had strong male qualities and strong female qualities. Each one was quite balanced in their energy field. The feeling of wholeness within each one was palpable. A Sirian holds the feeling of the wholeness of both male and female and can do the dance of expressing from either aspect, as both aspects are already in communion within themselves.

Also, you are clear in intimate relationship that there is no need for competition between genders. Who cooks, cleans, earns the money, etc., will work itself out within the wholeness of the union. The outer roles are not as important as the ability to co-create within the union. You have come to declare that wholeness exists already. We do not need another to complete us. We are here to co-create together, just as all the aspects of our individual selves know how to co-create from within.

Sirians do not understand all the fuss around feminism or men needing to explore their feminine side. You recognize that these have been valuable stages in human evolution based on the polarity of gender differences. And you are here to carry the living example of the true Blueprint of male and female operating in co-creative wholeness within to open the door to co-creation between two people. You truly bring the better way in the world of relationship and relatedness. This is truly an example of advanced technology in this world for a couple to move beyond co-dependency to deep communion in love and wholeness.

The downside to this can come as a feeling that you are so whole and complete in yourself that you need no one else to "complete you." This could be a problem if you desire to be in an intimate relationship. Sirians must remember that you don't need relationship to feel whole and it is wonderful to create relationship for the more "advanced" levels of co-creation like sharing and magnifying our gifts of wholeness, or for the purpose of sharing the joy of living in the playground of life!

Bringing peace versus war, bringing creation versus survival, are core ways for Sirians to bring the better or best way possible. Wholeness in creation is truly an advanced technology for this world.

To truly bring forward one's mission as a Sirian is to consciously, knowingly choose the high road in service and never sell out, or settle for, anything less, and never betray the greater whole. For a Sirian the better way is the easy way, for it is aligned with all you agreed to bring to this world. And it is aligned with the purposes of your Soul Family from Sirius. Your actions are clearly for the purposes of serving the galactic picture. Your mission is one of dedication to a broad outworking based on advancement.

Sacred Feminine Councils: A Branch of the Sirian Family

Another asset of the Sirian world that has appeared in the last five to ten years is the re-emergence of balance between the male and female energies in our culture. One very particular way this is coming through are in the Sacred Feminine Councils that the Sirians established. Those Souls who have trained with these councils carry Sirian characteristics. They are developing collectives who work together to establish the true power of the feminine, and to assist in bringing the spirit of co-creation between male and female as was originally intended.

The Sacred Feminine Councils established by the Sirians were born out of the Sirian commitment to teach about the balance and wholeness of the male and female aspects of creation, so they can better work together. The Sirian way of balance and wholeness between male and female is in stark contrast to the "battle of the sexes" that has been in operation here.

There are four dimensions of the Sacred Feminine Council: the Hi-Qua Priestess, the Warrior Priestess, the Eagle Priestess, and the Psychic Healer Priestess.

The Hi-Qua Sacred Feminine Council is the one most represented here at this time in history. As a Soul you may have spent some time training with these Sacred Feminine Councils before coming here, especially for this incarnation, while your dominant Soul Family is from another star system.

The Warrior Priestesses such as Joan of Arc, Helen of Troy, and Xena, warrior priestess (from television fame) give expression to the right use of masculine energy within the feminine field of power. Through the Warrior Priestess energy, the ability to make one's own decisions without having to seek those outside oneself out of self-doubt is emerging.

The Eagle Priestesses are women doing sacred work as their focus here. They are great mystics such as Mother Teresa, Mary Magdalene, Quan Yin, and the Virgin Mary.

The Psychic Healer Priestesses are women empowering the psychic realm for healing. Caroline Myss and Doreen Virtue are examples.

The Hi Qua Priestess

The following are words from a friend in the Hi-Qua Feminine Council who will speak of the strengths of this body of feminine power.

"The Hi-Qua is a small group of galaxy travelers who have done great works in many places. Those who have trained in this Feminine Council like to physically travel throughout this world. We never lost awareness of who we are and why we came here. We are usually very psychic. As women we carry a feminine energy that is slightly different than that of the Earth Goddess energy. We are naturally powerful in the world, which is often interpreted as being more masculine in energy—we are often out in the world taking action and doing things. We are whole and complete in ourselves, carrying the total energy field of the masculine within the feminine. We are here to seed these codes of wholeness within the divine feminine here.

"There can be friction, consequently, with men who are not balanced in their male and female and who will feel threatened by the Hi-Qua power of wholeness. This can cause power struggles or abusive situations. It may take time for the Hi-Qua to find suitable partners who can match and support their work in the world. We cannot compromise our mission to be with a man or masculine energy that does not fully support us.

"Joan of Arc carried not only the Warrior Priestess energy but also the Hi-Qua energy. She is an example of a feminine Soul who never compromised or sold out. She was directed by spirit and wouldn't lessen that, even though she was killed for doing so. She used the power of the collective feminine force and did not use the power to overthrow the existing system. This ability to effectively use this true feminine power is what is being established now collectively, through women and men accessing the true power of the feminine.

"With this true power source in place there is no room for manipulation, backstabbing, misused sexuality, or survival mechanisms to get what you want for yourself or to keep a man.

"The Hi-Qua Sacred Council Mission is to raise the vibration of the planet. In so doing, we had to step out of the familiar structure of the female in a way that can't be measured by the usual standards. I see this happening collectively. Most Hi-Quas are unwilling to hide our power, which means we live life on our own terms as people and are clear about following our natural inner-feminine guidance. Hi-Qua tend to be women who are out in the world stirring things up. We aren't the 'stay at home,' inward facing aspect of the nurturing mother feminine energy."

The Feminine Sacred Councils are seen as an advanced spiritual technology that the Sirians assist in bringing here. These purposes are parallel. The Sirians are also here to heal duality and bring it back to natural polarity. The Feminine Sacred Councils help to do this in relationship to the wholeness of male and female collectively.

The Sirius star system, called the Dog (God) Star, was also named Isis, a powerful feminine figure in Egyptian times.

Historically speaking, the feminine energy was such a threat on the planet to the dominating, misused masculine "power over" energy, the Hi-Qua energy field and influence went underground and were inactive for a while. It is now resurging.

This powerful, balanced feminine energy of the Hi-Qua Priestess and the other Sacred Feminine Councils can be accessed and called on anytime now by anyone.

The Sirian Proclamation: There is a better way!

12

HADARIAN

Love is the essence of life and creation.

Star System Location: The planet Hadar within the star system of
Beta Centauri.

Soul Characteristics:
* You hold the Soul stance that Love is what matters.
* Your view is "What else is there?" You value connection, commu-
nion, and creating together as Love.
* You hold what we define as divine Love.
* You are playful, creative, and live from the heart.
* You have come here to explore the facets of the diamond of Love
that exists in the Blueprint for human experience.
* You have a sensitive heart and deeply feel the lack of Love that
exists here.

Well Known People:
Julia Roberts
Gwyneth Paltrow
Goldie Hawn (also Mintakan)
Princess Diana
Mary Magdalene
Marilyn Monroe (40% Parallel)
Barbra Streisand

Elizabeth Taylor

Jennifer Aniston

Penelope Cruz (40% Mintakan)

Mother Teresa

The planet Hadar's hallmark throughout this Universe is that it has been deemed the planet of divine Love. This beacon for divine Love that Hadar is has been held for our Earth, and it has been held for many other star systems and worlds for an immeasurable length of time.

Hadarian Hallmark of Divine Love

This frequency of divine Love in our human experience feels like the beauty and grace and abundance of divine heart connection and the sacred nature of communion with the Beloved. Divine Love births the riches of co-creation between beings. In the Hadarian experience, the sharing of Love happens as naturally as breathing and is, in essence, all there is to do. Life there is about being Love in all its possible expressions. You beings who have lived in the Hadarian world know deep within your bones and Souls the experience of sharing in the collective expression of Love. You know what it is to operate in the magical flow of a true collective. You can't imagine creating otherwise. Hadarians don't quite jibe with the strong desire for individuation that we strive for here, especially since that individuation usually entails a competitive edge of comparison and competition. For Hadarians the truth of individuation is merely appreciation for the unique, divine spark each one of us is, all born of Love. We are all here to serve Love, as distinct variations of all the facets of Love. It is the collection of the facets of the diamond of Love that gives the diamond its incredible strength, brilliance, and beauty. This is what Hadar is like. It is a place of many connected facets in continual expression of Love as purpose.

My Hadarian client Susan stated how vital and real the nature of community is in Hadar. "By moving beyond this world and uncovering the exquisite nature of Hadar and how it is such a core part of me, I was able to finally feel what a sense of community is all about. I no longer feel alone and am now able to create relationships that are more meaningful and fulfilling to me." Most of us long for community to blossom in our world. We can have it if we focus on the essence of the Hadarian world and let that grow inside to bring forth the bounty of the authentic spirit of community that the Hadarian world has always carried in this Universe.

As a Hadarian, you have tremendous knowledge of co-creation—especially the Love and joy that emanates from creating together. Co-creation between two people means that both benefit equally. This is truly what you strive for in all your relationships.

Hadar holds a true example of family in its original essence, which the spirit of co-creation depicts. Serving Love looks and feels like playing together and enjoying the abundance of Love and the joy of endless possibilities for connection and communion. Co-creation in Love is the joining of different divine sparks together. The kaleidoscope of Love's expression is unlimited.

You Hadarians are very playful, creative, and hold a childlike nature that is refreshing and compelling to be around. It is the same innocent and magical essence of Love in creation that we adore in children at play. You are always fresh, alive, and full of wonder, saying through your hearts, faces, and bodies, "What do I wish to create as Love now, naturally and easily?" You connect and commune here in order to co-create. This is life! And Love is the force animating creation.

Feel right now what it is to know Love for another human being. Take a moment to imagine the beauty of a spring flower bursting forth in the freshness of spring, the feeling of warmth when a loyal dog stands wiggling its little behind as you walk in the door. There are so many ways to know connection and communion in the vast array of the expressions of Love here in this world.

You Hadarians have explored the galaxies to discover and magnify the multitudinous expressions of Love waiting to be known. You see through the eyes of Love and view everything from that perspective. That is your inherent purpose. What a gift you bring here to a world parched and starving for even a drop of the rich commodity you hold. For you, the Earth holds a potential for Love's robe of many colors. You have come not only to assist us to remember the look and feel of divine Love, but you have come to play in the playground of life.

This life is designed to be Love in expression through the physical, mental, and experiential capacities we have—the feeling of Love known as sunlight on our face, when chocolate touches the taste buds in our mouth, when birds sing a mating chorus in trees overhead. This world is ripe with the natural expression of Love everywhere, and it is forever etched in your heart memory: the sensations of your grandmother reading you a story and tucking you in the first of many times, the glow that lives in every cell in your body from a Lover's first kiss. We are blessed to have such an array of Love's expression to behold through all our senses.

The Movie *Cocoon:* The Hadarian Way

The movie *Cocoon* depicted the Hadarian essence well. Divine Love was the elixir for eternal youth that was in the pool where all the elderly men and women swam with the large cocoons that they discovered. There was a scene in the pool in which a brilliant Light was transmitted from a young woman (she was said to be from the planet Antarean) to an Earth boy she met. This transmission energy from her was what Hadarians naturally create all the time. This is your natural state of radiance. This is the true essence of co-creation you lived from in Hadar. The magnification of divine Love was your purpose for existence in Hadar and is now your purpose on Earth. In Hadar, when you exchanged the Light of Love with another Hadarian being, everything was magnified. And then you moved on to the next opportunity to exchange Light as Love with another Hadarian, each with their unique facets of the diamond. Every minute of the day. Very simple and exquisite.

This is also meant to be the purpose for connection between everyone on Earth. We are together to magnify divine Love in all its diversity of expressions. You Hadarians have come to re-instate this divine experience of the truth of Love's power and purpose through its ability to create connection and communion for each and everyone you touch. When we co-create with another person based on this energy frequency, it magnifies who each of us are as divine beings. Love is the greatest essence there is for spirit and Soul growth. You Hadarians embody this radiantly.

The Container for Love

This planetary container for Love was held by Hadar for a very long time until relatively recently. It held a place for the sureness of Love within this Universe. Recently this frequency overflowed from the Hadaraian container and is now available throughout this Universe so that the possibility for this high-magnitude expression of Love can be deeply known in worlds beyond Hadar. It can now be shared throughout this solar system and galaxy. You have come here to inspire and re-activate Love as the governing frequency for the Earth Blueprint. We welcome these beings with open arms and open hearts.

Because of this and other evolutionary shifts that have occurred here, divine Love is once again in the Earth-field. It has always existed in the core of the Earth, like a constant flame. It has only been missing on the surface of the Earth, where we humans have continually chosen to ignore it, abate it, and even destroy it.

This flame of Love has always burned brightly as part of the Blueprint for Earth. Love has always been in the design for specific communion between the heart and the core of the earth. You Hadarians have generously come here to remind us that Love always was here, and is ever-present now. It is the eternal galactic frequency on which existence and creation are based. We can re-ignite that connection and communion for ourselves anytime by visualizing a connection between our heart and the heart flame of Love at the Earth's core. To be alive means Love is flowing through us! To breathe, it means Love is always with us, igniting us at every level. You have come to remind us of this simple fact. Connection, communion, and creation are what all our hearts long for, and this is what makes the world go round!

The Heartache Factor-Challenges

One of the challenges that Hadarians face more deeply than most is your heartbreak for the collective choice here to live outside of Love. You weep inside to see and feel all the evidence for the individual and collective choice to exclude Love, for the choice to be fueled by energies other than Love. Those substitute choices for Love are mostly fear and all its variances. Hadarians feel the emptiness of the absence of Love. Your hearts are highly sensitive to this emptiness, personally and globally. Your hearts acutely register the absence of the feeling of communion.

Your Hadarian challenge is your sensitivity to the lack of Love. Your gift is your ability to bring Love into any situation or any moment because

Love means everything to you. "What else is there?" is the word from the Hadarian heart. Your mission and purpose is to bring Love and ignite its fullness in human experience, to sustain a galactic presence of Love so that its variety of expression can continue to be transmitted everywhere. That is the macrocosmic view. And the Hadararian view also pertains to the microcosm: that divine Love's expression can be known through the hearts of the beings on Earth again, in each moment, so communion and co-creation are alive and well here.

Filling the Empty Places with Love

When you feel the empty, lonely, unconnected heart experience, you feel a sense of a hole or pain. You feel this sensation relative to yourself, a friend, or for humanity. You can see it as a creative void, instead of a black hole or bottomless pit of sadness and heartache. The key is to remember this sensation is actually a longing for Love. This is your call to action. You can breathe Love in where you feel its absence. This time, in this space, Love will prevail. This time your choice is for Love, not its absence. You will activate your heart and Soul purpose through filling that void and bringing reconnection to divine Love. You have the essence of Love in your Soul memory bank to draw on. You have connection to divine Love in all that you are and know from the Hadarian essence, and you can draw on that now. To bring divine Love as connection and communion is the Hadarian Soul's destiny fulfilled. This is not merely caretaking Love or an overextension of your own sense of personal, individual sympathy. This is the creative command that you have much Soul know-how in delivering. "Let there be Love" is your continual divine proclamation.

I often find that the heartache a Hadarian feels can be completely rectified if you take a journey to your home world to activate that divine Love connection in your heart. A big part of a Hadarian's heartache comes from the sensation of disconnection to this glorious existence you have known prior to incarnating here. This can be rectified easily, thank goodness.

Here is a wonderful depiction of this very scenario described by a Hadarian friend.

"I moved from Colorado to California three years ago. It was exactly what I wanted and I was very happy, but for some strange reason I felt very disconnected. What was this about? I was surprised how deep this was, but how relieved I was to get beyond this debilitating downer feeling. Susann and I did a session that took me to the very point of my Soul's home world. I will never forget it. In my visualization of my home world of Hadar, I was an embryo in waiting. The scene was like a hotel. Each of us was in a room, and there was a big vestibule in the middle that was swarming with activity like a beehive. I was like a puppy in a dog pound. When I had developed enough, Souls from the Hadarian world came and I loved them. I wanted to be a part of their spirit and world. They were so filled with Love and they were so connected with the Universe and each other. My Soul mission had begun. I felt so filled with everything wonderful. It was ecstasy! I brought this memory back with me to the present and presto: I felt so connected to my new world and so ready to get creative with my work and my life. This will stay with me forever."

Anyone who you Hadarians bring into your intimate circle is present to experience communion with the divine Love that your Souls carry. It is vital that you know this, so you take care in who you invite into your sacred heart. This precious level of communion that you innately extend must be honored and not allowed to be taken advantage of. You who bring this gift of holding the true power of Love must insist within yourselves on keeping your "umbilical cord" to Love and communion with your Soul world that is based on Love. Then your relationships here will be an extension of your gift of holding divine Love as your very essence and nature. As a Hadarian, you are truly connected and in communion with the divinity of Love you know from your home world existence. When you insist on being primarily fed through that "umbilical cord" to Love, your relationships here will be born of this pure connection.

Being fed by what truly nourishes you allows you to co-create in the frequency of the Earth plane. It allows you not to expect something that not everyone can fully give you as yet. It helps fill in those empty spaces you feel that you wish others could fill in. They aren't quite capable. And yet, they are capable of assisting you in exploring the variety of expressions of Love that are to be known and shared here like no place else! The Hadarians declaration can be voiced in the following way. I have gifts to bring of divine Love here and I want to connect and commune with others and their gifts to magnify Love flowing through their facet of the diamond of creation.

Here is an example of how the connection to divine Love fuels our very existence and health. This story is from a Hadarian.

"For the month of July, 2004, my body was completely overwhelmed by a mysterious illness. My personal history is free of illness, so it was a huge shock to experience symptoms of uncontrollable chills, high fever (104 degrees), hallucinations, and various altered senses (taste, smell, etc.). After three weeks, the symptoms subsided, but I was left thoroughly exhausted, depleted, and unable to function. I needed to rest after the smallest activity. Even having a coherent thought seemed too much effort.

"I had contacted Susann, who, after hearing of my experience, suggested a session. I seriously doubted she could help me with this one! But Susann assured me she had done immune system work before, and a session would be beneficial. We did the session later that day, and

I spent the rest of the day sleeping as usual. The next day, I woke up to find myself energetic, clear-minded, positive, and even strong enough to get grumpy! I was myself again, after having lost all my strength and most of my hope!

"This is what we did. As we went into the session I saw that my heart was filled with black. We created an umbilical chord and sent it to the sun. I became engulfed in it. I brought it into my heart and the black disappeared. Susann explained that the heart is directly connected to the health of the immune system. I totally know it now."

Pattern of Limitation in the Soul Memory

A very distinct sensation Hadarians commonly share is the fear of being taken advantage of. Coupled with this is the feeling of being imprisoned and limited here in the ability to bring the Divine through the heart. As a Hadarian, you want to know sacred union with Love in your heart, and you feel a sense of being held down from knowing that.

There is a pattern of enslavement that you know in your Soul memory that creates these sensations of limitation. We have all heard stories, possibly seen images, about a time long ago when temple goddesses would sit around pools together all day reveling in the beauty of the feminine. There have been many stories of how they bathed and took care of each other and created through song, laughter, and sharing as women. It is a luscious, exquisite picture of the feminine essence embodied in all its beauty, beingness, and creativity.

The nature of the Hadarian world feels quite similar to an idyllic garden in essence. It is a very feminine place. Hadarians can be viewed as goddesses and gods in the temple of Love and creation.

Beings from other worlds would travel to this world, out of curiosity, to explore the nature of divine Love as the Hadarians held it. For instance, the Alpha Centauris, from a star system close to Hadar, would come and bring their essence of infinite presence and absolute connection. They are good friends, sharing their diverse and complimentary aspects of the jewel of universal creation. The Hadarians were very welcoming of the exchange of Love that bringing together the Alpha Centauri and Hadarian energy field brought.

How the Absence of Light Exists

Indeed, there are Soul Families co-creating together to magnify the many facets of the Divine. And, at the same time, there were and are, in fact, races of beings who have chosen the absence of Light, darkness, as their source of power. This false power source fueled by fear, lack, or the desire to take Light from another, does not vibrate at the frequency of Light and creation, but rather as darkness, and the absence of creation, which is destructive in its nature.

As a Universe operating out of free choice, the choice for darkness sprang out of allowing the creative void, which is part of the matrix for creation, to be filled with something other than Light. Darkness ensued as the disruption of Light coming into creation. We know this in our personal lives whenever, in a moment of moving into the unknown, we choose fear instead of Love or conviction to life. We always have a choice in each moment of creation as the known moves to the unknown or the creative void opens the door for choice in creation and we are given the option, as it was originally intended, to make a choice for the nature of Light. What do I want to create from universal Light now? That was the original design for life. So, the creative void was viewed with curiosity. It was seen as a space for possibility other than Light, as an example of our ability to have free choice. When beings decided to explore he creative void beyond its original intention, darkness became a something. If it becomes something, we are putting creative energy around it and into it. We make it real. When we make nothing—the void just as it was designed to be (a space or a void)—into something other than simply a space of unknown, it can be disruptive. We are playing God for our own singular need to survive and we are changing the rules. That is using free choice with an agenda.

We've all had the experience in our lives of making nothing into something, emotionally. The husband forgot milk at the store and comes home. The wife discovers it, and all of a sudden their marriage is on the line around this void in his memory at the grocery store. This void becomes ground for divorce. Yes, this is an exaggeration to demonstrate the point. If any of us have gone into this territory of bringing disruption into the void, it makes sense. In hindsight, hopefully, we have realized we have made something, in the form of fear and anger and emotional reaction, out of nothing, due to a backlog of our inability to bring Light into our own present and past moments. We reenact "The Fall," so to speak. Falling from choosing Light in all its variations, colors, and radiance to choosing the absence of Light, translated into fear, resentment, victimization, power plays, etc. It's amazing how quickly these little scenarios can snowball into huge disasters, internally or externally. Internally, when we feel the void in our self, in that moment, which we translate as the husband's lack of love, respect, integrity, etc., we act to destroy the perceived "enemy," which comes out as attack, hurt, rejection of the person for the void felt and perceived by the wife in that moment. Imagine if in that moment that feels like a void of Love and respect, we tap into Love and respect, instead of attack and pain, which is what the wife feels. The moment of creation might look more like, "My dear husband, I love you and respect how full your life is right now. I want to respect myself and ask you out of your own sense of self-respect how you want to handle your memory lapse and what I see as your agreement to respect my request for milk. Thank you."

This is an example of how we can, in practical terms, bring Light as Love where the old habit of re-creating "The Fall" from Love exists, where we contribute to darkness and destruction in place of Light.

Beings of Darkness Stealing Light

Imagine the temple goddesses by the pool. That's easy. Now imagine other races of beings coming to explore this glorious feast of the creation of divine Love. Remember, there are some groups of beings who have deliberately chosen to bring darkness and disruption instead of Love and creation. But they also want to experience Love and creation because they want it all! Remember each one was birthed as a divine spark of Love in their original existence as a Soul. And, in fact, their reason for wanting to co-mingle with the Hadarian energy of Love and creation is because ultimately that's what even the worst "bad guy" wants. They just have devious means based on personal agendas outside of the design of our Creator to get it. Because each one was birthed as a divine spark of Love in their original existence as a Soul, even Souls bent on destruction have a Soul memory of their essence of Love. In their development they chose to magnify its absence, but that divine spark, no matter how small it is, lives within them or they wouldn't exist. That is the universal principle. So they've been playing in the realm of destruction as their primary choice of how to get Light. They have even amassed others around them and can now be considered a race of beings fueled by disruption as their force for manifestation. They have learned tricks like how to be wolves in sheep's clothing. All the fairy tales, myths, and modern day tales in movies depict endless ways the bad guys try to get what the good guys have and how they will try every trick in the book to achieve this goal.

The wolf in sheep's clothing decides to go see Little Red Riding

Hood, or the witch tries to get the sweetness and joy from Hansel and Gretel to make it her own. This is the eternal tale of those lacking Love always seeking it out. In the Hadarian story, there are actual races of beings from other worlds who go to Hadar to get their divine parts.

In contrast, the Alpha Centauris came to Hadar to share the diverse gifts of Love and truth as part of universal co-creation. But in the Hadarian story there is a race of beings, known as the Draconians, from the star system of Eta Draco, who came not to share their gifts for the purposes of co-creation, but to take the goodness from the Hadarian "Little Red Riding Hood," so to speak. They arrived looking like powerful forces and tried to disguise themselves as Alpha Centauris, whom the Hadarians love and trust. The Draconians showed the Hadarians a little of their power. It was a false, dominating power over other kinds of energy. The feminine world of Hadar was intrigued by this new dimension of what they supposed is part of creation. Why would they have seen it differently? Weren't these beings operating from Love just like all the other beings they had shared with as they traveled the galaxy to explore the multitude of the varieties of the expression of Love? The Hadarians didn't have any concept beyond pure faith that every being was an expression of Light. So they blindly trusted the Draconians.

But the Draconains were filled with a power to possess, not a power to magnify the creation of Love. The Hadarians forgot to check with larger universal sources of true power to make sure the power source of the Draconians was clear in its intention to connect with the pure essence of the Hadarians. If the Hadarians had stayed connected with Creator intelligence, they would have known that the Draconian energy wasn't clear in its desire to commune with Love. Love without this truth is left disconnected and unsafe. So the Draconian power play over the Hadarians was designed so they could possess Love. They enslaved the Hadarians to hold their gifts prisoner. They took the divine Love the Hadarians collectively emanated and claimed it by force to be theirs.

We can all relate to this to some degree. Typically it would look like the following. When we have chosen fear of Love instead of Love, we end up fighting to get Love or desperately holding on to someone to fill the place of Love we were afraid to hold for ourselves. We all know this experience of choosing fear, resentment, and anger, but underneath is a heart longing to know connection, communion, and creation. These qualities of experience have just gotten lost by the Soul's continual choices for destruction of that connection in order to belong, to be liked, to feel a part of things, etc. So the Draconians chose destructive power over other beings to receive reconnection to divine Love, which is their greatest longing underneath all their outer enslavement patterns. And it goes against universal principles and cosmic law and order for a being to receive divine connection through another being. It's stealing.

We are each designed to receive this energy freely and continually as an umbilical cord to the Divine. This is the design. So for beings to go against this design and attempt to possess Love through another does not allow them in fact to receive this divine principle, even if they have the Hadarians on a ball and chain. They can only bask in the glow but never really have the Love they are going after. Love cannot be claimed or possessed. It is a universal law. The Draconians, like all of us, must connect to the one source of divine Love ultimately, to truly know it. It is vital for all of us to remember that. This is what the gift of the Hadarian world is returning to us. The truth is that divine Love is all there is, and it is our divine right to be connected to that and live it thoroughly. The Draconians and other races bent on taking various aspects of Love and Light through disruption and attempted possessions of another's energies have continued this mischievous pattern to this day. This is one reason we have so many in this world who are bent on possessing and destroying other individuals or countries.

The Enslavement of Hadar

The Draconians enslaved you Hadarians while you were in your explorative innocence and desire to commune with every aspect of creation. You learned in hindsight that not everything that existed was held in divine Love. And you discovered that it is always essential to stay connected to a larger aspect out of which you came, that is absolutely trustworthy, which is our Creator's presence, when communing with others—even if you know you carry pure connection to Love. You Hadarians must remember that just because you hold pure connection to Love does not mean that everyone does. The lesson for the Hadarians was, and is, to stay connected to the infinite presence from which Love was created and then test any new frequencies that come into your field to see if they resonate with that infinite vibration of Love.

This enslavement pattern is held around the Soul of every being who has spent time on Hadar. It is a challenge for you. Remember that just as it can be recognized, it can be released. It is often reflected or felt in the body as a limitation of the heart or breath, physically, experientially, or energetically. You Hadarians carry to varying degrees a sense of subtle or gripping limitation around your ability to live as divine Love. Your Soul inherently knows how to live as Love. But because of the Soul enslavement pattern you carry, you feel limited in your ability to know Love as fully as you know is possible in your life. This can show up in heartache, inability to have deeply satisfying intimate relationships, breathing or lung difficulties, endocrine or hormone struggles, or any sort of physical female difficulties. You Hadarians are not alone. There are many Hadarians I have worked with who have not been able to receive answers to these difficulties through the medical community or through simplified relationship counseling. I am glad to say that it is possible to release these Soul imprints entirely.

Emancipation from Enslavement

An example of the Hadarian enslavement pattern and its impact on personal life is well stated in the following words of a Hadarian client of mine.

"All my life I have had occasional attacks of chest pain near my heart. The attack, lasting two or three minutes, would feel like a severe muscle cramp, and breathing would be painful, if not impossible. Outside of the attacks, I often felt a shot of pain if I simply took a deep breath, so I became accustomed to breathing with very shallow breaths, and even holding my breath for periods of time.

During my childhood, my terrified parents rushed me to a doctor repeatedly, only to be told nothing was physically wrong with me. As an adult, if these attacks happened around other people, they would be highly alarmed and would want to call an ambulance. It was hard for me to reassure my companions that although I couldn't breathe (or talk!), the attack would pass.

Then one day an attack came as we were talking on the phone, and Susann said she could help me. I was highly skeptical, but did the session anyway—and never felt the pain again. It's been four years now. How did this happen?

Susann helped me connect the dynamic of Hadarian imprints to this chest pain I was experiencing. We took a journey to Hadar and the remembrance I had of being held captive by beings that wanted my precious Light. This time I brought in my connection to divine Love and moved his energy out. We moved the energy into that space so that my chest was literally lit up with Light and absolutely no fear! The pain was gone. It never came back."

Affecting the Passage of Time

You who have spent substantial time in the Hadarian world have a fascinating ability to let time work for you. It is the ability to bend time. You bring this skill with you, and many Hadarians have been able to use this while here on the Earth. Hadarians laugh when I tell them this, because they inherently know it can happen, sometimes because you want it to consciously and other times it just happens as a pleasant surprise. For example, if you know it usually takes an hour to get to the theater you are going to, and circumstances dictate that according to the clock you have just forty-five minutes, you can gently stretch the notion of time so that you are able to get to the theater in just forty-five minutes. We all have the ability, in fact. Hadarians remember it and remind us all what is possible. I've tried it. It works when my intention is pure. It's fun to play with and good to discover more of our natural abilities when we are living from our Soul heritage.

Often for you Hadarians, the people you have the most authentic degree of Love for are other Hadarians. There is a natural connection that is pure and real that allows you to rekindle a sense of true home in your heart. I always encourage Hadarians to find ways to connect with others from your Soul Family.

Your inherent gift of Love is what is longed for here so deeply. I can explain and assist in freeing these enslavement patterns that have been such limitations to your life fulfillment here in large or small ways. It is vital to do this, so that the essence of divine Love can be present and known through the expression of life again as it was intended to be in the Original Blueprint for planet Earth. This gift that

Hadarians bring is your heart's statement of Love embodied in your life. The Hadarian heart and Soul presence of Love can be called upon any time and by any of us who want to reconnect to that pure essence that exists here and universally for the asking.

The following is an interview with a Hadarian friend.

Susann: What is it like to come here and bring the design for divine Love?

Penelope: What this means to me is that Love is all there is. Everything relates to Love. Everything responds to Love and everything is created because of Love. And in bringing this feeling and thought into the planet, I feel that the planet has a chance to survive and to grow and prosper, to be again like the Garden of Eden. Out of Love, everything else follows. It was created first and it is a divine thread through everything. It is crucial that we have Love on this planet.

Susann: When you think of the quality of Love, how do you describe that? What is the dimension of Love that human beings here have not touched yet?

Penelope: I equate the terms connection and communion as terms to describe divine Love. I also equate divine Love with the Christ Light. Jesus had the Christ Light; Mohammed had it; Buddha had it. All the great beings on this Earth have had this Christ Light. It is the high, pure quality of Light, Love and wisdom combined. It is essential that we all know how to tap into it. Personally, every morning I spend time in meditation, and I ask for the angels, the Archangels, the master teachers, and my spirit guides to bless me, and I ask for any knowledge they wish to impart to me and to guide me every day to learn how to spread the Light better and how to spread the Love.

How I live from Love is simply to let go and let my spirit guides who continually hold a place for Love with me to be fully present. They will always be with me and protect me and open the path that is much greater than anything I could imagine myself. The best way to know Love in this world is to hold communion with the divine Light that I described, merge with it, and know union with it in my heart and deepest cells.

Susann: I understand that one of the challenges for the Hadarians is the Soul pattern you carry of enslavement by other forces that claim to be larger than Love.

Penelope: Through meditation and in life I have found that what I truly know in my heart and Soul is valid and nothing can diminish that. This energy of enslavement I feel is definitely around, but because I know I am guided and protected and focus on that, I am impervious to these influences. It is healthy to be aware of these energetic influences attempting to limit my expression of Love, but it does not mean they guide me. I am aware of the fact of this disruption in the world, and it reminds me to focus on Love to break the bondage that comes when one is out of Love. The enslavement pattern can only come when you agree somewhere in your Soul history to be lead by something other than Love.

I want to infect others with the desire to spread the Light. I have been given guidance to create music CD's so that the voice of the frequency of Love can be heard. If we listen we are given so many tools to bring the Light of our Soul into manifestation.

Susann: I understand that Hadarians feel deeply the heartache of Love not being part of this world and they feel that heartache very acutely when this high frequency of Love is not known personally for themselves or with others.

Penelope: It's funny that you should say that because it seems that every psychic I have gone to has said there is sadness in my heart. My life is good and I am happy in my life, but there is a Soul-level sadness you speak about that comes through. It is the sadness that on this planet there is such a lack of Love and that does make me sad. As I am with family and friends and groups who are interested in holding a place for Love, that sadness is lifting. When I feel the sad, the empty, the tear in my heart, all I have to do is feel the connection, appreciate the Love for someone or something, and fill my heart with this healing balm. This healing brings that Love into the void so my heart can remember its true deeper place for holding Love.

Susann: As you bring that connection and communion into your heart, at that moment you are actually re-seeding divine Love into this world where the absence is most strongly felt. That's why you came in the first place. As you bring Love in you are declaring that it can be turned around.

Penelope: I like to connect to what I call the Christ Light grid above the Earth. It makes me feel deeply connected to the group of Lightworkers who are here on this planet and invisibly on the grid around this planet to help us in so many vital ways.

Susann: So you are able to feel that even though you are in this world that has much separation from Love, you are connected to this sphere in the energy grid above the Earth, which has always been connected to Love?

Penelope: I am optimistic about how we can bring this in. It is here to be touched and known to our very core as we continually choose it as our beacon here. I look forward to seeing a world of peace and joy, abundance, and happiness in every way.

Susann: As a Hadarian, a large part of the adventure of your mission is to explore the varieties of the expressions of Love. You have moved around this galaxy not only to explore but also to experience how Love is done in a multitude of ways. Many Souls have come here to be part of planet Earth's Original Blueprint for the experience of Love simultaneously through the physical, mental, experiential, and spiritual. In a nutshell, we are to experience Love moving through the six senses. Coming into this world in this explorer mode, how have you known Love as the expression of joy and enjoyment and appreciation?

Penelope: I ask that Light shine through my eyes so people know there is something special going on with me. That it is not just a ho-hum life, but there is way more to this existence going on. I ask that people receive messages through the energy imparted from my eyes, and I think it is an easy yet profound way to communicate the joy of knowing Love in this reality.

I express Love through my creative artistry. I am a painter and songwriter. I impart Love through my artwork and singing. This is Love moving through creation. This is the joy of being alive as Love in motion.

The Hadarian Proclamation: Love is the essence of life and creation.

13

ALPHA CENTAURI

*I am here. I have always been here. I will always be here.
I am Creator source for my world.*

Star System Location: The Alpha Centauri star system.

Soul Characteristics:
* You are deeply compassionate towards the Earth mission.
* You are devoted to protecting us from and helping us move beyond the influence of negativity here.
* You are assisting the Earth to come to self-sufficiency.
* Your stance is that Creator source lives within me.
* You are visionaries and idea generators.
* You are fearless in the face of destructive influences.
* You hold a high mental ability.
* You live from a large viewpoint or perspective.

Well Known People:
  Sting
  Robert Redford
  Martha Stewart
  Richard Gere
  Barbara Walters
  Gandhi
  George Washington

Dustin Hoffman (40% Blueprint Deliverer)

Bruce Springsteen (also Sirian)

Tom Cruise (40% Blueprint Deliverer)

Colin Farrell

Jude Law

Clint Eastwood

Hilary Swank(also Sirian)

Morgan Freeman (also Pleiadian)

Byron Katie

Larry Byrd

John Elway (also Blueprint Deliverer)

Archie Manning

Peyton Manning (also Sirian)

Elijah Manning (also Sirian)

lpha Centauri is the closest star to our sun at 2.5 light years away. Alpha Centauri is our next-door neighbor!

The Compassionate Neighbors

Those of you who herald from Alpha Centauri have come here exuding the qualities of being great neighbors—its in your very personality make-up. Not only do Alpha Centauris make great neighbors, but your Souls carry an inherently compassionate nature. You are deeply understanding individuals. Your message in coming to this world is, "We see that you on the Earth have gotten yourselves into a few messes by making some choices untrue to your internal compass guided by connection to your Creator and Soul knowing. How can we help you get turned around?"

This understanding compassion is akin to a fatherly kind of understanding that can occur when his teenage son is not keeping his grade average up. With understanding, he realizes that it would be more productive to help his son with his school needs rather than just punish him. That is the quality of assistance that describes the compassionate, understanding nature of the Alpha Centauri.

You Alpha Centauris were called on to help here because you recognized that some of the pitfalls we were falling into before you came were due to our naïve, buy-in to disruptive energies. Most of this buy-in was out of innocence or lack of education by young Souls here.

Any of us with children know how much compassion and patience is required in watching a toddler learn to walk. Parents know this process includes a few falls, maybe even tears or a bump. But it is essential for the child to learn for himself how to walk. It develops his inner strength and inner guidance. If we constantly hold his hand or just hover over him, he never learns to be self-directed and parents become more other-directed and less self-directed themselves.

So, you Alpha Centauris who have been around the galactic block know that "stuff happens" and it especially happened when Souls first came to planet Earth. This assurance and compassion are such welcome aspects in this confused world full of Souls that are always looking for someone else to make their life work.

The Spirit of Self-Sufficiency

You Alpha Centauris bring the spirit of self-sufficiency to this equation. You hold the energy of absolute, unwavering connection to universal Source. It is the absolute within the dance of creation. It is knowing that all is well because the truth of connection is present and will not be violated or betrayed.

Self-sufficiency means that God or Source lives within you. As you're connected to universal Love, you are completely in tune with all that is. Your heart and Soul expression of life is utterly free to create with diversity like ribbons of abundant, color-filled Light from the maypole of almighty connection. This is the message you Alpha Centauris bring.

Your Alpha Centauri essence knows that the spirit within guides your life. One challenge I often see that follows from this knowing is your lack of asking for anything outside yourselves. This can include not allowing others to play a part in fulfilling your needs, as you may believe that you don't have needs. This can also include not nurturing yourself since you don't believe you are here for anything other than to hold a place of absolute connection and be of service. Period. You might question where self-care even fits into your formula.

The downside to being focused on self-sufficiency can appear when Alpha Centauris have a problem. You have a tendency to withdraw completely, like a turtle pulling into its shell, to resolve the problem. For you, the truest way to go about problem solving is to simply go inside yourself and reestablish the absolute connection to Source that you know in your Soul and then bring the fruits of that connection into the situation at hand. That would be the ideal means for finding a new vision of a problematic situation. Instead, there can be the tendency to go inside and let the problem stew and forget the purpose for going inside, which is to bring connection into that moment. Remember Alpha Centauris, the only reason to go inside your shell or cave is to re-establish absolute connectedness to your Soul purpose and bring it with compassion into the situation that is at your fingertips.

People feel quite safe around Alpha Centauri energy because, as an Alpha Centauri, you possess an inherent space of planetary protection. This feeling of protection you exude is due to the absolute connection you hold. Nothing can rock you off this center of connection so we know stability and security of spirit in your presence. You are here to remind us that true protection comes from our own individual holding of absolute connection to our Creator Source, moment by moment. This connection allows us to relax into knowing that all is well in our world because our Creator holds it. This is what the Alpha Centauris have come to re-establish to the world's awareness.

Help Release the World from the Grip of Disruption

This protection element that is so strong with you is also due to your keen sense of responsibility for releasing this world from the grip of disruption that we have naively bought into. As you Alpha Centauris help raise the frequency here so people feel their Creator Source within, those who bring the negative use of power through their personal agendas for the use of Light for disruptive purposes become impotent and dissolve. The disruptive use of Light and power "creates" negative power fields that are present to deliberately diffuse Light's potency.

You Alpha Centauris have come to help stop these negative power fields from having such a strong influence here. If these negative power fields aren't being used, they become useless. The Alpha Centauri approach is to amplify the power of Light here through our collective reconnection to our Creator Source. As each one reconnects, in the spirit of self-sufficiency to our Creator Source within, Light in this world is amplified. When the power of Light is turned on, where does darkness go? It ceases to exist. We cease to buy into disruptive power as a way to get where we want to be. We trade in our beliefs feeding disruptive power and replace them with ones that support Light's presence here.

Influence of Draconian Race

There has been a particular race of beings called Draconians, from the star system Eta Draco, that have spearheaded disruption here. People from this world that we would know are Adolf Hitler, Osama Bin Laden, and Saddam Hussein, to name a few. They all believe it's okay to take the life blood of others to serve their purposes for greater power for themselves. They have used our moments of feeling helpless and powerless to pull us into their web of illusion that they hold the power that we are lacking at that time.

Sometimes we forget the best Soul choice is to increase and expand our connection to our Creator and creative sources for furthering our Soul fulfillment. We sink into powerlessness and hopelessness and from there we can get into trouble by innocently looking to disruptive sources of power to help us feel powerful again.

The Draconians are a collective of beings who live to take advantage of such situations. They appear to be powerful individuals, but they are true parasites who steal and drain Light from others so they can have the life force they need for existence. They are the least self-sufficient beings around, even though they give the false impression of strength. Draconians give others a feeling of superficial power and make them addicted to the hope that someone outside themselves has what they are looking for. True codependence in action. Also, because taking life force from others (it could be labeled spiritual murder) is against cosmic law and order, and against the reality of free choice and free will, beings like Draconians do not have permission to get their life blood from others. Draconians are continually hungry, like vampires, and are dependent on others for their life blood.

You Alpha Centauris have watched the Draconians play these tricks in other worlds and know energetically how to stop them on their disruptive influence. You help beings here come into their own power of self-sufficiency. As you teach us to be powered by our own Light source, we aren't drawn into the deceptive power play of Draconians.

Alpha Centauris Are Fearless

The Alpha Centauris that I work with all concur that you aren't the least bit afraid of terrorists or any other threat based on destructive motives. You know where the true power lies and you recognize a false sense of power is not worth being afraid of. You are bigger than that game. This is what it means to stand in one's truth. This is a tremendously important position the Alpha Centauris hold for this world.

Since Alpha Centauris are not afraid of illusional power, you are in the perfect position to help dissolve the illusion that this disruptive power can be helpful to anyone. You Alpha Centauri's are familiar with this dynamic. It's a large part of your mission for coming here. You help dissolve this illusion of power just with your presence, even if you haven't consciously been active in this regard. It is one reason why you carry such a strong essence of protection. You want so much to assist this world from being overtaken by this disruptive nature.

What this looks like on the outside is that you are here to dismantle the destructive power that controls the systems that we all count on, such as medical systems, legal systems, drug companies, and oil companies. Uncovering the corruption operating within the Enron Corporation is a prime example of the dismantling of these negative uses of power in a large system that influences all of us. I was aware of the Alpha Centauri energy around the whole exposé. I have no doubt that we will be seeing much more of this large-scale reckoning in the days ahead.

An example of one of the most known Draconians is Adolf Hitler. Because many believed it was okay for him to say, "I can colonize what I see to be a weakened spirit in the German population. I can take advantage of them. I can circle them around my campfire. I can delude them that I have power that they don't have and that I'm going to help them." Many were looking for a means to be more powerful

lives and bought into Hitler's claim to be able to take them
e was able to take advantage of them because they bought
into his illusion of power.

So every time we buy into the idea that someone else has a greater
connection to power than we do, we feed the sense of dependency
on someone else's power. If that person lets us do this they are taking
advantage of us. That is the destructive use of power. This is where the
trouble starts and "evil" gets perpetuated. We say no to Light and yes
to darkness, simply stated. That is where we have gotten into trouble.
That is how we start to develop what I call "barnacles on the Soul."
These disruptive Soul imprints keep the Light of our Soul from shining at its optimal brilliance. The Soul is pure, but it can acquire these
barnacles, which cloud the Soul's ability to bring forward its gifts in all
their splendor. Consequently, we need bright lights such as the Alpha
Centauris to remind us that the true source of power is born of our
absolute connection to our Creator.

Uncovering False Power Sources

You Alpha Centauris are privy to the Draconian game plan of
stealing life force from others. You have the ability to expose this lie, so
that the Draconians are left impotent. Exposing the lie is like opening
the curtain on the Wizard of Oz, revealing that his almighty power
was just hype, just a machine to cover up his feeling of powerlessness.

Another example is Saddam Hussein and the world he controlled.
For years many succumbed to his destructive ways because they felt
powerless to do anything to change their situation; Saddam's empire
was being fed by everyone's fear of going against it.

When the Iraqi war first broke out in 2003, because there were
enough people all over the world who were interested in creating peace
as an alternative to war, the frequency of peace had a creative influence

even in the midst of this initial war effort. So the dismantling of power there occurred swiftly, with minimal destruction to the land, or bloodshed to the people. This part of the world that had been under the hand of disruptive forces was freed up to make different choices, and the option for Light was reinstated as another possibility again.

This dismantling of the power forces was able to happen because of the creative influence of many forces, both visible and invisible. The Alpha Centauri know-how and fearlessness to catalyze the freeing up of energy imprisoned in darkness was instrumental.

We didn't have to kill Saddam Hussein to get rid of his influence. We just said, "You can't do this anymore. We have recognized you, we've identified you, and you can't do this anymore. We are going to amp up the faction of Light in this world, and your power will have no more say." And, because the Iraqis stood up for themselves and said, "You're out," they created a collective agreement to the possibility of dismantling Saddam's power play over them. When the Iraqis said, "You're out," he became impotent. He was no more a force of evil. He had no more power. And he was found like a homeless bum in a cave.

This is an example of how the divine formula of Light displacing darkness works. We do not have to go to war with what we hate or fear. We just dissolve its impact by its displacement with Light.

Here is a declaration from a client, Eric, of his opportunity to remember his true stature as an Alpha Centauri.

"I know I came here from Alpha Centauri. When I developed a cough and tight chest condition that mysteriously appeared each night when the Sun went down, I decided to see how this related to my Soul heritage as an Alpha Centauri. We discovered that in my coming here I left a certain power source behind. Let's roll back the tape. The universal picture of my Soul was large, free, and fearless. That was great to experience. Then, as this Soul coming to the Earth to explore and help, I became overwhelmed with the inner struggle I felt. I had deep compassion for those who were so lost here. I could feel the pain in my heart and constriction in my breathing just thinking about it. And I felt if I took on this mission to save all these folks, I would be destroyed in giving myself away. That felt overwhelming. I felt my life would be consumed. Again, I felt the constriction in my breath.

We returned to that place of the Alpha Centauri dimension of my Soul: free, large, and fearless. This time as I took the journey to the Earth I made sure I stayed connected to the large Alpha Centauri field I existed in. It felt like being connected to and surrounded by a radio wave frequency that was solid, true, and absolute. This time going into the Earth was totally different. I remained free and fearless. I simply walked on the Earth and those who were available to receive my truth were blessed. It didn't matter how the transformational power I brought happened or what the results were. I lived fearlessly and freely and knew that was enough. I stayed intact and connected. People here got it or didn't. I still knew I made a difference. And I could breathe and my heart was open and at ease. Huge. This is how I was meant to live."

Here's a fun piece of information that is unique to the Alpha Centauris (and Hadarians). You feel very comfortable with the idea that they actually traveled here in physical ships. It's fun to mention this to my Alpha Centauri friends or clients, as they all seem very comfortable with this concept. It feels very true to them. And science fiction is not "fiction" in their minds at all. I always say to them, "Who do you think wrote all these science fiction stories like Star Trek and Star Wars?"

Natural Visionaries

You Alpha Centauris have high mental abilities and the capacity to hold a high level of consciousness and conscious awareness of another perspective here for this world. You are visionaries and great at seeing the big picture and the large perspective. You are constantly coming up with new ideas, new inspirations, new formulas and possibilities as you have a dominant personality as a seed planter rather than the one who follows up on a project or idea. You believe that growth for you comes through your movement into new fields continually and not through plowing the same field over and over and over again. If you are in a company, you'll let other people do the groundwork. You will be drawn to doing the higher-level work. You love to bring the new vision. Others are here to catalyze your vision coming to fruition and completion. That's not the Alpha Centauri strong suit.

Your strong suit is holding the place for and absolute connection to our Creator Source while being alive in an individual human form. You are passionate about bringing the people here to this place of self-sufficiency of spirit. With deep compassion you open the doors for others to find the creative ways to bring their gifts of universal magnitude to fulfillment in life in this world.

The following is an interview with an Alpha Centauri friend, James.

James: I think it's true that Alpha Centauris are dismantling negative-energy power forces. Draconians believe they have the right to take the power source from others, to take advantage of others' naiveté, and even take over whole groups of people to beef up their own power sources. The Alpha Centauris are here to help dismantle this ability, which goes against free choice.

But I also believe that they're here influencing a lot of other lower frequency vibrations to raise the vibration to a higher frequency. And in doing so, there's more bandwidth available now that it's not being used by the negative energy sources. We can now utilize this energy that was once used for negative influences, to now be used for positive influences.

Susann: So what Alpha Centauris are protecting is not just the people here, but also the one universal source of energy.

James: I'll get more specific. A Soul who has lost connection to our Creator Source in some fashion is someone who has their energy in limbo and without direction or purpose operating in that part of their Soul, so this Soul can be influenced very easily by forces looking to consume random energies for their personal agendas.

Susann: Yes. It is thought that if we shine our Light brightly we will be hurt for it, and that's not the truth. It is our strength of Light that's being sought, but it is the weakness in our Light field that occurs due to fear that opens us to the power of the negative influences that we might innocently choose in a moment of weakness due to disconnection. This is how it works. In a moment of confusion or fear or need we made a choice for something other than Light and that stays with us as a weak link. For instance, we might believe that if we hide from an enemy, he can't hurt us. If we are hiding we are saying that we don't want anything to reach us and that includes our connection to spirit. We are actually unavailable to our spirit and its connection to Light, which is the true safety.

James: So those with personal agendas for power can easily trick a young Soul who doesn't understand the choice for destruction that is so prevalent here. When you turn on the TV you see those influences that look like they're powerful. You see scenes of a bank robber grabbing somebody and putting them down on the ground and tying their hands or making them drop to their knees. That looks like the bank robbers have some power, you know? I think the Draconians purposely operate in that way, because it's really easy to attract those lost Souls to that frequency of disruption that takes power from others. The Draconians, like the robbers, are going for the goods that they are lacking. The robbers are going for money and the Draconians are going for the power of Light. They are stealing it at the level of a person's weakness or lack of understanding of devious deeds.

I think the real challenge is to get the people who are operating at a lower frequency to attune themselves so they can receive higher frequencies.

Susann: Yes. And the purpose for advanced Soul Families like the Alpha Centauris is to help people here attune to that vibration. And that is the simple nature of what a person's purpose is in coming from another star system that vibrates at a higher, purer frequency, to be a tuning fork for that vibration and that possibility of what others could be.

James: My question is, "How do you make an impact in this world at a higher frequency? Just by telling your child that you believe in him, or by a simple act of kindness, or being a better person holistically?

Susann: Don't you think that it's a matter of trusting that every time you emanate that vibration it has a ripple effect, like a pebble being dropped into a pond? A true vibration has a huge influence beyond what we can see. That has to be trusted and perceived.

James: Sometimes I feel like I don't fit here because of the intense nature of my energy. I mean it feels like Lighting bolts in contrast to the everyday vibration here. Sometimes I feel like my own physical body cannot understand this intense energy, so how could others around me understand it. And because the way the emotional realm is used here is so foreign to me, I sometimes have a hard time letting this intense energy into my life expression without it coming through in a distorted way because the emotional realm does not quite make sense to me—and I am not sure how to use it well. Since the emotional realm is not being used now the way it was originally intended for the Earth Blueprint, and as an Alpha Centauri I want to align only with what is true (and that includes the truth of the Blueprint), I have a hard time buying into not only trying to understand the emotional realm but wanting to put time and energy into using it well.

I have to be careful not to let this create isolation for me from others. An example would be an Alpha Centauri walking into a room full of people with negative energy, let's say. And immediately, you say to yourself, "Well, I'm not supposed to be here. It doesn't feel good, I should get away." The real truth is that you are supposed to be there to emanate your energy. And I find that if I just stand in that space the negative energy immediately dissipates. Either other people start to leave or the whole energy of the room will change dramatically.

I realize that as an Alpha Centauri, I may find myself in some very isolated or what looks to be isolated situations because of large energy fields full of fear or emotional reaction of some kind that can feel like that is where the power is because the majority buy into it. And the truth is that I am where the true power is. It is vital for me to remember that place of self-sufficiency and hold to it and not be afraid to be my most potent self, and then I can be available to inspire others to live from their most powerful, self-sufficient heart and Soul.

Susann: Alpha Centauris are protectors, and are redefining what we call protection. You are bringing in the energy field of absolute connection and safety and stability. There is thus a feeling present of the remembrance of what it is to be held by something larger, to remind us that universal presence or our Creator has always held that for us. It's bringing a candle into a dark closet. Where there's Light, there is no darkness. That's the true nature of protection. The protector does not go to war to defend but embraces from a place of Love-filled truth. What we have termed protection is a defensive stand against something and that just creates a warring vibration that fuels the very element we are trying to keep away from.

You're wired to use your truth and protection to benefit the Earth system. You are simply coming and bringing what it looks like and feels for a person to embody universal force and be self-sufficient in bringing that frequency here. The Alpha Centauris are here to remind us that we are the God source and you are here to teach us how to stand in our inherent power.

James: I would agree with that. I don't think you're ever going to find an Alpha Centauri being a TV Evangelist that's preaching to large groups of people, telling them what to do, telling them what to believe in. I think the Alpha Centauri is more of the quiet person on the street that walks up to you out of nowhere and says, "Who are you?" They speak directly to the Soul of a person and bring the depth forward and ask them in their inspirational presence to take another step in living from that place. The Alpha Centauris play a substantial role as the silent teacher. The Alpha Centauri energy is telling or showing the world to just sit quietly and listen to the subtle things that are happening around us.

Consciousness is created to exchange energy fields and merge frequencies for a greater purpose in each moment. The use of the mental capacity gives us the ability to consciously focus energy, exchange energy, and bring attention to where our energy is directed.

Susann: I see why Alpha Centauris are considered seed planters, because they carefully plant seeds of new ideas, new possibilities, new relationships of energy dynamics continually. Others are here to water the seeds and harvest the seeds. You will start with planting a seed that usually has a high conscious focus, which consists of plenty of ideas, plenty of energy patterns being brought into thought form into the physical reality. And it's for the people here to decide what to do with this plethora of new ideas or thought forms once they are planted. Alpha Centauris whom I speak to are always relieved to hear that they're the ones who plant the seeds, and someone else cultivates those seeds. They have been accused of not being good at follow-through, but it's not their job.

James: I know that a lot of Alpha Centauris definitely struggle with the completion of tasks and projects. And for me, the ease has come as I have seen that it's not necessarily that I need to come to a completion with a project, but I need to understand that the completion of that project is starting another one.

Susann: So let's talk a little bit about the whole compassionate nature of the Alpha Centauri. From this place of absoluteness, there is compassion for all that has lost aspects of connection. There is a compassionate understanding that you will "Forgive them, for they know not what they did."

James: I think within that compassion for all things is an Alpha Centauri's core characteristic of being nonjudgmental. Therefore, you will always be given a chance, and a second chance, and a third chance, and a fourth chance. No matter what you do in your life, if you are presented with an opportunity to do well, the Alpha Centauri will always make that available to you. I think the Alpha Centauri compassion is the Great-White-Father aspect of compassion, not so much the mothering side of compassion. It's the hand-on-the-shoulder reassurance. It's the father on the sidelines saying "good job." It's the grandfather who comes by and says, "I will always take care of you, James," or whatever. It's not the loving, caring, nurturing, mothering aspect.

Susann: Would you also say that the compassion relates to understanding how people here have bought in innocently to negative influences? There's a compassion that you hold because you understand how Draconians or other types of negativity have influenced them as well. Out of innocence, we make mistakes. So there's an understanding that mistakes are made, and there's an understanding back of the mistakes that there is this core place that everyone can return to, no matter how much mess somebody has gotten into; they always have that core remembrance of their true connection to the all that is.

James: I think that's the ultimate truth.

Susann: Yes, and that's one way that the Alpha Centauris dismantle the negative power sources; it is by saying, "You don't have to buy into it anymore. It really isn't real, and it's okay. I understand how you bought into it out of innocence and ignorance, and you can just say goodbye to that influence and not give it power anymore. Instead of having to go to war with it, you can declare that it doesn't carry weight with you anymore."

James: Wow, it sounds so easy, doesn't it?

Susann: It just occurred to me that a woman that I was speaking with last month who is an Alpha Centauri is very protective of her property and all it carries, which relates to being protective of the Earth. This is the piece of the Earth that she is responsible for, so she's extremely protective of it, and, for instance, wants to make sure that in her will this property goes into the right hands. That's a really good example of an Alpha Centauri female and how they use protection.

James: She's a steward of that place, which is a reflection of her stewardship ultimately, of the whole universe. The Alpha Centauri in a female form, if you're looking in today's world of things, is going to be women who are in a place of power. They're going to be corporate women, heads of organizations, or leaders in their community, maybe even spiritual counselors. But I think they're going to have a very masculine energy to them and a strong protective side. You're going to feel very safe in their presence, much like being with a big, powerful mother versus a lovey-dovey caring type of mother. They would be somebody who can wrap their arms around you.

Susann: I'm thinking as you are speaking about how each of the Soul groups have come here with a specific key to the equation of bringing forward the power of Light, which dismantles any frequency other than Light. The Alpha Centauris showed up to say with their spirit of absoluteness, "Of course, this could happen."

James: The Alpha Centauris piece is to align the groups to come together because they are familiar with providing leadership for group movement. They know throughout this Universe how to bring the teams together.

With such diverse spirits working on a similar project, another key is the way different Soul groups are connecting together now and realizing the good neighbor spirit that we Alpha Centauris naturally bring. The Soul groups know each other because they are working on the project together. This is the common thread or purpose.

Those with personal agendas don't know how to band together, because they don't trust others' intentions. The fear factor keeps them separated, and separation weakens. In this view they are saying, "How do I know another is on my side?" Anyone having a personal agenda for themselves won't usually have another person on their side. There is no solid platform. Those working for the common good have a common platform that is a shared intention that can be trusted. Negative groups have fear as the commonality. Those of Light or common good base their connection on the Love that is already inside them.

Susann: Dismantling the power stations is actually dismantling the fear stations.

James: Yes. That is how the station for power for destruction was assembled. It was based on fear. We are bringing in groups of Souls to dismantle with Love something based on fear. Love displaces the fear factor collectively.

If you look at a government as a source of power, they originally were brought together to govern the people by the people. It was a good thing. We were working for each other showing how we could leverage each other's skills. "I can help you do this and you can help me do that." Free trade was present and there was fluid motion between all the people.

Then fear came in based on personal agenda. "What about me?" "How will I survive?" or "I'm not strong enough to survive. Maybe I'd better collect more power. Maybe I'll do what I need to do to build a source of power so things work for me. I better try to change the system to get what I need."

In the government based on common spirit or collective good, needs are met for the individual and for the group. Each facet is taken into account. If we are working out of Love, we know if we give and others are in this same intention, we can trust it will all work out for me and everyone involved.

Security means trusting what you believe. "I am secure in the thought that Love will prevail. My home is secure because it is based in Love. That I can trust."

In God we trust. This shows up on a dollar bill. If you were secure that God is within you then the phrase would be "In myself I trust. When I put out this money, I trust it will come back."

We have lost the ability to find the truth for our self within our self. Why do I take the word that I hear from someone else as the truth?

Susann: The truth is that the true power sources for holding Love have always been here. When we reinstate that place of power within our self, this common key will simply unlock the means to dismantle anything that doesn't resonate with that Love. So you are here to embody self-sufficiency yourself and plant seeds without the need for anything from the outer world to recognize you for having done so.

James: I'm planting the seeds of the connection, and I'm self-sufficient in bringing that frequency here, no matter what happens around me.

Susann: What is the one proclamation that an Alpha Centauri would state to be able to come back to the vibration of remembrance of what they have to bring as an Alpha Centauri Soul into this world? What would that proclamation be?

James: I am here. I've always been here. And I'll always be here.

The Alpha Centauri Proclamation: I am here. I have always been here. I will always be here. I am Creator Source for my world.

14

PARALLEL

I am in sacred union with the one, the all that is.
I exist as everything, everywhere.

Star System Location: Parallels come from and live simultaneously in univeses parallel to this one.

Soul Characteristics:

* You bring the ability to live in a number of existences all at once and all the time. This ability brings the knowledge of how to live in multidimensionality to this world.
* You hold a divine spark of universal connection to this and a number of other universes.
* You hold the truth of being one with the all that is.
* You carry natural awareness of the legions of beings we are all a part of.
* You have Soul experience of what it is to live in the present moment continuously.
* You know the truth of the purpose of the emotional realm: to experience the feeling sensation of the bounty of life.
* You bring the knowledge of the essence of sacred union with the Beloved.

Well Known People:
J. R. Tolkien

Peter Jackson (producer of *Lord of the Rings*)

Elijah Woods (Frodo in *Lord of the Rings*)

Charlize Theron

Russell Crowe

Diane Keaton

Michael Jackson

Meryl Streep

Tina Turner

Nicole Kidman

Anthony Hopkins

John Lennon

Michaelangelo

Leonardo da Vinci

Picasso

Thomas Jefferson (40% Mintakan)

Deepak Chopra

Eckhart Tolle (author of *The Power of Now*)

John Nash (his story: *A Beautiful Mind*)

Madonna, the performer, is a great example of a very modern Parallel being. She also is Pleiadian (40%), but her Parallel dynamic shows in how she has lived so many different existences and will continue to. She has been a huge archetype for the freedom of the expression of the feminine, as a singer, a dancer, actor, wife, mother, and writer. All her roles have changed the face of the feminine and how women see themselves. Women embody the remembrance that we can be all these things. Women live through many aspects of existence in a lifetime. Parallel multidimensionality teaches us that we can be many aspects of the expression of the Divine. The possibilities are endless.

There are universes that exist parallel to this Universe, in another dimension. Simply put, these Parallel worlds are way out there! They are not on any astronomy maps. So how do we know they exist? And how do we know that there are Souls here who come from these worlds and are here to bring the gifts of their Soul experiences in these worlds into human consciousness and experience? I became aware of these Parallel worlds or universes by meeting various clients and knowing of people like the ones I will describe in this chapter, who hold the Soul characteristics from these Parallel universes. So very many times I have described these worlds to these precious beings that have come here from those extremely far away places. Every client understands exactly what I am talking about and agrees about how real these existences are to them. And they are deeply appreciative that someone knows and understands who they are as a Soul and what they are about as a Soul.

We can learn from Parallels that many aspects of experience can exist simultaneously. This especially pertains to our ability to live from our Soul or spirit at the same time that we are productively functioning in this Earth existence. Parallels live in and experience different universes simultaneously. We have a similar experience on a smaller scale all the time. We may experience a sore muscle, a sad emotion, a clear idea of how to help alleviate the pain of the muscle, and feel a thankful connect to spirit all at the same time. They are all unique levels of existence living within us simultaneously. This is to say that we can live in multiple existences at the same time. The Parallels lesson to us is that all things exist in parallel, and there is so much more here to be experienced than we know. I have been able to discover this dynamic of Parallels through clients, students, and friends as well as through understanding well known peoples in this world who herald from these realms to do specific work that is needed now. There have been the collectives who were Parallels that we are all familiar with and who have come at various vital times historically to plant their valuable seeds. The widespread seed planting from Parallels coming solo to assist with the Earth project only began 2,000 years ago as compared to the entrance of many other advanced Souls coming since around 250,000 BC to assist here.

Historical Evidence of Parallel Collectives

Throughout history many have come from Parallel universes and very definitely left their mark. Mayan Indians, the Hopi Indians, the Anasazi Indians, and the Aborigines are the best known. They were all seed planters who came collectively to bring forward advancements for civilization. They brought the seeds for collective expression of co-creation in their unique ways. The Mayan ruins hold an incredible energy of ritual and sacred foundation that capture the attention of many to this day. The Anasazi cliff dwellings are magical and mystical. How did feathers from birds living only in South America get there? How did the Anasazis leave this world en masse without any trace? There were no bones, no burial grounds. Parallels come here through what can termed dimensional doorways—something our physical bodies, tied to this gravitational field, can't do. To the Parallels I see now, you have no question that you knew how to fly, or teletransport. Parallels know this is an inherent ability of their skill set when the gravitational field is not so dense as it is here now.

You Parallels have the ability to transport yourselves through energetic portals from this Universe to your other universes. The various energy vortexes people love to go to like Stonehenge in England; or Sedona, Arizona; or Crestone, Colorado are actually energetic dimensional doorways to Parallel universes. There are whole civilizations living in parallel to any of these energy spots on the Earth.

The crop circles being discovered around the globe are evidence of current energy vortexes that are being created to open dimensional doorways from Parallel universes to the Earth world.

A few Parallels I have spoken to feel they could accomplish natural ascension by leaving this Earth through dimensional doorways but have chosen to make their exits a little more palatable for family and friends. They are very conscious about choosing when and how to leave this sphere. One person I know exited through a short, painless time of cancer; another exited through the flu that turned into to a death-related illness.

Parallels Live in Multiple Existences

A very unique dimension for you Parallels is your ability to live in three or more Parallel existences all at the same time. You do this naturally while you are here on Earth. This may not make sense to the linear brain, but we all probably have had something of this experience ourselves.

A parent, and especially a mother, knows what it's like when their child first goes off to preschool or kindergarten. I remember when my daughter first went off to kindergarten with a teddy bear tucked under her arm how I was partly present in my day and partly aware of being with my child where she was. Daydreaming is another example. I can be fully aware of being in a chair and in a dream world at the same time.

It may look to someone studying you who work from the Parallel existences that you have a disassociative disorder. Commonly it feels like you are out of your body, "somewhere else," spacey, or not very present here. One client described to me that she feels she is often walking around in a fog. It feels that way to the emotional body, but there is a better way to understand this phenomenon.

You actually have only a portion of your existence anchored here, on purpose. You hold other aspects of your connection and energy field for creation in other Parallel universes. When you appear to be "someplace else" you are in fact focusing more attention on being in one of your other realities. It is vital for you to do so. You are fed by these other worlds and the gifts of spirit you have to bring here are from there. So you must access those worlds to deliver your gifts here. You have a divine connection in this Universe, like everyone here, and you have divine spark connections to each of the other universes. For you, it is like living in New York City; Bozeman, Montana; Capetown, South Africa; and Los Angeles all at the same time. Literally, it's not just about owning houses in those four places but being in all four places simultaneously. I call you Olympic multitaskers. This ability brings the gift of what it is to live multidimensionally here.

We have not done very well here with our ability to live out the Blueprint for the planet. This Blueprint was originally centered on the advanced capacity to explore and create through four dimensions together. We let go of the spiritual penetrating and igniting the three-dimensional existence, so those from Parallel existences can help us open to our natural spiritual abilities while having an experience in a body, consciously experiencing creation. Our present goal is to remember that we are spirit taking a 3-D form to magnify the Soul's expression of creation as life. We can exist in numerous planes of existence at once. This is what the Parallels have come to seed into the Earth consciousness. Besides, if Parallels existed with only this 3-D existence, then your incredible gifts would not be accessed and brought here. We need to allow Parallels and some dimension of all of us to be "out there."

Another form of multidimensionality the Parallels bring is the reality that you are simultaneously connected to many aspects of spirit, as expanded parts of you. This is true for all of us. Like a tree, we are the trunk and there are many branches and leaves that are a part of the tree of "I." We are so much larger than this physical form. "I" is the aspect of Soul that has chosen to be in a human form while the other invisible aspects work in conjunction, or parallel to each other. We have legions of beings with us at any given moment. We can be aware of this, as we stay connected to the reality of the oneness of all that Parallel beings embody. You are here to remind us we can embody this truth also. The Parallels I connect with are very aware of these troops of beings that are ever-present with them.

My client Carrie described her return to a Parallel existence this way:

"Everyone was filled with Light. Each was special and unique, not better or worse. There was an absolute appreciation between each one and a deep appreciation for all life in this existence and the existence of planet Earth. All life has meaning. No aspect of life is bad or good. Each aspect of creation plays the music of our Souls. Together we make such beautiful music, and we help let the music of others come forth. One Soul purpose is to appreciate all beings. When I appreciate others I assist them in appreciating themselves.

I am going to do a ceremony of appreciation for each one in my immediate world, for the music of each one's Soul. Then I will feel the harmony of our music together, making a third music as a symphony of Souls."

The Parallel home is universal, not just of the Earth. To live from many existences expands and broadens one's sense of the foundation of home as a universal one. To feel that the whole galaxy is our home is so very freeing! We can move beyond feeling the sense of limitation of being trapped in a mere physical existence here. It was not meant to be that way. The brave Souls from Parallel worlds are here to remind us of how expansive life here can be. It is essential for you Parallels to rekindle that experience while here so that you can bring it as your Soul purpose to others.

Often, if you Parallel beings are having a challenging time here, which definitely happens since this dimension of density is so very foreign to you, you naturally opt to shift your focus of attention to one of your other existences. This helps you feel nourished, connected, and understood, and gives you a new perspective on situations in the Earth field. It makes sense also for you to go to those worlds where you have advanced understanding of the working of spirit. You go there to absorb these substantial gifts, so it's a nurturing thing when you "leave." Moving your attention to another existence can give you fresh input or just plain relaxation when you feel out of sorts with this dimension of existence. I know we all feel that urge to "escape." Parallels show us that we can simply move out of the seriousness of feeling limited here by physicality. We can keep one toe in the water of connection to this world, and the rest of us can exist in the spiritual dimensions our Soul knows well. Spirit bridging into form is how life was designed to be. You Parallels are bringing experiential data from other aspects of the totality of self. We can do that too. This is true divine proportion. Just show up and let Light take it from there! One drop of pure Light creates an ocean of influence here.

Part of the work that I have done with Parallels is to help clear the dimensions of their Soul so that they can travel to other existences while here, without the disruption that they have allowed to come into their lives due to the illusion that they have to be part of this polarized existence. This clearing helps them move freely back and forth between existences while here.

A unique piece that beings from Parallel worlds have is what I call a divine spark that they share with this world and with other worlds.

All human beings have this divine spark within the heart chakra. This spark of life is the connecting point within you to all of universal creation. Those who work in Parallel will have a divine spark in this world, and also divine spark in other universes. This is something unique to the Parallel beings.

Translation Needed Between Parallel Worlds

It is important for each of you Parallels to have a translator being put in place for you, so that the guidance you have from Parallel universes beyond this Earth can be translated into language that works for the guidance you have in the Earth field.

Here is a story from a woman who has beautiful connections to her Parallel worlds, but needed help in translating those realities into her life experience here.

"A notable session with Susann involved the resolution of my difficulty in holding the Light—my life force or essence—as I interacted with others and participated in life. I was going through a difficult period at work as the only female partner in a business organization dominated by men. The structure of the organization was not supportive of left-brain style of management, and was primarily non-inclusive and rigid, with constant power struggles that left me drained and frustrated.

In my session, Susann led me into a deeply meditative but conscious state, and guided me to the source of my issues pertaining to my inability to hold my own, my truth, and my Light in challenging situations.

In the session, I found myself out in space, somewhere in the Universe, amid stars and distant planets. I felt myself more as energy than a physical being. I'm holding a golden orb or globe, made of Light energy. I sense that I'm supposed to take this golden orb safely to my destination. I'm now on the edge of a field of debris in space, with wisps of mist or smoke and what appear to be dead or dense physical objects floating about.

A nearby planet on the other side of this field is brightly lit and completely covered with human bones and skulls. There are some large, dark shapes lurking in the shadows and I believe they are waiting for me to enter the field so they can snatch the ball from me. I also believe that if they succeed, I'll end up a pile of bones on that planet across the field. I am afraid and angry that I have been left here without support and guidance. In the distance I see a blue-green planet—my destination. I'm wondering if I can find a clever way to outfox or outrun these hungry shadows. But I'm too afraid and angry to even try.

I hear a voice behind me saying clearly and calmly, 'The shadows are as big or as small as you want them to be.' Susann reminds me that they are also there or not, based on my choice. I decide that they are small, the size of little mice, and only one or two in number. Now I feel big and the orb I hold is bigger and brighter. I'm not inclined to hide it, whereas I was trying to keep it concealed before.

In confidence, I zip through the field to my destination of planet Earth, which feels safe and sound now that I have the bright, shiny orb or Light. But once I enter the outer fields of the Earth, all is gray and dark, and I'm once again afraid of shadows, that they are far bigger than me and will try to steal my Light away. I have forgotten that it is my choice as to whether these dark shadows exist and have any power over me.

Again, I feel as if God, spirit, the Universe, my guides have all abandoned me and left me with an impossible task and very little help. I am defenseless.

Susann guides me back to where I first got the instructions and the orb. I find myself in a well-lit space of light and warmth. I'm given this wonderful golden orb of Light and told that the only thing I have to do is to hold it tightly at all times. The golden Light has transformative powers but only if held in its entirety. I'm excited at the prospect of transforming dark places and as I fly off to find them, seemingly friendly and partially lit beings are approaching me. Their light is fragmented, and they are saying that they can show me what wonderful things I can do with the Light —a piece of it here and a piece of it there can really light up dark places. And forgetting that I must stay connected to that which emanates pure Light, I get into exchanges that fragment me and replace pieces of my Light with darkness. And therein lies the source of my fear—that if I reveal the Light, I will be attacked and pieces of me will be ripped away until I am bloody and bruised.

This translated for me into a day-to-day experience of my withholding my true essence in my workplace, and other areas of life, for fear of being attacked and ripped to pieces. I had to conform to the world order 'as is' or be attacked and unsafe. Again, the choice appeared to be no choice at all.

Susann helped me to see that the fear of probable opposition and challenges were a result of the belief that I was abandoned. And this perceived abandonment was merely a reflection of my having abandoned my authentic self in order to conform to forces that were darker and that I believed were stronger. I had forgotten that if I held the Light and merely held it tightly, it could transform the darkness, for darkness cannot survive the Light—Light always overcomes darkness. I no longer had the daunting task of fighting the darkness or running from it. I only had to stop running from myself."

Life from the Present Moment

Parallels know the formula for living in the present moment. The present moment for you Parallels includes within it past, present, and future. This may not make sense to most of us but for the Parallels the past and future are contained within the present. Your inherent ability to live in the present moment paves the way for your natural ability to purely experience life because you are fully present in it moment by moment.

We were designed to experience the creation of life in each fresh and new moment. Knowing this helps cut through the illusion that we need to live from the trauma and drama of the past and the fear of the future. The reluctance to simply experience being fully alive now has created an epidemic bipolar state that consists of the human swing from manic hyperactivity as a way of falsely feeling alive to the polar opposite state of depression. Imagine the experience of the bounty of life coursing through our veins, our hearts overflowing with joy, and our minds clearly focused and directed—in our Soul purpose. This can only happen from the place of the present moment. We long to have this experience, but we collectively have hunkered down to buying into our need to cope and survive instead of living from our birthright of creating and experiencing from the vastness held in the present moment.

The Parallel home is universal, not just of the Earth. To live from many existences expands and broadens one's sense of the foundation of home as a universal one. To feel that the whole galaxy is our home is so very freeing. We can move beyond feeling the sense of limitation of being trapped in a mere physical existence here. It was not meant to be that way. The brave Souls from Parallel universes are here to remind us of how expansive life can be. It is essential for you Parallels to rekindle that experience while here so that you can bring it as your Soul purpose to others. It is understandable that you feel very limited in the idea of just living within a physical world. Like others, you can get caught in the state of separation that is prevalent here. And your greatest gift is the vast connection to so much that you know. It is vital for you to re-open that connection so you can bring it like a bridge, to this world that is so hungry for its long lost friend called Oneness.

The Power of Now

Eckhart Tolle is a very fine example of a Parallel who is currently planting valuable seeds of reconnection to oneness. He has written the book *The Power of Now*. As a Parallel he knows in his Soul what it is to live absolutely in the present moment. *The Power of Now* is very much about living in the present moment. One of Eckhart Tolle's Soul gifts is to bring the power of the present moment into focus again, as it has been very much lost here. The power of now is all we have, and the vibration he carries of this in his book is one of being able to reconnect people with that possibility in their lives. *The Power of Now* carries the accurate design for existence in the realm of the present moment and the oneness of the all that is.

I suggest to Parallels I work with that their reason for reading this book by Eckhart Tolle is different than for most. You are to read the book to connect with and magnify these truths that you already know. This will spark and encourage you to bring your gifts more fully in this world. *The Power of Now* proclaims that there is a great opening for the understandings of Parallels to be received here. I am so appreciative of the evidence through his book and many others of the collective receptivity to these pure states of being that Parallels bring.

In *The Power of Now*, Tolle speaks of our return to the pure experience of life. Our outpouring of the pure experience of life is the original way we were designed to give expression to life. We are given six senses through which Light can manifest as the myriad forms of life in full bloom. We are created to bring forth such essences as joy, power, magic, love, and aliveness through the sensations of connecting to life as it is created now.

The emotional body, which Tolle calls the emotional pain body, is a distortion of this design for experiencing creation through life. As we simply create and then experience our creation of life, our need to produce an emotional reaction to life will fade and then vanish.

It is vital for all of us, but especially you Parallels, to remember the knowledge of what it is to do life from the place of pure experience through the six senses, so that you don't fall into using the emotional body the way most do. It is your job to remind this world what else is possible.

For instance, joy is the feeling experience of a heart in full bloom in the moment. The emotional body is comprised of emotional reactions and responses to an experience or state of existence. Imagine that you are creating a heart that is open and blooming. The emotional body decides to feel scared in response to that sensation. Or it feels sad because of past feelings of hurt attached to the heart. Or you are angry that he doesn't love your heart in full bloom like you want him to. Emotions only distort the original creation of the heart.

The emotions, in being utilized to help us return to the pure state of experiencing life, are really gateways to pure essence. Play with this! Fear is the gateway to the magic and curiosity of life. Sadness or grief opens the heart to know its birthplace for Love and joy. Anger is the gateway to return us to our power and our truth. As you Parallels remember the blissful reality of the pure experience of living, you can help others find and utilize the gateways provided by any emotion to return to the true state of being in life in all its potency of expression.

Examples of Parallels with Us

In the movie *A Beautiful Mind,* Russell Crowe plays John Nash, which was quite appropriate because Crowe is a Parallel being on a definite mission. John Nash's genius wasn't understood, so he was harmed for it. He was a genius who brought advanced formulas in the world of physics. He brought this information through from his other existences. It terrified people because their brains couldn't understand how he got this amazing information. The movie also depicted how a Parallel is seen as schizophrenic from the scientific perspective. He did in fact have an amazingly creative and beautiful mind, which was not understood or appreciated here. For John Nash, as it was depicted in the movie, the deep, abiding, unconditional Love of his wife and tremendous belief she had in him held such a vital and strong vibration that he was able to be in life without medication or tremendous pain. His gifts were given room to breathe into this world to a certain extent. His life truly opened a door, as painful as it was, for the gifts of Parallels like himself to begin to be received. There still aren't many from Parallel universes here now, relative to the entire population, but many more are appearing.

A Parallel named Harry Palmer designed an excellent course on self-development called Avatar,® which allows a person to learn highly refined tools as a means to truly master experiencing life in the ever-present moment. Harry Palmer is on a mission to bring the Avatar course to people worldwide to help reinstate the pleasure of experiencing the natural abundance of life as it was meant to be. I have taught this course for over ten years and it never ceases to amaze me how the tools that were created bring you back to the simple, but grand ability to be the creator of your universe. As it should be!

Deepak Chopra is also a Parallel. What a tremendous seed planter he is for the consciousness of mankind, as he continually describes real steps for living from a path of success in the manifestation of all that one is. He came as a world teacher when the world was ready for his gifts. For years he has introduced so many true dimensions for health and well-being that go way beyond the medical model this world has felt strapped to. He has changed the face of medicine many times over. He came to plant seeds of possibility for living from the inherent state of well-being that we all carry in our cells. He is keen to teach people how to open up to and use more holistic approaches to health. He is highly regarded for the methods he offers to assist people to remember that wellness and happiness starts within. He's been fully received, very generously by many, and never questioned for his approach. Quite remarkable. I believe that is because his timing for being here was very orchestrated. He came when the world was ready for his gifts, and he will leave when he has planted all of the seeds that he needs to as it relates to his Soul destiny plan for the paradigm shift of creating health as an internally driven state of being.

It has been scientifically proven, for instance, that prayer positively impacts surgical procedures and is being used in all the finest hospitals in the United States. This is just one example of the fruition of so many seeds Deepak Chopra has planted in bringing high frequencies into the field of health care. He has brought a far greater value to the state of wellness as an internal barometer of our happiness in being alive as Souls here than has been known before.

You Parallels feel that you have the ability to transform anything you connect with, even death and darkness. You learned this ability in your other worlds, so that anything of creation you connect with can become a part of you as part of the oneness of all that is. That reality and ability works well in other universes, but does not translate well into the gravitational field of planet Earth. In this world, Parallels cannot inherently transform everything they touch because the Earth is a denser field to work in than other universes. A Parallel must learn when they have a desire to transform something to give that request to the beings that work with them and let these higher resources bring Light for transformation where it is actually welcomed. Parallels are meant not to get so directly involved in the transformational process they know is possible in other dimensional worlds. In essence you must radiate Light wherever you are and let the Universe manage where it will be utilized best.

Many of Our Children Are from Parallel Universes

I have discovered that many young children born since about 1996 are from Parallel universes. Their presence gives me evidence that whole new possibilities of living from the higher realms of spirit are now possible. These Parallels in young bodies are coming to speed up the process of mastering our Soul journey here collectively. They are coming now because we here have done our work of Light to pave the way for their expansive presence.

More Parallel Resources

Those from Parallel universes are here to clear up the pattern of polarity on Earth and throughout this Universe. You hold the Blueprints for oneness. Oneness is what exists to be known beyond polarity. Polarity first appeared in a particular Parallel universe, so you feel a keen sense of purpose in rectifying that pattern and bringing oneness here, where polarity has created warring, judgment, and divisiveness. You can remember to bring in this frequency of oneness by tapping into your Parallel connection any time you find yourself caught in polarity and want out of it.

You Parallels also have knowledge of the secret to manifestation. That would be stated in this world as holding sacred union with what one wants to be or become. You have the inherent ability to change the raw materials of existence to the life forms of your choice. This is the secret of manifestation. Thought forms can become the reality of what moves through the heart and Soul. Deepak Chopra conveys these secrets eloquently in a number of his books.

Souls from various Parallel universes have brought a plethora of spiritual resources, as I have described. You were very drawn to come here to experience the bounty of resources that are available. There is a great exchange going on, which is natural to life purpose everywhere. You came to partake in the diversity and abundance of life forms that have been created as nature in all its glory and incredible display of the exquisite beauty and endless variation of creation. Nature is the exemplification of Love made manifest in life forms of magnificent diversification. The animal, plant, and mineral kingdoms are all teeming with brilliant displays of magic. There is no place like this anywhere in the galaxy. So you can see how Souls from Parallel universes that love to explore, adventure, and experience would choose to come here just to be part of this magical kingdom!

In this vein, you who exist in numerous Parallel universes while here would be wise to remember that when you are having feelings of isolation or disconnection to the oneness of all that is, which you know deep in your Soul, that nature itself holds the vibration of oneness with all that is.

I have discovered that for you who are Parallels, to ground yourself 100 percent to the Earth to find stability is not really appropriate or satisfying. You don't naturally find stability with this Earth energy field as you feel it from where you stand in oneness. The Earth surface doesn't hold that vibration of oneness at the surface where we find ourselves. At the same time, there is oneness deep within the core of the Earth that can be touched by each of us. This frequency out of which the Earth was birthed is the fire of divine Love continually creating life in absolute connection to universal Love and oneness. That line of Love can always be connected to for stability and knowingness while things swirl on the surface and feel to you like the sensation of separation and disconnection.

There seems to be a lot of experience in the last ten years of you dreaming more about dimensional doorways and portals to other universes, because you are feeling more of a connection to the beings from your home universes. At the same time, those beings from your home universes also have greater influence here because you connect with them and receive their gifts, which gives them a presence here. This is the natural outpouring from the state of oneness.

It is quite real for you Parallels to understand what it means to travel energetically between universes on a regular basis. It is no surprise for you to feel the presence of many other beings traveling alongside you as you move freely between and within the various universes. You feel genuinely connected to a sense of oneness with all that is. This is a reality for you, not imagination. The seed of connection to this oneness you plant here helps deeply to raise the vibration of this world from survival mode to a mode of creation on a much bigger playground.

You beings from Parallel universes know the true balance of energies, which is true polarity, as they existed before there was the distortion of polarity we now know. You are here to help this world return to that more inherent state of existence, which says there's day and there's night. One is not good and its opposite bad, which is the way of polarity as we know it here. True polarity exists to differentiate essences. Night is a distinct vibrational field compared to the quality of day. Up has a directional dimension that is different than down, for instance. This is the simple description of the truth of polarity. Existences are distinct and they have relational connections. Parallels understand this and are helping to bring the truth of polarity back into the Blueprint. This balance of energies in the true make-up of polarity allowed us to have the ability to experience endless possibilities of energies and keep those possibilities in balance so that wholeness would always exist. In the energy field of true polarity wholeness was maintained while expansion occurred. The distortion of polarity that we now know is a way to limit creation and the endless possibilities in creation.

Feeling Separation Is the Challenge

The key challenge for you Parallel Souls is the sense of separation you feel so deeply. You know to your core what it is to exist as part of the oneness of all that is. You know the sense of connectedness of existing in the eternal, ever-present, omnipotent oneness that exists everywhere, with everything. You feel the essence of existence, which is all there is, and out of which everything springs. You have come to this world to plant the seed of this remembrance that lies within us all, and within every cell of the planet.

Consequently, for you to be in a world that dominantly exists from the place of separation makes little sense to you. You can't understand the human choice for separation, so life here feels confusing to you. But you also understand that in spite of the choice some people make, the oneness of existence can still be received by others. Separation is a challenging concept for Parallels, but fortunately, you have come to help dissolve this overriding illusion, because you know the power of union and oneness.

Sacred Union

The deepest aspect of the Parallel gift is your experiential knowledge of sacred union with the Divine, the Beloved. To know this oneness is the secret of our deepest heart longing. What do I choose to be in sacred union with in each moment? This is the question that Parallels raise in our consciousness. The presence of you Parallels here allows us to remember the experience of being in sacred union with all that we create, which brings forth the experience of passion and purpose to our lives. What a blessing this is.

As is true with the Soul essences of all the Soul Families, the gifts of the Parallels can be drawn on by each of us at anytime. This is why they have come to replenish the Earth, so that all here can access the memory of sacred union with the oneness of all that is. It is the birthright of everyone.

The following is an interview with a Parallel.

Susann: My understanding is that you are getting information directly from the dimensions and beings of your Parallel universes as a means to assist you in living from an expanded place and to help others to get a feel of how to live from this expanded place. How would you describe the ways that your connection to Parallel existences benefits your daily life?

Patty: I would say that this applies to the many things that I know, but that I was never taught this lifetime—from cooking to some of the healing work I do, to just the sense of having a huge amount of knowledge to draw from that makes my life work in ways that don't seem to be natural for everyone. I have no idea where it came from, but I am grateful for it.

I think when I was younger I felt like I was out of my body. But now, even when I'm in another dimension or universe, I know it. But I'm still here. It's interesting. Sometimes I have the knowledge that whatever I'm bringing or saying is coming through me but I don't call it channeling. It's just coming from this other dimension of me.

Susann: You as a Parallel are one aspect of numerous aspects of being, operating in a unified manner to show how oneness looks to the human eye. How does this capacity play out for you?

Patty: I truly believe that there are hundreds and thousands of spirit guides everywhere. They're not all-powerful. They need us to be able to come into this dimension as much as we need them to go to other dimensions. But they can't come in unless we invite them and allow them to be there. So that's why I have never been afraid of what other people perceive as spirits, or haunted places, or things like that. I call these beings my cosmic committee.

Susann: Speak to me about how your ability to know connection to oneness and union with the Divine teaches you how to deal with the limitations you encounter here.

Patty: I can remember many years ago when I had an astrological reading. The woman said to me, "It's not that your mother didn't love you. It's that your mother didn't love you in the way you knew love and connection." I feel love from a lot of different sources. When I was younger it bothered me a little bit. Then I thought, well why should I be bothered? Because there is as much Love out there as I want to take in. If I want a thimbleful, a cupful, or whatever I want, it's all there. So whether one person likes me or loves me doesn't make any difference.

Susann: That's a huge gift that you can bring here. I work with people at a psychological and emotional level all the time and that's one of the biggest wounds that people here hold. They feel that if a person doesn't love them, they don't know Love. Love is much bigger than an emotion. It's an absolute connection to all that is. You can help people just by carrying the vibration in your healing work. You are opening portals for them to other dimensions of possibility for their lives. If they can receive that they can bring it in for themselves. This absolute connection to oneness you bring opens the door to our chance to experience the large range of diversity springing out of oneness that there is to be known on Earth. How do you find this world to be an expression of the diversity of oneness?

Patty: Right now I'm experiencing touching the chair. I'm experiencing that I am thirsty. I'm experiencing that I'm glad for our connection. Every moment gives me the chance to experience the endless diversity of life there is to be known. It is all connected to the oneness that I know deep within my Soul. There was a man that I worked with when I worked at a mental health center in northern Maine. And he was a whittler. He whittled things all the time during sessions or when we were all doing some group activity. And he had this phrase he repeated: "Feelings aren't good or bad, they just are." I always took that to mean, "Yes, we are not what we're feeling in that moment." Some people get into the feeling and they get stuck there. And that's why there're so many therapists out there. We're a vessel. Life comes through us. This whittler reminded me of the simplicity I know for the formula of life without the drama and trauma we seem to love to attach to it.

Susann: It's your gift here that you know the formula; that you have what it takes to truly do life here. If you don't bring it, it won't be brought. You remind people of that aspect of the Blueprint. And in exchange you have the opportunity to experience the sensation through the six senses of the joy of living, held in the bounty of nature all around us.

Patty: Yes, it's an amazing place here, like no other. I am very happy that I came.

The following is an interview with another Parallel.

Carey: Everything is now. From my experience, when I move in that reality, I have this point of reference in myself as being my flagship self. From that reference point I have the ability to move pretty fluidly in physical and conceptual spaces.

Susann: Bringing your gift of knowing the connection between existences helps inspire and remind people that separation does not have to exist between the different dimensions of physical, mental, emotional, and spiritual. They are meant to be one dimension and different dimensions at the same time.

Carey: And because it is one, that quite literally creates the power to choose. You can choose to be in a more limited experience or you can make a different choice. You can choose to be in primarily a purely physical experience, or an emotional one. You can choose to isolate those experiences because actually they all co-exist.

Susann: Do you have difficulty with the way that we separate our experience here, especially in the way we disconnect our Soul from our physical and emotional experience?

Carey: Oh, absolutely, because it's incredibly limiting. And you know from many peoples' personal experiences, and mine in particular, that limitation becomes very crushing. Because it is so limiting here, we get very disrupted from even our own understanding of the expanded place of Parallel existence.

Susann: So the challenge for Parallels is trying to understand how it's done here. You want to help but are caught in the different understandings of what wholeness is about. It's like being caught between two worlds. You know what's real, but here, the illusion of separation is so strong. The question becomes, "Do I function the way they do in order to belong and to be able to operate here? Or do I function from the multi-dimensionality that I already know, which isolates me and makes me feel misunderstood?" And that choice can be fraught with complications.

Another gift of Parallels: there are dimensional doors that can be opened from this Universe to your parallel one to help us come back into greater and higher frequencies of possibility for wholeness. There are vortexes around the world that exist, such as Stonehenge in England, to help bring in the frequencies of Parallel existence. And more and more are opening. For instance, when the World Trade Center Towers came down, and people prayed for help from the heavenly realms, dimensional doors were opened through which help could come from Parallel existences. Because of what happened on 9/11, new avenues were opened providing connection to larger realms holding oneness, for all here to benefit from.

Carey: I absolutely agree with you, being one who was there. I understand exactly what was rewoven in that place.

Susann: Can you explain how you were there even though you were here in Colorado?

Carey: I'll try. In the weeks preceding that morning, some others and I already knew something was up on a large scale. We didn't know cognitively what the specific event was, but we had an understanding that there was something large occurring that we could feel energetically in the works. There's almost no language for it. It's an intuitive process. You feel something coming, and you know something's happening, but you don't know what it is. That's a really simplified way of stating it. A larger part of me was present. I knew I was conferring with and meeting with other people in other realms. And perhaps for some, that would come through in a dream. For me, it was as real as me sitting here talking to you now. It's not that I just had a sense about this event in the works... I was participating in it.

That morning I woke up and I knew that I wasn't fully present for myself in my human experience. I physically got up and took care of what I needed to do, but my awareness was not fully present in my experience. And then I just knew that I needed to turn the television on and get clued into what was happening in this physical world.

When the 9/11 events occurred, I wasn't horrified like most people were. I was in a complete place of acceptance. It was like a bell going off, or the phone ringing. You just get a call. You know that you are getting a call and that you are answering it. It's like you're picking up the phone and saying, "Okay." And there were many from other realms on a conference call.

This is the only picture I have given to people about it. But the truth is, I have other pictures I'd love to share. But it's like a large part of my consciousness had been disembodied. I went to the place where the energy of the event was happening. The Earth grid, we'll call it. I literally became part of a certain small group of people who were there to facilitate the process of reweaving the matrix in the area of the Earth grid connected to Manhattan.

I sat down in my apartment and I closed my eyes, and I just wasn't there anymore. Instead, I was in the atmosphere above the Earth with a number of other individuals, and we came together, each with our own task in the group, to facilitate the breaking open of the Earth grid and reestablishing a new connection. It was working with Light and frequency and vibration, so it wasn't tactile. It would be similar to taking a weaving and cutting a hole in it, and reweaving around that space to make a new pattern. But it's done, as I said, with Light, with tone, with vibration, with frequency. Some of us were reweaving and establishing this new portal. Some of us were caring for those who chose to stay but were harmed. That's a strange reality for most to understand - to be an angel up there and still be a physical human here.

I believe that the people in those towers at the time of the event all chose to be there. And those who died all became columns of Light that replaced the World Trade Center. Each person became part of something larger, and created with that energy the essence of self. They created the material, the new yarn to weave with.

In my consciousness, I even blend with the others. I am still aware of myself, and yet the presence of others becomes a part of oneself.

Susann: It is strange, but for many of us, we do know what it is to be here and be aware of a loved one on the other side, for example. Or to be here physically and be closely aware of a husband or friend across the country, as though we were there with them.

Carey: Referring again to 9/11, I was energetically part of the event to hold a clear space. And in doing that, I could also observe everything that was going on around me. Now, had I chosen at that time to violate my own mission, to compromise my path, not to hold that space, if I suddenly decided that I was going to go do something else that would have caused harm to that overall mission … well, that kind of choice is completely impossible for me. I would have not been able to do that.

What the general population doesn't understand about people in Parallel universes is that we don't actually have the capacity to do a whole lot of damage because we are not capable of it, except to ourselves. That was a choice we made before we got here. So we came with that encoded. When we get to this place of being in choice and teaching choice, we have to confront ourselves when our own choice confronts us. If I do something outside of my own integrity, it's devastating very quickly. And then I have to confront the fact that I chose this, and in effect, I am harming myself with my choice. And it forces me to stop.

If you're suddenly compromising your path, a path of Light, and allowing it to cause harm, then for Parallels, that flashes back instantly. I can't allow myself to create harm for others.

And that doesn't mean I'm perfect. I've done things that have harmed people, but never in the capacity of a Parallel, always in the capacity of a human being. As an emotional human being I have caused harm because of my emotional state. Getting caught in the separateness, I have caused harm, just like any other human being can cause harm. But as a Parallel, operating in the fullness of that multi-dimensional state, I have never harmed because I cannot choose something that will harm from my Parallel self.

Susann: How does having information about things outside yourself become a challenge for you?

Carey: This creates problems for us because it intimidates people to have information about them. They feel like we can read them, or know intimate processes about them or violate them. We could read their minds; we could know the bad things they've done. But we won't because we couldn't be here without a certain integrity. And if that integrity breaks down, we are affected to such a degree that we can't function. It's a fail-safe. If we abuse the process, there's an automatic shutdown and we can't get to it anymore.

Susann: That's a really excellent point. We don't have free choice as it relates to anybody else, or anybody else's energy. There are built in ethics that apply with free choice that say this.

Carey: In the realm of free choice, and being who I am in this Parallel Family, I've made the commitment that I will not try to violate someone else's free choice just because I can see certain things going on with them.

Susann: What would you say is the largest influence that disrupts you, or the most poignant one, the one that really gets to you?

Carey: There's a belief system here that includes good and evil, black and white, right and wrong. This is the polarity dynamic that operates here. We believe in God and Satan, and then we apply moral values to that polarity. And the truth, as a Parallel knows it, is that this is only a system. And though we're choosing to experience all this physically, by being human, we don't have to buy into the belief system that attaches morals to the polarities. Even as Light workers, there is a tendency to define our experience. Good, bad, Light, darkness. But the truth beyond that is that we all just are.

People are threatened by our clarity and our acceptance. As an example, I totally accept that beings have come here with a personal agenda that does not have to do with bringing Love. I totally accept that and I do not believe that is an evil agenda. I just don't see it that way. What I do see is that I do not have to choose that agenda.

Susann: You don't have to be influenced by it, which is the bottom line.

Carey: And therefore, I'm not. But what making that choice does for me, as someone in the Parallel Family, is it puts me into a different dimension. Hence, I feel the isolation from many here. And I am still walking, talking, interacting, and interfacing with this environment and with the relationships I've created. Others simply don't understand me when I say that it doesn't have to be this way, or it doesn't affect me. And they get angry and jealous and disconcerted because I'm not affected.

Susann: Tell me how you are able to bring your gifts from Parallel worlds to transform this world of emotional reactions to a world of truly experiencing what we create in each moment.

Carey: I see emotions in a very particular way. Take the feeling of fear, for example. When you take the reaction to the feeling experience out of it, it's simply a frequency. And like the bands of frequency in a radio, you can just change the channel to change the frequency. It is that simple to utilize the experiences of a feeling nature that exist and allow them to simply be an experience of a frequency.

For instance, I don't want to get pregnant. That is a deliberate frequency I am creating. I don't use birth control. The frequency that most would use is fear of being pregnant as protection against pregnancy. I use that frequency in my body as the energy form of a shield or filter that deliberately does not allow pregnancy. This is not about the emotion of fear about getting pregnant. I am using the knowledge of possible pregnancy as a frequency to choose to not accept pregnancy.

Susann: I had a client who works in Parallel dimensions say that she just gets so much information that she gets concerned about what to do with all this information. She doesn't want the responsibility of all that information, especially the information that pertains to other people. How would you assist other Parallels to learn how to perceive and be intuitive without getting overwhelmed?

Carey: What Parallels forget is that we have the capacity to store information and allow it to unfold.

If I hold in my awareness that I have all this information, but it's not up to me in my human experience to process it all, I'm much better off. The human experience says that we have to work it out. But for a Parallel and for many people who are beginning to operate in this more expansive state, that's not the truth anymore. The truth is that I don't work it out. I don't have to process it. And simply knowing that reconnects me to an access code for this information.

You can put all this information in a box, a storage container, and request that it process itself and that it be delivered to you at the time that you need it. This information is for global influence. Often times what we forget is that part of our job is to connect with other Souls who aren't necessarily in physical form, and we disseminate this information through them. So a lot of times we bring this huge amount of information through awareness, which is meant to have a global impact or effect, but it's not up to us as a single human individual to apply it. It's up to us simply to hold it and then, the next time we meet with other Souls from other universes, we work together and it becomes transmitted here as it needs to be.

So for example, I'll reference the 9/11 situation again. For weeks before 9/11, I knew what I knew about the event. But you see, as a human being with my mental self, I didn't have to know that 9/11 was going to happen. Because as a human, that would have caused me a great deal of trauma to walk around knowing three weeks before the event that it was going to happen and there was nothing I could do about it. Or to be one of the nut cases who calls the police up three weeks before the event and says there's going to be a terrible bombing at the World Trade Center. It helps nobody. Not only that, it victimizes me emotionally and mentally. It also has the potential to victimize me in external systems. If I am that person who calls up, then once the police are looking at me, they're hauling me in and asking how did I know, and where did I get the information? And pretty soon, I'm on the FBI's most-wanted list!

So instead, as a Parallel who was aware that this was going to happen, I didn't have to know. All I had to do was bring this information and hold it, and kind of talk to people a little bit, because I have my releases. I can share with people, something's going on, I can feel it, something's happening. And that heightens people's awareness to their own mission in this if they have one. It's a process that Parallels forget, because we take it on as a human, as an Earth-based experience in separation, rather than in the multidimensional aspect of wholeness.

Susann: I would Love to hear something of your experience around this idea that Parallels know the past, present, and future as one dimension of time.

Carey: For me this relates to our karma and how the past affects the future. Today, right now, I can sit here on my porch, and I know, because everything in my history tells me, that a car hit me. And I have serious physical limitations, mental limitations, and emotional limitations as a result.

Okay, that's my past creating my present. And my present is now affecting my future. Because in my present, I'm operating as if I've been hit by a car. However, in this present, if I know that something about that past was different, I change my current experience. So this is a leap of faith.

In this moment, sitting here on this step, I have an experience in this moment of knowing that I have chosen to experience at a knowing level that a car never hit me. And in knowing that, I create and change the past, and create a different future. I know that's an extreme example.

Susann: Yes, but it's a good one to use, because it's real.

Carey: Take the present, where I am right now. I know right now, in this moment, for example, that I will never be in another accident. I know. It's a cellular knowledge, so deeply seated in me that I know it. There will never be another accident in my future, ever.

I know this. I know I never had an accident in my past. But it doesn't line up with my historical experience in the mental and physical realm. So that creates a tangle in the past, because my knowing it doesn't make it not so for others. All these people have documented it. All these people remember it as so. But guess what? They remember it until they don't.

Now, it's getting down to fine points. Throwing out the fine points of my experience, what I'm trying to convey is that our present moment changes everything. And for me, it's not always congruent with my memory process, and this is a specific issue for Parallels. But for others on this planet, it becomes their memory.

So for example, tomorrow morning you could wake up, and it's possible that there could be no war in Iraq going on. And you would not have a memory that there ever was a war in Iraq going on because you would have shifted yourself to a place in this experience where there is no war going on. And therefore, changing your point of reference in terms of the strength of who you are, you would have literally changed your location on this plane. That would then draw energy to that experience, and your experience in or this dimension would then cease to exist. And the war would simply go away. It would not be happening for you.

Susann: Exactly. Just because we hold it as a reality, does not mean it is a reality at another level. It is just our reality for the moment.

Carey: Right. And again, we've heard this, and this is already out there in the matrix, in the Universe, in a different teaching. Where awareness goes, energy flows.

Susann: How would you describe your experience of actually transforming your reality and it having an impact planetarily, while you are in the human form?

Carey: We don't have to work for peace. We don't have to change what's going on. We simply have to take our energy to the place where peace is happening and war will just fall away because it can't exist without feeding it. We are all operating in the freedom to choose what we experience and therefore feed. We don't have to base our lives on emotional reaction. We can simply shift our reality and choose where we are and what we see. As we change our perspective, our world changes. I believe this is a major reason for those of us from Parallel universes to come here. We can show others the simplicity of what it is to live from a different, more expanded, connected reality of oneness while operating in this physical dimension.

The Parallel Proclamation: I am in sacred union with the one, and all that is. I exist as everything, everywhere.

15

ARCHANGEL REALMS

Each Soul comes to the Earth to contribute its gifts, talents, and knowledge from various locations in this solar system and beyond.

As a Soul enters this Earth field it chooses a primary Archangel Realm through which it works to add Soul personality dimensions to its mission and purpose. Each of us picked a realm, which is called an Archangel Realm, to clothe our Soul's personality. We picked a primary way to express that spirit so that we don't have to be all things for all people. It's like creating a designated spiritual profession with particular characteristics that we can focus on and excel in.

There is a vast array of angelic realms. Each realm brings into focus an aspect of spirit. There are many colors to spirit's definition, and they are ever expanding in creation as there are more words in the dictionary every year. For instance, there is an Archangel Realm that brings into focus splendor and purpose. When most of us first incarnated here for the first time many thousands of years ago, splendor and purpose were not viable energies for us to focus on. Back then life was about survival, so our focus gravitated toward bringing healing, balance, and the ability to get to a more powerful foundation on this planet. We are only now moving from that evolutionary stage to a new one where we will magnify joy, splendor, purpose, magic, wholeness, and exploration. The children incarnating now are bringing the higher frequencies of joy and connection as never before. They don't have to experience the Soul pain and heartache of coming to Earth feeling separation from a Universe held by our Creator's Love and truth. If they don't have to spend a lifetime healing separation in this three-dimensional reality, their purpose can include far greater frequencies that can establish the vast array of spiritual dimensions here that were intended. Splendor will become a household term, ecstasy a common experience, and abundance the natural state.

The Seven Archangel Realms for Soul Personality

There are seven primary Archangel Realms that are specifically utilized by Souls to assist them in defining their Soul personality and purpose during Earth incarnations. The Archangel Realm each person chooses often strongly correlates with the Soul's heritage mission for coming here.

Each Soul has chosen one primary realm that it has utilized for all its lifetimes here. Each Soul continues to gain expertise in its chosen fields of strengths in service. It learns how to bring forth the gifts of that particular realm and, at the same time, evolve beyond the challenges that are part of that realm. In this polarized world, we seem to have both strengths and challenges. By knowing the attributes and challenges of each realm, you can have a better understanding of the "job" description of each realm. You may feel a kinship to more than one realm; we each have a primary realm and we may explore or train in a secondary realm. Because these energies are aspects of spirit, a realm doesn't delineate what outer job you have, such as a doctor or lawyer. It denotes how you most valuably express your spirit and gifts in this world.

For example, I work primarily through the Archangel Realm of Raphael, as a healer through Love. My Soul gifts come through the avenue of healing Love. I chose that realm to bring blessing and growth to all I touch. This does not describe what outer job my Soul must perform. It describes the energy field my movement in this world must carry to bring my heart and Soul's purposes to fulfillment. As I do, feel, think, experience my life as healing Love, my Soul's treasures expand in my life. I have deliberately signed up for this realm for many lifetimes. This most benefits myself and all here, and it is designed to be equally personal and planetary fulfillment.

I also have a secondary realm. Sometimes Souls take on a secondary realm for a portion of a lifetime, so the energy field of that particular realm is accessible for them in a strong way, as needed. Usually a realm will be added to serve planetary fulfillment, not merely to fulfill personal purposes. But it will benefit both.

Ten years ago my Soul elected to open to the Archangel Realm of Gabriel. I'm sure this was all set up by my Soul ahead of time. The basic outline of contracts and agreements for my Soul's destiny plans were laid out to choose from. My Soul knew that this was about the time I would move into teaching, followed by writing. Communication and teaching are the hallmarks of the Gabriel Realm. Through this realm's connection, I am surrounded by and infused with the strength of expression to utilize in my work and life. This realm provides divine mentoring, training, and education as do all the Archangel Realms. You may find alignment with a number of the realms, if not all of them. That is not surprising. In the Original Blueprint, we may have chosen a more primary realm and we had access to each of the other realms for our growth and fulfillment. We are in touch with a wealth of resources that are available through the Archangel Realms. These realms are designed to assist us in bringing qualities of spirit into form through our life of service. By design, all the realms "should be" fully activated through us all the time. Consequently, you will discover pieces from each realm that you value and you either desire to have more of in your life or feel are already engaged in you. We are never alone, nor do we have to create our life path all by our self. We do not have to take decades of time to learn and incorporate these realms. Our heart and Soul are being trained continually as we open to receive the energies from the realms we signed up to live through. As we become more attuned to the Archangel Realms we dominantly chose, we can feel more free to express our heart and Soul robustly through those characteristics.

Ultimately, we are all designed to operate through all seven Archangel Realms, at all times. This is our birthright. So we can all develop a real and strong connection with each of the seven realms. And we are free to call on the energies of each of the realms whenever we choose.

Well Known People and their Archangel Realms

Michael

Paul Newman	Michelangelo
George Harrison	George Washington
Bruce Springsteen	Sting
Michael Moore	Al Pacino
Richard Gere	Tom Cruise

Gabriel

Nelson Mandela	Robin Williams
Jim Carrey	Michael Jackson
Oprah Winfrey	Bette Midler
Tina Turner	Louis Armstrong
Barbra Streisand	David Letterman
Marilyn Monroe	

Raphael

Meg Ryan	Marilyn Monroe
Charlize Theron	Courteney Cox
Julia Roberts	Dean Martin

Auriel

Goldie Hawn	Princess Diana
Mother Teresa	

Zophkiel

Kevin Costner	John Lennon
Buddha	Thich Nhat Hanh
Tom Hanks	Kevin Bacon
Eckhart Tolle	

Zadkiel

Bill Gates	Mick Jagger
Madonna	Robert Redford
Brad Pitt	Christopher Reeve
Gwyneth Paltrow	Susan Sarandon
Elizabeth Taylor	Jack Nicholson
Diane Keaton	Benjamin Franklin

Kamiel

Bill Clinton	Johnny Depp
Barbara Walters	Martha Stewart
John F. Kennedy	Martin Luther King
Jennifer Aniston	Ringo Starr
Halle Berry	Angelina Jolie
Russell Crowe	Frank Sinatra

Archangel Michael

Archangel Michael brings to focus the realm of the protector and spiritual warrior.

You who work through this realm are here to stand for truth. You are protectors of truth and spiritual warriors for truth. You have chosen to work through the energy field of truth to bring forward true and clear perspective, ideas, and inspirations based on truth, and to allow the actuality of the vibration of truth to have a place on the Earth. Paradoxically, you hold the perspective that there is no such thing as one absolute truth. What each one sees from his or her vantage point, aligned with their heart and Soul, is what carries the viewpoint of truth for that moment. You who work in the Michael Realm are here to teach this perspective. You show it through living example and inspiration. You speak in absolute terms. "This is the way it is," fills the tone you carry through your words, voice, and action. "This is how I see things in the situation, in relationship to another, or as it relates to a larger world scenario." Your challenge comes in how you deliver this absolute view and how it is received. You are often perceived as "black and white" in your delivery, which can feel rigid, hard-edged, and uncompromising to those you are addressing. It can also feel so absolute that there is no room for another's vantage point. In fact, when you stand for truth, which your Soul compels you to continually do, you want to draw forth truth from those who are with you. You desire to have your truth honored by each and every one and in every life experience.

As protectors of truth, others feel very safe with you. The safety that the Michael Realm emanates is not a safety from what is dangerous. It is not a safety based solely on comforting. It is the safety that says, "You are safe to be your true authentic self. As you honor your stance of truth you will be honored and protected in turn." You are a warrior for truth and will stand by others absolutely and hold their truth sacred as they uphold your forthright stance. You stand by them and they will stand by you.

It is not so much what you believe to be true that matters but rather your Soul ferocity to support truth wherever it is held. Do not get caught up in whether your view is right or wrong. Others may feel your ferocity discredits their truth. It is your task to teach them to have the same ferocity for their truth. This is what "Michaelites" wish to bring forward in this world. The truth is true and all is well; unconquerable life prevails.

In this world, truth is not particularly held in high esteem. Therefore, you Michaelites often carry the challenge, to varying degrees, of not feeling (or even being) heard when you stand for your truth.

For instance, if a boy stands up in class to report to his teacher that the formula she has written on the board is incorrect, what usually happens? The teacher feels embarrassed and tells the boy to sit down, or even worse, takes away a privilege for putting her in such an awkward position. His truth is not seen as respected, and he consequently "learns" that in order to make it in this world his stance will not be honored and must be withheld. His stance for truth sours and curdles and turns into resentment and anger. When later in life he meets people whom he feels honor him, most often a spouse, his pent up anger gets unloaded on her or him. A spouse would be wise to learn to duck somewhat when his demonstrative nature feels threatening.

As a Michaelite, your loved ones will be rewarded as you deepen your presence in truth and integrity. You do not let anyone else decide what is true for you. This is your gift to this world—to show what it is to come from a stance of individual truth and hold to it and be true to it. To have someone else tell you what your truth is goes against everything you stand for. So how do you deal with this dilemma? Your presence draws forth truth-seeing in others, so it is natural for those with you to be truthful in your presence. It would be useful for the Michaelites to honor truth wherever it shows up. That is your purpose. So in this situation, when a friend speaks to you of what he sees to be true for you, you can acknowledge to yourself, or out loud to him, "Thank you. I honor your truth. I honor your truth for you." It is not seen that he is trying to name your truth for you. It becomes a truth revealed for the other person's sake. That is what the Michaelite can honor and stand for.

The Michael Realm is key in holding a space for the heart's expansion. This realm can be called on any time for those who are expanding in their heart and Soul's expression in their lives.

The Michael Realm can also be called upon anytime one feels a need for the energy of spiritual warriorship or protection during life's everchanging influence on our growth. As we call upon the spirit of truth that the Michael Realm stands for, we are naturally honoring our Soul path and purposes every step of the way.

Archangel Gabriel

This is the realm of communication, sound, vibration, and the written and spoken word.

This realm brings the teacher, speaker, and communicator who desires to give knowledge and information to many. As a "Gabrielite," you are quick to stand up and speak your mind. At the same time, if you have felt held back in bringing out your voice, due to various life experiences, you will be very reluctant to speak your heart.

Your means for bringing your Soul into life is done most strongly through the spoken word. You are very verbal and even love to hear the sound of your own voice. To problem solve in emotionally charged territory you will want to talk your way from A to B, from unresolved to resolve. This is the way you get information and knowledge to teach.

It is important for you to be with people who listen to you, because talking is the way you work through life situations. When you feel heard, you feel your Soul is appreciated. It is more about feeling your words are honored and listened to, then the importance of speaking the words.

The realm of Gabriel loves honesty, integrity, and truthfulness. You abhor lies and untruths or half-truths. You have difficulty with systems such as the legal or judicial systems, which purport to uphold truth, but often don't.

You are known to shoot from the hip and tell it like it is, honestly and directly. You are here to ferret out lack of integrity and honesty. If others are not living their truth you will sniff it out and often call them on it. You are great teachers for growth to those who are longing to stand in their truth. You are tremendous supporters of what is real and true in those you care about.

In many instances, you Gabrielites are better employers than employees. Or you are best working for yourself. If the boss or manager is not being upfront or acting in integrity, you will not hold back on calling them on their lack of honesty or integrity. That may not go over so well with the higher ups! Your challenge is to learn to be diplomatic. For instance, before you blast forth with whatever you are thinking or feeling, it could be useful to ask the recipient if they would like to hear your vital knowledge and information. Learn how it serves others first, and it will serve you most in the long run.

Speaking from the heart in authenticity is a great gift of Gabrielites. Your Soul gift will be received by others most potently when this is the case.

The largest part of the Gabrielite's art of communication and teaching is to teach the right use of judgment. In this polarized world that categorizes everything into right and wrong, good and bad, detrimental judgment swirls around endlessly. The right use of judgment is something entirely different. It makes the statement, "This is the way I see it now." We all have the divine right to express who we are in this and every moment. We have each chosen gifts we desire to bring through our heart and Soul into life. We all have the right to state how we perceive or discern a situation from where we currently stand. This is the truth of the realm of judgment. Gabrielites are here to remind us of this reality.

As a Gabrielite, you have a tendency to judge others or yourselves if you aren't clear in how to use this realm most productively. You will get on the other end of judgment and judge others or be self-critical when you feel attacked or simply not received for your expression. It is important for you, when you get caught in being critical about yourself, to return to the remembrance of the truth of judgment. "This is how I perceive my vantage point of life in the moment now. I am willing to view life differently in the next moment." It is much easier to change your judgment than to beat up on yourself or another when you don't feel supported in your truth, internally or externally. As teachers, you have much to impart and proclaim, and you wish to share your knowledge wherever it is available. You risk criticism for "standing on your soapbox." Being yourself takes courage, trust, and standing up for yourself.

As we let these teachers speak, we will be inspired to bring forth our own greatness and depth.

This is a revealing story from a Gabrielite:

"I was working in a small office with a number of other entrepreneurs like me. We were all quite creative and good at what we were doing. But I found myself having some difficulty being a subordinate or just a team player. I kept making what I considered to be legitimate suggestions to co-workers that I thought would help them be more creative or more powerful and focused. They didn't welcome my suggestions and I felt left out and unappreciated.

Then I discovered that my Archangel Realm is Gabriel and that this is true for a number of my colleagues! No wonder. I understand now that my desire to express myself through words is great, but I need to be more diplomatic and ask people first if they want my input. And I'm now my own boss for my business. And that works so much better. I love working with people, but I have to be in a leadership position. If I'm in a group where someone else is the leader I have an unconscious tendency to be a leader, and it can feel undermining to a boss. I feel much more free knowing that my Soul chose to come through the Gabriel Realm, and thus my words are powerful and are meant to be used wisely and with due consideration to others."

Archangel Raphael

This is the realm of healing Love.

As natural healers from the heart, you who carry this realm innately project blue healing rays through your hands. As a Raphaelite, the way your Soul emanates its gifts is through this healing energy. You don't need to do anything outwardly for healing Love to be radiated to others. Raphaelites have a tendency to overexert this healing influence unnecessarily. It works on the level of being, not doing. In essence, healing naturally occurs wherever the frequency of Love is present. You Raphaelites can overextend yourselves based on your feeling that everything needs healing, feeling that it's your job to bring that healing Love wherever it is lacking. That is an endless, exhausting, fruitless task. Love is the same energy as life force.

You are here to help us to return to the natural state of wholeness through the power of healing Love. You are always present with understanding and care. You are loving individuals who have a tendency to deplete yourselves by attempting to fill the seemingly endless needs of others. Your challenge is to discern who is part of your Soul plan to extend your energy toward and how to do it in a way that does not leave you depleted.

You are here to show people that Love is an infinite commodity universally available. It is not yours to personally give to others. When a Raphaelite feels the need to personally give the divine Love they inherently feel connected to, to another, as though it belongs solely to them, it can become a caretaking exchange, which is disempowering to both people. This caretaking level of love is different than the frequency of divine Love. Healing as Love is not meant to be at the level of caretaking. It is not for you to say, "I'll give all I have to you, because it feels so natural to do so, and it doesn't matter if I get anything in return." This state can lead to the expectation for others that you are here to fill their needs for Love. The Raphaelite is here to remind us that divine Love is the healing force moving through everyone. You must visualize or feel an umbilical cord from your heart to the source of divine Love. This is how Love, in fact, feeds us all. The channel from our Creator to our heart is filled with divine Love. When we feel thanksgiving for the eternal presence of Love, it ignites the miracle of healing that hasn't held a place for Love. We can co-create as Love with those around us freely and appropriately from this place and this place alone.

Remember healer to heal yourself first in this way and you will have much to give and will be rewarded joyously in return for that gift.

The Raphael realm can be tapped into any time by anyone requesting the healing balm of Love that is vtal to our life nourishment. We are designed to know this healing Love as a natural flow of our heart's expression.

Archangel Auriel

This is the realm of compassion and unconditional Love.

This realm carries us to the healing magic of Earth Mother and nature. You in this realm are extremely compassionate, unconditionally loving, tolerant, and patient. You are exceptional as friends, partners, parents, and mates. You bring the essence of unconditional Love in a world that is sorely lacking these gifts.

You will listen to and receive those you care about with ease and generosity. You inherently know this world craves what you have and feel it is your humanitarian duty to be available 24/7. You constantly feel the longing to know unconditional Love everywhere you turn. Many will be drawn to your loving presence unconsciously because your Soul emanates such a pure, generous, receptive energy field.

Mother Teresa and Princess Diana are great examples of those who lived through this realm. The whole world loved and revered both of them. Princess Diana had the biggest wedding and the biggest funeral in history. We can't help ourselves in inherently loving the generous, genuinely loving expression of the loving Earth Mother and sacred goddess archetype Aurielites embody.

Beings from this realm adore nature in all its aspects. As an Aurielite, you help us connect and know the treasures of the natural world. You would be wise to place your compassionate nature only where it is joyously received. You have a tendency to have loose boundaries because you are so attuned to the huge need everywhere for your gift of an unconditional loving presence. You can easily be taken advantage of because of this.

You can call on the mother lioness side of yourself to protect and care for what is valuable to you. It also brings forth your qualities of vulnerability. The mother lioness is the fiercest animal there is. The lioness can rip to shreds anything that threatens her cubs. This lioness energy is equally important for protecting what matters most to your heart and Soul. As that is fiercely protected, then others can't take advantage of an Aurelite. Others will still be able to be inspired and uplifted by your loving presence and giving nature, but will learn how to know unconditional Love for themselves instead of relying on you to give those qualities away to them.

There is nothing quite like having an Aurelite as your friend. It allows us to authentically connect with the essence of unconditional love we all long to know and truly relish.

Archangel Zophkiel

This is the realm of balance, harmony, cosmic law and order, art, beauty, and perfection.

Balance is the hallmark of this realm. Zophkiels are continuously focused on what brings greatest balance and harmony to any particular moment, situation, or relationship. As a Zophkielite, you see the beauty and artistic dimension that is present in any situation or will do whatever you can to draw it out. You love to blend the arts and sciences either through your work or your personal interests, like an engineer who paints watercolors as a hobby or an interior designer who studies astronomy on the side.

As children you were the ones to stand in the middle of the teeter-totter to feel the sensation of bringing both sides to balance and equality in midair. This strong desire to bring balance and equality has become your nemesis. You can hold this middle ground with control and perfectionism. You can become rigid and uncompromising to create the sensation of harmony, which is really "my way or the highway." In this world of diversity, which births differences, balance is an artistic component of bringing diverse elements into a harmonious whole.

This middle ground that Zophkielites stand on brings peace and reconciliation where there has been polarity and war. As a Zophkielite, you plant seeds of harmonic convergence. You will see the holographic nature of the Universe, the world, and the moment at hand. Your challenge is to bring balance and harmony without being rigid and perfectionist. This can happen if you feel out of balance in your personal world. The middle of the teeter-totter is a fluid and moving place, not a static holding zone. A better picture of harmony could be seen in the movement of a swing. It is a dynamic and flowing balance. The holographic back and forth movement of the swing brings balance through creativity, fun, and playfulness. Perfectionism for balance can be a means to limit or merely manage. Harmony can mean bringing a whole new perspective into a locked scenario.

You bring the gift of being able to bring out the best of all sides or the inherent complimentary nature of both sides. You thoroughly enjoy looking at all points of view from the place of the middle ground. You teach us to see all available points of view and to appreciate the diversity of creation. It also reminds us that the whole is much more than the sum of each of the parts. You play an essential part in any group dynamic, from family to business to any community function or team endeavor.

John Lennon is an excellent representation of one who brings the riches of the Zophkiel realm. His essence brought harmony through his music, be it the beauty of balance between two people or world harmony and peace: "Imagine all the people living for today… and the world will be as one." These are exquisite lyrics that allow us all to feel the possibility of harmony, balance, and peace in this world.

Thich Nhat Hanh, the Buddhist leader who has traveled around the globe for years holding prayer gatherings for peace and harmony, excels in his Zophkiel nature. He is tenacious in his ability to hold a place of harmony, regardless of the circumstance he is experiencing. He truly knows how to carry the knowledge that the sum of the whole is greater than the parts. He honors the beauty of the divine balance that is always there to breathe into in a moment of meditation. He knows it exists no matter how our human entanglements try to convince us otherwise.

Archangel Zadkiel

This is the realm that proclaims that abundance is the natural state.

You are tremendous creators and your creation is a direct reflection of that truth. Whatever you put intention on, whatever you direct energy toward, and whatever you have a feeling connection to will be real for you and bring forth fruit in your world. To work in this realm you are stating that you know what is true and you want to assist this world in living from this divine state. You want the potency of the riches of spirit to live fully through your life on Earth, and you believe this is fully possible in any moment.

Zadkielites are teaching us how to bring our needs, desires, visions, and dreams into reality. The saying "Heaven and Earth are one" clearly states this. There is no separation between the invisible and the visible world. Those of you who have trained in this realm and have the purpose of bringing the teachings of this realm here have the Soul ability to turn metal into gold. You believe that this gold, the wealth of Love and Light, is always available to be harnessed to transform even the most "metallic" situation. You know you do not have to be stuck in a heavily gravitational, merely physical, world, devoid of the influence of spirit. The gold of spirit is always available to transform, uplift, and lighten. If you know it, put your intention on it, then it is so, unquestionably. This assurance comes through those who work through the Zadkiel realm in clarity and trust.

The phrase, "We create our reality," heralds from this realm. You want the potency of the riches of spirit to live fully through our lives on Earth, and you believe this is fully possible in any moment. It does not mean you are responsible for or can change someone else's reality, but we are responsible for our own reality and our world. You from the Zadkiel Realm know that you are meant to be natural at manifesting. Yes, your thoughts are powerful! Be careful what you think. This realm reminds us of the potency of the connection between thoughts and what plays out in our life, whether it is positive or negative.

Sometimes Souls who purposefully have signed up to bring forth this realm have been influenced by negativity to varying degrees. Your Zadkiel Soul continues to hold the truth that you have the gift of being powerful in your ability to manifest. In my work with those from this realm I find some people who are great at manifesting but are manifesting negatively or against themselves, through a pattern of self-judgment, self-doubt, and self-sabotage. You naturally manifest whatever you have conviction in, whether it is a creative or destructive conviction. You are potently creating your reality based on self-effacing patterns within you. But this can be turned around as you remember the higher path of this Soul gift, to bring the abundance of the gold of spirit into your life in any moment.

As a Zadkielite, you also carry connection to all matters of birth and growth. You are naturally helpful in all aspects of the birth process and any area concerned with inner or outer growth—physically, mentally, or emotionally.

Unifying the spiritual with the material is the task of those who assign themselves to this realm. You must remember the great benefits of turning everything you touch to gold. You may have had past experiences of being harmed for this, or thinking you are above the crowd and so you imagine you are violated or misunderstood. It is essential that you reconnect to the truth you inherently know at a Soul level: that abundance at all levels of life is your true birthright, and you are the ones to reestablish that divine reality in this world.

Archangel Kamiel

This is the realm of light, power, and energy.

Kamielites are here to teach the right use of power. Kamielites are instruments for creative transformation. As a Kamielite, you are here to remind us that we can always be in our greatest power. Each Soul is given the birthright to be the powerful expression of the Divine that they choose to be. We are meant to be masters of our Soul journey and destiny. We all signed up to bring our unique gifts and spiritual capabilities. The Kamiel Realm reminds us that Light is the core power; it is the true source for any of our actions or endeavors. We always have the choice in any moment to be our most potent, power-filled selves.

Kamielites love to draw forth the best in every one you come into contact with. You love to find the most potent, Light-filled way possible in any situation. It's like you are holding a lightning bolt in your hand at all times. This lightning bolt holds the essence of transformation, the energy of Light. You are natural transformers with everything you touch. You are dynamic individuals and your energy is a catalytic one. The Kamiel nature leaves no stone unturned. If we find ourselves with a Kamielite as a friend, business partner, or associate, they will truly allow us to launch our dreams.

You are also great hands-on healers and energy workers. Healing for you is transformative, which is different than the warm, soothing healing influence of the Raphael energy. Your presence naturally emanates a power field. Even if you try to lessen it or stay small, those who come in contact with you can't miss this potent core place being held by you. When you live from this place you reveal that it is the power of divine Light energy that fuels all creation. It can be the true fuel for life for each of us if we choose.

Kamielites are here to show us how to be the most powerful we can be as sources of Light, without being abusive of that strength and without withholding our power due to fear of using it unwisely.

If you are one who has worked in the Kamiel Realm in other lifetimes, you were involved either in situations where you misused your powerfulness or you were afraid to use your power. This incarnation can either bring a shyness to be in one's full power or a reluctance to stand for one's strengths and beliefs because of past behaviors. This is the lifetime to utilize your gifts of transformational power, as you have more reinforcement for standing in your power now than ever.

In your presence, others will experience their own relationship to power. Some may feel they want what your powerful Kamiel presence has. Others will be intimidated by your Kamiel core presence. This can be a challenge for you. It is essential for you not to take personally others' responses to your "lightning bolt" presence, nor to be triggered by another's inability to be fully in their personal power. Your presence can activate another's issues around their use of power or their lack of feeling aligned to their personal power. You can learn to use your power to teach people by example. You can hold space for their true power to come forward. If others are nervous, do not get unsettled and chatter just to be at their level so they are comfortable. It is essential for you to hold your own sense of self and let others come to vibrate at your level if they choose. You will find that they will actually get excited and come to you. Teaching people how to be in their power is about meeting people where they are and drawing out what they are passionate about and focused on. Your purpose is to ignite their focus with the energy that says, "Yes, you can be powerful in the ways that you choose to be."

My favorite example of someone who works in the Archangel Kamiel Realm is Bill Clinton. He commands people's attention. He is not afraid to stand up for what is important to him. He cannot be easily intimidated. When he was president and working in international circles, I noticed that people would listen carefully when he spoke, and he always commanded a leadership position. He knew how to work with power and was an inspiration to many in this light. And, yes, his challenge as a Kamiel was his misuse of his personal power. He misused his power with Monica Lewinsky and that hurt him and many others. Yet he continues to find ways to have a transformative influence wherever he goes.

A Kamielite is here to help transform the way power is currently used in most parts of the world. Power over others, power over a situation, or power struggles are the common way power is utilized in relationships, business, and political, even religious, domains. Kamielites are here to proclaim that true power is not meant to represent this warring, struggling, survival-oriented position. It is meant to be the fuel for the creation of our heart and Soul's mastery and the collective, unified expression of the power of Light through the creative diversity on Earth.

Right use of power does not mean that if you are feeling the energy of movement as a force for change, you use it as anger against someone or friction with an outside source. If this same energy of force or power within you moves, right use means you hold it within you and allow it to fuel your movement forward and with a greater sense of power of self. Then you have truly transformed that force from one of destruction to one of creation. This is the right use of power that serves in a much more productive way.

The Value of Archangel Realm Knowledge

Here is a story of a woman's discovery of how her knowledge of her Archangel Realm has helped her:

"I realized that I was having trouble working with the co-workers in my office. I wanted to respect their viewpoint, but I didn't feel that they understood my perspective at all. Then I realized I was also afraid of letting them know my viewpoint. What a bind I was in. I knew it related to not understanding how power works in this world but I wasn't sure how to unravel this locked-up mess and get clarity on how to be my most powerful self, especially around men.

"Susann and I had a session and took a journey back to the time just before I first incarnated here and discovered that I was a new Soul to Earth. I was very excited and a little naive. When I saw what looked like a gray cloud of all the human suffering I got really scared. How was I going to change all this? I was excited to make a difference here and show people how they could transform anything with the power of Light that is available to all of us in this Universe. It is really the power of our own connection to universal spirit. But this felt overwhelming and too scary to manage. I forgot that it wasn't just up to "little old me" to turn this mess around. There I was standing in fear, disconnected from my own inner power source of Light, thinking I had a task ahead that was too big for me.

"In our session I got reconnected to my inner Light source and amazingly my whole perspective changed. I began to radiate Light naturally and I could see the Light burning through the gray cloud of the human choice to be powerless and suffer due to their disconnected state. I wasn't afraid of these lost Souls anymore. They were actually afraid of me deep inside. I saw the men in my life so very differently. I was the powerful one because I had the Light source that they wanted. I could make choices now based on that. I could connect to my co-workers where Light was present between us and not give away myself where they were being gray, dull, and disconnected. I have so much more self-respect and honor for the true power I carry and my natural ability to inspire that connection in others without giving myself away to get them 'lit up.' Such a relief. I can walk more easily in my job and my world. My physical breathing is way easier, too!"

Discover Your Soul Portrait

Each person has developed unique Soul qualities and characteristics based on their Soul heritage. As you dowse or divine what Soul Family or Families make up home for you and add to that the Archangel Realm that describes your Soul personality, you will discover the magical characteristics and gifts that make up who you are as a Soul and what your Soul purpose is. This is your Soul Portrait.

For instance, if you come from Hadar and live through the Realm of Gabriel, you would be here to give expression to and teach about divine Love.

If you spent a large amount of your existence in Sirius and live through the Zophkiel Realm, you might describe your purpose as finding the better way of balance and harmonious co-creation in life.

If you are a Blueprint Deliverer and live through the Raphael Realm, you would love to bring the healing energy of Love to open the door for each person's success and fulfillment.

If you come from Alpha Centauri and stopped off in Mintaka and express your gifts dominantly through the Realm of Michael, you would be focused on providing what it is to live in the truth of being completely guided by your inner Light. Your purpose is to bring this world back to the truth of self-sufficient living from Light as the only choice to ignite each individual's unique expression.

Your Soul will understand what your unique formula is—it is your specific, chosen Blueprint. You designed it. It is a special combination of Soul qualities and expression that makes you who you are.

Spirit Guides from the Archangel Realms

Our guides are with us to help us bring forth our Soul destiny plan. They are our mentors, for life. Our guides help us to access the gifts, or Soul agreements, we made to bring into this life. They activate our strengths, our Soul gifts, and what we most love.

They are the divine ones who help us see clearly, speak our heart and our truth. They are our ever-ready friends motivating us to be the powerful self we are. Our spirit guides believe in us 100 percent. They know we can do anything we put our heart and Soul to, and mostly they are the ones who love us and support us unconditionally. Take the chance of asking for and letting yourself receive the Love and guidance being channeled to you through your guides.

This life holds a great design. We choose beings to participate with us as actual aspects of us, in our life purpose and heart's desire. These guides are designed to hold our spiritual mission intact. They agreed to be with us to bridge our spiritual self to our three-dimensional self. They are the firm foundation we look for in this world where nothing is a sure thing. The effects of the planetary field of separation and polarity that exist here have plagued each of us. Our guides are here to help us re-awaken to our inherent wisdom. They remind us that we have always been connected to our Creator and our Creator's Love, regardless of what the prevailing belief system says is true.

Spirit guides come from the seven Archangel Realms. Spirit guides are with us throughout our lifetime. We chose our guides based on our plans, what we want to accomplish, and what qualities of spirit we want to be most strongly guiding our life. They are an aspect of us, bridging our Soul to the universal aspect of our Creator from which we are born. Because we as a Soul choose our spirit guides, we have a very intimate connection to this part of ourselves and all that we choose to create while we are here. As you establish intimate friendships with your guides, more intimate connections and friendships of a spiritual caliber will manifest in your life.

To discover which Archangel Realms your spirit guides come from, you can use dowsing with a pendulum, applied kinesiology (muscle testing), or your own intuition. You can use the same method that you used to discover your Soul heritage and your Archangel Realm. We have access to all of the seven realms of guidance on an as needed basis. As adults, we usually have an average of three or four main guides we have chosen to escort us through our life, for particular assistance with aspects of our Soul that are most essential to our purpose in this lifetime.

Our guides know all about this world. One of the unique features of spirit guides is their history. They have done many Earth incarnations. They know planet Earth and how it works. They are close by, studying it all the time from the invisible realm. What most know as master teachers, angels, archangels, and ascended masters are really beings who have not done more than one Earth incarnation (if any at all). This is why spirit guides play the role with us that they do. They know this world well and they have a large investment in this world and its purpose within evolution and the universal scheme.

Often, a spirit guide has been with you in other incarnations. You're traveling together in life once again. You can see how special this relationship is and how easy it is for you to feel that it is a part of you. This relationship is designed to be even closer than having a twin or a Soul mate. Spirit guides are literally a part of us. They have merged with us. They are working with us and for us, whether we are conscious of it or not. They have been with us since we made our plan to incarnate and invited them to be with us.

When we are born, one or two of our guides come in immediately with us. Then at puberty another one shows up. It is designed this way because as little children we only need a primary guide or two to keep us connected to our Soul essence and Soul purpose. The Soul is still in the developmental stages, so not as much reinforcement is needed. Puberty is truly about our Soul incarnation. It also definitely includes hormone shifts and matters of individuation. It is a time of an expanded desire to learn and see what we are made of. But behind all these outer patterns of growth is the larger internal shift, when our Soul comes fully into self-hood and we begin to open up to and take hold of its blossoming for this incarnation. This blossoming continues throughout our lifetime, but the seeds we began with are given a huge opportunity during puberty to be planted more firmly in the vision of our life direction and passions.

Around 21, we usually enlist a third or fourth guide. It is no accident that the world is aligned with this significant rite of passage. Age 21 is a landmark in our Soul development as we begin to step into this world and declare who we are and how we want to shape our purpose and gifts in the world. This guide works with us on our inner growth and is a mentor for bringing our inner dimensions in balance with our outer direction. It lines up the development of our spiritual world as we take on the material world. And we may bring in one more guide along the way for a specific purpose that was not subsequently present.

We have other significant rites of passage for our Soul's incarnation throughout our life. Astrologers speak strongly of the "Saturn return" we each go through around age 28 to 30. Then there are various points that we have termed "midlife crises," depending on the timing of various outer events in our lives. And menopause is another. Each of these junctures opens a gateway for the deepening of our Soul's union with our divine heart and its emergence pouring into our lives. *Soul Mastery is this journey of mastering our life movement from the Soul's vantage point.* Our guides are present to facilitate our Soul's masterful emergence into our life expression.

How Guides from Each Realm Assist Us

This is a broad sweep of the guides from each Archangel Realm and their contribution to creation. Each guide adapts to you and your needs.

A guide from the Archangel Michael Realm helps us see truth clearly and simply. This guide protects us and holds a place as a spiritual warrior for our heart and Soul's highest movement.

A guide from Archangel Gabriel Realm helps us to express our deepest heart and deepest truth. It helps us in matters of communicating and teaching so that our Soul purposes are brought most valuably into the world.

A guide from the Archangel Raphael Realm is here primarily to bring us healing Love. It is also a mentor for us in ways that we bring healing to others, personally or professionally.

A guide from the Archangel Auriel Realm opens us to nurturing and unconditional Love. It teaches us to give and receive this Love.

A guide from the Archangel Zophkiel Realm brings the way of balance and harmony to us. It teaches us how to look at all points of view and value the diversity of creation.

A guide from the Archangel Zadkiel Realm allows us to connect with the means to bring our dreams into reality. It assists us to be in touch with manifestation and abundance.

A guide from the Archangel Kamiel Realm guides us and teaches us to be in our greatest power.

Requesting Further Assistance from Guides

We can ask our Creator for another guide whenever we connect to the Soul's need to have one. We can ask that it be brought into alignment with our Soul plans and purposes and be an expression of our heart's connection to our Soul's Blueprint. We can ask that it be in agreement with the beings of our Soul Family that work in conjunction with our incarnation. But if our request is part of our personal agenda, it is unlikely it will be fulfilled.

We may ask for guidance from any of the seven spirit guide realms that I am speaking of. This is part of our Creator's gift to us. Our guides help us to live in the material world from a spiritual dimension, unifying the two dimensions. Because our guides are aspects of us inherently, anytime we ask for assistance they will be up close and intimate with our true needs.

You can ask for a guide from the Realm of Archangel Michael, for instance, as a permanent feature or temporary plan. It's your choice. That guide will utterly protect you.

A Raphael guide is helpful for any kind of healing need. A Kamiel guide is a great asset to your power point presentation or talk. Simply look through the attributes of the different guides and discover how they can be of value to you in your life.

For instance, if we choose to make a life-path change, say to something such as nursing at midlife, it would be natural to bring in a guide from the Realm of Raphael who works with healing Love. It may not be a guide we had previously considered to be valuable. Or, if we decide to head up a company, take a political office, or become a leader in a way that brings an exponential leap to our mission, we may connect with a specific guide from the Realm of Kamiel to assist us in using our greatest power and establishing how we can use our power with greatest clarity, strength, and heart purpose.

Also, we may know that various guides show up to meet specific needs for a particular time. A Zadkiel guide can help us manifest an immediate desire. And a Gabriel guide helps us find the right people at the right time, as we communicate internally our needs.

From Mary:

"Wow! My guides sure know how to help me in my life! I was traveling with my daughter and I woke up one morning with a stiff neck and a big need for a chiropractor! I asked my guides to help me, as I needed to be very available for many people that day. I let my fingers do the walking through the yellow pages and called a man—just the second call—who actually had an opening that day and didn't need me to do extensive paperwork, or x-rays, or anything complicated that I knew wasn't necessary. He took me right in, adjusted me, and I was on my way. And I even ran into an old friend in the office who was leaving as I was coming in; that was an added bonus to the chiropractic visit. My guides did it again! Not only did they take care of me and direct me to the right doctor, but also they added their own icing on the cake so I could see this old friend. That was a great addition to the whole thing working out."

We Work as a Team with Our Guides

In this Universe, our guides are present to assist us to bring the gifts of our Soul heritage into our life expression. They want to be employed! We are meant to be here as team players, never alone. Our guides remind us of the natural connection we have to legions of beings throughout the solar system. I see and feel myself being much larger than I am physically as my team is with me wherever I am and they don't take up physical space. They can fit with us in any doorway we go through. In classes I teach I often have people practice moving with this awareness of having our guides energetically with us. This experience expands our awareness of who we are so that we move out of the little me to divine me. Remembering our guides helps us to live more from this larger dynamic. When we get in an emotional bottleneck or stressful situation we can even ask for one or more of our guides to step to the forefront to help in handling the situation.

I remember the phrase "give it to God" first spoken to me many years ago. Giving or sharing our problems and needs with our guides is highly acceptable and very encouraged. Their job is to share the mission of our life movement. They know that being on Earth has many challenges. Their presence is part of the inherent abundance present in the Blueprint for life to be known here.

From Lisa:

"I am a very responsible and loving person. I love my family and care about them so much. Here's the rub. I discovered that this is a wonderful quality, but it has its pitfalls. I didn't realize the correlation until I was uncovering why I was having trouble with sleeplessness at night. I worked with my guides in helping me understand this sleeplessness. I was so responsible and such a caretaker that I couldn't turn it off at night. I figured it was my job 24/7. My guides reminded me of one of the key reasons they are part of my life and why we are a team. At night I can leave my responsibilities and all that I care for in their hands. They were thrilled with this opportunity as an act of Love and service with me. So at night I started to give them the list of my concerns, responsibilities, who I thought needed extra 'TLC,' and my heart's longings for either healing or manifestation. They said they love working in the night when the worldwide energies are more settled. What a difference that made in my ability to come to rest and feel a sense of peace, drifting off to sleep. I also understood that I didn't have to wear myself out giving everyone around me my personal juice (or Light). I could employ my guides to bestow those gifts I wanted to share with others and I could keep my tank full. This way, I never was depleted and was much more valuable to my life and world."

I have found that sometimes clients' guides can be compromising to their progress. Before we incarnated we might have chosen to include a guide or guides who were designed for smaller purposes than what we are involved in now. For various reasons we might have wanted to stay small or just wanted guides to support our smallness and not advancement in our life purpose. It is like having a kindergarten level teacher when you want to move into calculus or international affairs.

Sometimes we come into life with an attitude that we want to stay small out of fear of being hurt. Or we start out taking baby steps in our Soul path to accumulate valuable pieces we left out in another lifetime before taking on a substantial mission. Or we knew that we wouldn't need more powerful guides until we raised a family and afterwards began a life of service to a worldwide cause, for instance. Then we would release those guides who have served with us lovingly and well. We call on new guides or a set of guides who are more adept at international affairs or a larger mission than the need required up to this point. Guides are happy to be released to move on to help others requesting their service. This works the same way in school. We have different teachers for basic addition and subtraction than we do for geometry and trigonometry. I have many examples of clients who have released guides and brought in new ones. Linda described it like this, "It helped me step up to the plate in my life. Something I had wanted to do for a good while, but wasn't sure what was holding me back."

Richard explains it like this, "I knew I had something of greater significance to do in my life. I'm no slouch. Having a whole new set of guides was like being jet propelled into the new territory I was seeking."

These are just a few ways our guides can help us with the specifics of life. They are truly at our service. They hold the truth of what it means to co-create in our life. It's a deeply rewarding experience to open doors for so many to this level of the innate design of guidance in our lives in this Creator Universe. I can see the broad energetic smiles on the faces of people's guides, too, as they are understood more fully. This recognition magnifies the vehicle for spirit in our worlds, which pleases the guides to no end. Their purpose is being fulfilled with greater consciousness and expansion. And awareness of union with our guides amplifies our heart and Soul fulfillment tenfold. I have witnessed this generosity of spirit in action over and over.

Guides are here to serve the larger picture. It is completely appropriate to do some kind of ritual of your own design when releasing these dedicated friends and bringing in new comrades. Appreciation is greatly appreciated! I find this is true any time I am drawing on my guides for specific instances. And I always thank them for being present with me first thing in the morning and last thing at night. This is a wonderful, intimate, loving relationship I cherish, and my appreciation for it is as natural as breathing.

Spirit guides are often in this role so they can assist from the invisible realms and also so they can take a break from physical incarnation, but at the same time keep their investment level as high as possible in relationship to this Earth mission.

All of our guides are here to bring the spiritual dynamic of our Soul's purposes into alignment with our outer endeavors. They are truly the best mentors available. They allow our life to have meaning, value, and purpose as we outlined it to be in our Soul's Blueprint for this incarnation. Of course they are now saying, "We're just doing our job." That's true! They feel we are equally deserving of honor, praise, and acknowledgment for being the ones to do the human incarnation aspect. They know it is no small feat! And they are very happy to play their designated part for our personal Soul fulfillment and for the planetary advancement that they are so dedicated to.

Ask for What You Want

Our spirit guides are protectors that keep us out of harm's way.

Our guides advise us on whether to speed up, slow down, or redirect our efforts.

Our guides are deeply comforting and nurturing.

Our guides nudge us toward our heart's chosen goals in life.

Our guides assist us in healing whatever we need to heal to allow us to live from our greatest place and bring our deepest gifts.

We call on our guides in times of pain, fear, and confusion.

The key here is simple. Just ask.

From Alice:

"I have learned how to be specific in asking the Universe and my guides to provide me with exactly what I want. Then I had to learn how to receive it.

"A few months ago I was invited to an event I would have to travel to. I had a friend who invited me to go with her, but our timing for leaving to go to the event did not match up. Should I try to make the scheduling work that my friend was set for or decline the invitation? I was reminded of a third option. Clarify in myself what would genuinely work for me, which meant a ride coming from another (unknown as yet) source on the exact time frame that worked for me. Then communicate all this information to my guides. Ask for this request and trust that it would show up. I asked, and it showed up."

You do have this much loving support available and more. Allowing yourself to receive this Love and support makes reaching your goals and fulfilling your heart's longing so much easier.

Our Soul challenges come with us as we incarnate. We must change these patterns while we are in a body. We can imagine how great it would be if we were able to clean the slate of our past doings after we have died. But it's not set up that way. Between lives we do have the opportunity to see from a higher vantage point how we tripped up, or what we might do differently in the next life time, but the new plan and agreements cannot be set in motion until we come back into a physical body to activate those plans and agreements. There is no heavenly auto body shop to fix up the barnacles we have created in our life. But we are guided in how to best utilize the next incarnation to rectify whatever we choose to. We may opt to do a simple lifetime of forgiving someone, or choose a huge lifetime of high level mission to serve mankind dramatically. This will influence the choice we make of the spirit guides who will assist us in our life. We decide what is important to us and what level of transformation we want to engage in personally or planetarily. Then we select guides who are qualified to help us with what we value most in our life.

Be persistent. When it feels like you have bitten off more than you can chew, remember that you have spirit guides, councils of beings, and a myriad of teachers assigned to help you with your Soul plans and purposes. They are continually doing whatever they can to remind you that "we are all in this together," and universal wisdom for anything you are challenged with is present for the asking.

You create how your guides work for you, and what your relationship to your guides is comprised of. That is the joy of developing your connection to the world of guidance! It is up to you to find the name of your spirit guides. It's possible for me to determine from which Archangel Realm they come. But the name has a personal, dynamic quality, best left to you and your guides.

Things have shifted exponentially on the planet since 9/11, and we can choose to see this from a spiritual perspective. There is nothing secure or safe. There are no easy answers, no obvious villains to eliminate so all will be well again. It is impossible for anything outside of ourselves to grant us complete and guaranteed protection. Even the most vigilant mother cannot stay glued to her child 24 hours a day for her whole life to make sure they are safe. We just can't mentally come up with enough outer plans to make sure all we love is protected from harm. This shift since 9/11 is asking us to look internally to our ever-present spiritual self to meet our needs for Love, safety, peace, and assurance.

I have found that our spirit guides are the very aspects of ourselves that can hold the eternal lantern of assurance that all is well for us. I have seen personally and through the stories shared with me that as we allow space in our hearts for our guides to be with us, we are able to experience a direct manifestation of safety, security, peace, and Love from our very Soul permeating our life experience. This is their job. It behooves us to keep them employed for our own health and happiness. They are the bridge that allows all that we are connected to of our Soul Families and home worlds to be with us on a daily basis.

16

INTUITION

You are becoming more attuned to your Soul's gifts and the precious connection you have to your Soul Families and your spirit guides. You are opening to receive the abundance the world of your Soul heritage has to offer continuously.

Utilizing your intuition is the best way for you to communicate and commune with this vast aspect of your Soul that is invisible, but very present with you. Just as the Akashic Records is an open book for you, so is the book of your Soul's life open to you through your guides, teachers, and Soul Family connection. Opening your intuition is opening your book of life. Your intuition allows you to access your heart song, the gates to your passions, and the doorways to your purpose and direction. Your intuition is the vehicle that connects divine Love to your plans and purposes so that your life ignites as the focus point of your Soul. This is Soul Mastery manifest.

Intuition Is Our Natural Gift

It is within our very Soul makeup to be intuitive. Originally, human beings were capable of telepathic communication and had constant telepathic connection to our Creator and our Soul connection to our home worlds. This was all part of the Blueprint before separation occurred between our spirit and Soul to our physical reality. It is our intuition that will open the channels again to our inherent capability to allow spirit to move through our heart and Soul. It is our intuition that creates the bridge for telepathic connection to our Soul Families and larger invisible worlds.

It is known that whales and dolphins have always been masters of the invisible worlds of connection. Humpback whales used to be able to communicate across entire oceans with subsonic pulses. Today the ambient noise from machinery prevents this. African elephants can use subsonic calls to reach each other from many miles away. Again, without human-generated noise interference, they could call nearly across the continent. If you are standing near an elephant using these calls, you can feel them in your body, even if you can't hear them.

If other mammals have what we might deem to be super powers, so do we. Intuition is an innate skill that we are born with. You only have to trust it and practice it. It is a sacred gift. It allows us to believe in our deepest self. It allows us to connect to the part of us that loves to see our life fulfilled. You can awaken to what lies within you and begs to be given expression, if you set your intention to truly want all that you are as a Soul to ignite, if you really want to kindle the fires for the abundant manifestation of your heart and Soul's destiny plans for a magnificent life, you will.

Steps for the Intuitive Process

Here are a few aspects that comprise the formula for trusting and engaging in your intuitive pathway that I find to be tried and true.

The first step is to connect with your heart. Your intuition requires a divine connection, and the heart is the space through which universal wisdom and guidance comes into life. This is the key. We may get many intuitive visions and messages through our third eye and upper chakras, but it is essential for the heart to be engaged to know that the intuitive information is true for our life. It's our Blueprint, *our* heart's truth.

Let your intuition be your inner lantern to light your way. Feel or see a connection between your heart and our Creator, or the divinity of your choice. You may call it universal wisdom or infinite presence. Be sure that this point or emanation you see or feel is one you absolutely trust. Create a visual or feeling path between that source and your heart that is filled with Light. Having done this, you can now know that there is an open pure channel for guidance to flow into to be received by your divine heart. This assures you that any guidance or information that you receive is connected to the source of divinity that you trust and aligns with your personal divine heart.

Now you can relax and allow yourself to trust your guides, who are a key aspect of your intuition, to work with you. Thank all those aspects of your spiritual self that are present with you. This allows you to bring your awareness to the largeness of all that you are and all you are inherently connected to. This can include your higher self, your spirit guides, any of your teachers, any beings from your Soul Families and Soul worlds. These are dimensions of you that your Soul and now your heart are inherently connected to. This is a great way to claim your divinity and largeness as a being.

As you hold that divine presence, that awareness, that connection in your heart, simply by saying thank you to those beings, they will return your heart connection by showing up and being with you in any way you request. Appreciation is a magical resource.

Now that you have their attention it is time to set your intention. Be clear which door you want to open, what you want assistance with, or what kind of support you are asking for. Know that you are now connected in your heart and Soul, so it is okay for you to ask for what you want. In this step of getting clear on what you want, it is important to *ask* your guides for assistance. Because of free will your guides will not act on your behalf, without permission. It is up to you to open the door for them.

Your guides only give you what is aligned with your heart and Soul, so what you are asking for will open doors for your Soul fulfillment and highest good automatically. As you take these vital steps you will not have to worry that you are being selfish, that you will get unaligned or disruptive information. Nor will you have to wonder if you can trust what comes through the intuitive channel being created.

Now you know where you want to go. The next step is to commit to it. Trust that your commitment is valid and valued, and your guidance will respond. Commit to opening up to receive the gift. Trust the wisdom of your spirit each step of the way. Commit to being seen, understood, and received. That is what your guides are here to refresh in your Soul memory bank—that you are seen, known, and understood. Your interaction with them is the way to confirm that. As you commit to opening your intuition so your spiritual self can give you input, be sure to surrender the question, situation, or topic. "Mail the letter!" This is a co-creative process.

If you are in your car driving to a destination you have to know where you are going and stay committed to whatever it takes to get there, including trusting that you will. The same commitment works with your intuitive process: commit to that intuition being a very real avenue for your Soul's expression and it will be!

Describe what makes your heart and Soul sing and open yourself to receive the gift of guidance that would allow that to manifest. Remember that your intuitive guidance seeks the most creative potential and outcome so that you can flourish. Intuition is the means available for you to realize that everything you need is within you. Listen from your heart to the guidance, to what is being given to you. As you listen to the words, the feeling sensations, the images, the metaphors that spirit is gifting you, all you have to do is take the guidance into the physical realm of action, which is your part in this team equation.

I had a client who was asking me about a wheat allergy she had and what it might be about. I connected, asked, and surrendered to what came up. I saw the words, "Wheaties, Breakfast of Champions." Very funny. So I shared that with her. She said, "Oh, when I wake up in the morning I don't feel very powerful usually. I could use the breakfast of champions!" As we played with it further, it came to us that it wasn't about physical food she needed. The Wheaties represented an energetic power source. It was a power source in herself that she wasn't allowing because she was afraid to be her most powerful self. She was "allergic" to it. The wheat she is allergic to represents this fear of being a source of power. When she listened to the spirit of this message she got it for herself. "When I'm not being my most powerful self, I have a wheat allergy that appears."

Your guides will give you one step at a time. As you follow with love, commitment, and trust, more will be opened for you. As you receive the gift of the first step to take, fully and with gratitude, embrace it. You want this world to receive the gift you've come all this way to give. Receiving gifts from your guides by opening to your intuitive self will pave the way for you to be received.

This is truly the formula for you to be the most powerful expression of Love your Soul is committed to being. This is a basic formula.

Intuition is not usually a black and white proposition or linear equation. I was helping a student, Mark, with his intuitive skills and we had great fun uncovering the creative avenue intuition is.

Mark was wanting clarity on whether it was the best use of his time and energy to sell a nutritional supplement he really felt good about, or put more effort into marketing his chiropractic business after a lull in the usual number of new patients.

He was frustrated with the guidance he was being given. "I just wanted to get a yes answer to one of the two options of whether I should be selling a particular type of supplements or do more marketing for my chiropractic practice. I did not get the straight forward yes or no I was looking for," he said. I asked him what he did receive. He said the guides shared with him that if he sold the supplements he would receive more short-term gain. If he put energy toward marketing his chiropractic business he would open a door to less immediate gratification and more long-term gain. He was shown that both options were viable, but gave different rewards. "We always have choice," the guides were saying. "What is it you truly want here?" was their question back to him. Then they assessed what he was truly wanting: more short-term advantages or long-term advantages.

This helped him understand how intuition works. It does not show up as a command to, "Do this, Don't do that." Intuitive guidance opens doors by which we can step through as we *choose* which avenue feels expansive, brighter, or lighter. Mark was being given a great education in intuition. There are always options based on what truly has the greatest value. In this case did he resonate with quick return or long-term gain? Which one *really* was his choice? Mark's story is just one example of the magical and creative resource our inherent intuition gives us to connect with the spirit of what gives value to our existence, moment by moment.

Intuitive Guidance Is Our Power Source

Authentic guidance is empowering, breeds self-sufficiency, and is gratifying. It opens doors. It does not make absolute statements of authoritative positioning. Intuition frees the Soul to move masterfully into our lives. It always feels expansive and is filled with blessing.

Intuition helps us allow our lives to work the best way possible, from our heart and Soul's perspective.

From Deborah:

"When my second son, Nate, was about 18 months old, and his older brother, Jesse, was about 5, my first husband, Ken, and I visited my brother-in-law, Keith, at Cape Cod. Keith is a golf pro and he took Ken and me to play golf and give us some pointers. It was a beautiful spring day, still a little chilly, but we all bundled up and headed out to Keith's club. Not too long into our lesson, I looked over to see Nate and Jesse standing on the next green, playing. They were a little ways off, but I could see them, so I returned my attention to my game. When it was my turn to tee off, I looked down at the ball and before I could swing I was filled with an overwhelming sense of dread. I looked over to where my sons had been playing and they had disappeared over the knoll and were no longer in sight. Everything in my body became alert and I felt my inner voice urgently prompting me to run. I dropped my club and began sprinting to where my children had disappeared. Ken, a fit athlete, could not even keep up with me, but followed behind yelling, 'It's okay! Everything's okay!' But I knew it was not.

"When I arrived at the top of the knoll, to my horror I saw a water hole at the bottom. Nathan was turned upside down in the water, his head completely submerged, and his little legs up in the air. Jesse was frantically trying to right him but did not have the strength. I raced down the hill and pulled Nathan out, who gasped for air, but was gratefully all right. If I had hesitated at all, questioned or ignored the promptings of my Soul, my beautiful son could have drowned. Fortunately, because I acted immediately, Nathan had not been in the water too long. To this day I am immensely grateful that I listened to the inner promptings of my Soul and my guides, which saved my son's life.

"From that point on I always tuned in to my children through my intuition to assess their well-being, whether they were in the next room or away from me. I vowed to honor my intuition in all ways, and it has blessedly served me well in many situations. But this story is by far the most profound."

Utilizing Intuition Opens Your Soul Life

Listening to your intuition proclaims that you are increasingly interested in uncovering who you truly are. You are training yourself to focus on what is real for you. You are learning to honor the voice of your heart and Soul.

Your heart is the access point to your Soul. In listening to your intuition through your heart you will become free to express your authentic self, which includes your genuine needs, feelings, and desires. You will become deeply committed to loving your core self and the voice of your Soul. You will have much greater discernment in who you can trust and how close to let others in who cross your path in life. You will become more honest with yourself in this arena. You will know that you always have choices and you are in charge of your life, with a team of undeniable, unwavering supporters to assist you in making choices that are best for you.

As your intuition guides you to live from your heart and Soul, you attract others who live from their heart and Soul. By giving your spirit a voice, you will align with others who respect your voice and want to walk with you in life.

By allowing your intuition to be your guide, you will open your connection to the vastness and the assurance of the eternal flame of existence, the Beloved.

Your life will flower, expressing the abundance of your heart and Soul's sacred union with the Beloved.

You will know home. You will be home.

Intuition Is Our Creator's Gift to Us

Intuitive guidance is our Creator's gift to us. It is the collective voice of your higher self, your guides, teachers, angels, and the Divine. To receive such a gift and have it work for you, you have to value it by receiving it in your heart, in your being, in your consciousness.

Accept that your intuition is available to guide you, help you, inspire you, teach you, lead you, and support you. Your intuition is a loving force that will not override your free will, or your feelings and concerns. It will not direct you authoritatively, nor will it manipulate you. Intuition is your best friend.

It takes courage to direct your life from within and recognize that your Soul is your true essence and you can trust your true essence and your connection to source. By trusting your intuition you are putting your life in the hands of your Soul and its connection to our Creator. To trust feels like the safest, most sure aspect of life.

Intuition Brings Abundance to Us

Intuition here provides the means for allowing our Soul gifts to be accessed and given a valuable place in our life. There are many gifts that are yours to bring. The frequencies of those Soul gifts are contained within this book. Allowing your intuition to be a trusted, loving friend in your day-to-day life is truly the best way to stay in touch with those gifts and the abundance of ways those gifts may be given shape and dimension. Your guides, through your intuition, are also completely aligned with bringing you the thorough enjoyment of creation. Personal and planetary fulfillment is designed to go hand in hand. As you are filled with the Light of your Soul's gifts shining through you, the world around you glows. As you are open to be guided by the mastery of your Soul, so will the world become a reflection of our Creator's Blueprint and the Soul destiny plan for this majestic foundation for creation, as it was intended.

CONCLUSION

This is your time. This is your moment, to connect to your Soul's gifts and treasures. I honor your courage to open yourself to the power and majesty of who you are and what your heart and Soul have to birth here and now.

This world called to you. You chose to share your Love and divinity with this aspect of creation on Earth. You chose to play your Soul's song here and expand your Soul's experience to include the bounty of life's joyful expression, an opportunity that exists here as nowhere else.

As you access the gifts of your Soul and allow them to flourish in your life, Soul mastery becomes yours. Your Soul Family and guides thank you from all that they eternally are, for all that you continually bring.

RESOURCES

Discover more about the author's work at www.soulmastery.net. To contact Susann for a personal appointment or to schedule a *Soul Mastery: Accessing the Gifts of Your Soul* book event or a Soul Mastery workshop or training in your area call 303-546-9712 or email her at susann@soulmastery.net.

For more information on "Igniting Your Intuition: Your Greatest Resource for Mastering Your Life" workshop or teleclass email susann@soulmastery.net or visit her web site for her schedule of classes www.soulmastery.net.

For further information on dowsing:
Dowsing for Beginners by Richard Webster
Pendulum Magic for Beginners by Richard Webster
Medical Assistance Program (MAP) by Machelle Small Wright
    Appendix A: Kinesiology
Accessing the Akashic Records:
Akashic Record Dowsing: Addendium II, Vol. 1 by Arlen Bock. Email:
    habock@fone.net
Sunlight on Water by Flo Aveia Magdelena (p. 137 and p. 145)

CPSIA information can be obtained
at www.ICGtesting.com
Printed in the USA
FSOW02n1650290216
17308FS